O GAUGE RAIL-ROADING

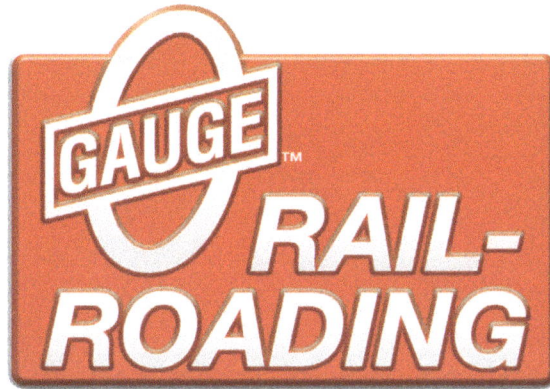

Building a Layout

by *O Gauge Railroading* magazine's "Backshop Foreman"

Jim Barrett

This book chronicles seven years of construction on Jim's world-class, three-rail O scale model train layout.

Production Design, Layout and Editing
Rich Melvin

ISBN: 978-1-7361500-0-9

FOREWORD
by Alan Arnold, CEO & Publisher
OGR Publishing, Inc.

This book is dedicated to the memory of Jim Barrett who was our friend and partner here at *O Gauge Railroading* magazine. Jim passed away unexpectedly on October 29, 2020. This book is a compilation of Jim's Backshop articles written over his last seven years with *O Gauge Railroading.*

Those of you who knew Jim will never forget his love of the hobby as well as his never ending willingness to help anyone that had a question or problem with regards to their trains and layouts. Jim had the wonderful ability to take what seemed to be a complex "how to do" project and explain it in very easy to understand terms.

Many of us met Jim through his magazine articles while others of us were fortunate to meet Jim in person. Jim always made an encounter with him an adventure mixed with quite a sense of humor.

An example of this was on one of my first trips to the TCA York Meet. While driving, Jim called me from his car to make arrangements for lunch. I was many miles ahead of him and wondered how long I would have to wait at the restaurant for him to arrive. Well, I was in for a surprise!

Alan Arnold
CEO and Publisher
***O Gauge Railroading* magazine**

As we got closer to our lunch destination, Jim checked in with regular cell phone calls indicating what mile marker he had just passed....holy cow, he was getting closer and closer to me rather quickly! This went on for a couple of hours and then in my rear view mirror I saw that big and mighty late model Mercury he loved so much. And there he was with that big grin on his face! He had to have been averaging around 100 MPH to catch up with me!

Then the phone rang. It was HIM! He said, "I am on your (another word for rear), follow me!" Then that almost 20 foot long car screamed by my little PT Cruiser like I was backing up, I pushed the petal to the metal like the little engine that could and did my best to keep up with him! Looking fearfully down at the speedometer, I could not believe my little PT could go that fast! Zippity doo dah we went and in little time we arrived at our lunch destination. We both parked with Jim heading to the door first while I worked to dislodge my fingers from my steering wheel! We were walking into the restaurant with limited conversation as I was trying to get over the warp speed we had just been going. As we sat down at the table, Jim said to me, "That little Cruiser amazed me! I can't believe you were able to keep up like you did!" All the while he was smiling and giggling (he had a neat giggle). He then started what became a "Jim Barrett Original" story that he told many times to others. He expounded about the time when some guy in a PT Cruiser was chasing him down the interstate trying to pass his Mighty Mercury! "That PT was losing parts as the air friction heated up the metal." he would say. "I could see the fenders and antenna de-materializing." he would remark with his typically funny comments and facial actions, all of which was very animated as everyone at the table was laughing. Little did I know that Jim was well known for his heavy foot while driving. Everyone already knew that a trip with Jim was going to be fast and furious, full of fun conversation as he blew the paint off every car he passed!

So, with this book, Jim's last forty-five Backshop articles will stand as a lasting legacy to one of *THE* ambassadors of our hobby...a guy who never met a stranger, and who touched many lives in positive ways.

Rest easy my friend, in that Great Train Station In The Sky.

Alan

TABLE of CONTENTS

CHAPTER 1 - Where Do I Start?

Having a model train layout usually involves spending the layout's entire life mulling over what you would have done differently if you had another chance. I've been blessed with seeing and photographing a great many different layouts in my travels for the magazine, and now I've been dealt a new hand in my own life which involved moving to a new location and starting a new layout from scratch.

The logical place to start is with a design on paper, even if it is nothing more than a sketch with some measurements on it so you'll know what you can and can't get away with. Sketch out the walls of the planned layout space and if possible use graph paper so things will be drawn to some scale. That helps you see how O72 curves can eat up floor space. It also helps you see what you might have to relocate, pole through, or work around to accommodate your plans. Don't forget to include doors, traffic patterns, and access to permanent fixtures like circuit breaker boxes and so forth.

With a plan in mind, focus on changes or additions that may need to be made to the space you have available for your layout and do this well before you start actual construction. The time to change or modify things above, behind, or under your planned layout is now, because once it is built, making major changes is difficult at best or even next to impossible at worst.

A layout, once it is adorned with full scenery, will absolutely swallow up light. There's nothing worse than a beautifully executed layout that can't really be appreciated due to inadequate or improper lighting. In addition to quantity of light, the quality of the light you use is also important. While full and intense fluorescent lighting is a help when building and working on a layout, that type of lighting is also harsh and generally unflattering. Incandescent lighting is much warmer, more easily varied for mood or effect, and less apt to induce fading of the scenery and train items. Have you ever visited a train store and noticed boxes for merchandise that have been sitting unsold for a long time? In many cases, the color of the box bleaches out over time if it has been sitting exposed to fluorescent lighting. That type of lighting can, over time, also affect engines, rolling stock, and scenic items, definitely not something you want to happen to your trains.

Because layout scenery and features literally swallow up light, a high level of ambient lighting is almost always necessary. In addition, an alternate and separate system of track lights with variable intensity floods, spots, and scene or mood lights is really the preferred way to go. For general construction, cleaning, and electrical work, overhead fluorescent light that floods the room will be fine. Home improvement stores sell very economical two-tube ceiling mounted fluorescent light fixtures for as little as $20. In my room, I placed a 4′ fixture about every 8' down the middle of the 12′ wide room (Photo 1). This turns an otherwise dark basement into daytime very nicely.

For lighting the layout, simple and efficient track lighting is available with 4′ and 8′ long tracks. I used 8′ tracks wherever possible, making the future location of individual lights flexible. Since you're putting in the lights way before you know exactly where you want them focused, this is important. You will probably need an electrician to install a couple of new circuits for these track lights, especially if you live in an earlier house built back in the 1950s or 1960s.

With ceiling related matters attended to, it's time to consider the rest of the available space. Don't let the current location of features such as household plumbing, hot water heaters, or even concrete block walls necessarily limit you in your new layout design. Believe it or not, those things can be easily moved or penetrated if you do it before you start building.

When working with basements, I hate the space that is lost just turning trains around so they can go the other way. Often enough, just on the other side of an existing wall, you may have a furnace using up a chunk of space for nothing but...well...a furnace. My current layout design calls for the train to go through that wall, make a loop around the furnace (nice use of O72 or larger curves), and go back through the wall to rejoin the main layout. That results in a couple of perfectly functional tunnels on a mountain face on the layout side of that wall. True, you may need a big concrete saw or a hammer and chisel to get the job done, but the result will be well worth the effort. I penetrated the wall where the track will pass through on two different levels (Photos 2 and 3). Both levels will turn in double-deck style around the furnace seen in Photo 4.

And while we're talking about the furnace, don't let the PVC pipe vents get in your way either (Photo 5). Those two vents were put in by the furnace installer with the least amount of creativity and labor. He can be forgiven because he likely never had the privilege of planning a train layout. Photo 4 shows what happens when you relocate them to accommodate some tracks at a future date.

Consider the hot water heater, too. I needed some additional space for access behind my water heater along the back wall for my train storage design. With the help of a plumber and about an hour of his labor, I relocated this appliance to where it needs to be to fit the layout better (Photo 6).

Photo 7 shows a very pesky problem sink drain coming from the kitchen upstairs, as well as an old dishwasher drain that had been abandoned in place by a previous homeowner. That sink drain will play havoc with a track going to a future engine transfer table positioned along that back wall, and the abandoned dishwasher drain (the horizontal line near the ceiling) is just plain ugly!

I couldn't move the sink drain line where it went into the basement floor, but that was below the level of the future layout. I was able to relocate most of the line that extends above the future layout by making a jog in the plumbing line (it will be unseen below the table). That shifted the location of the rest of the drain line as close as I could possibly get it to the back wall, which included going through the paneling and right up against the block foundation (Photo 8). That left so little of the pipe exposed above the layout that I could most likely hide it with a future scenic panel.

I saved the best trick till last. I learned this while photographing a number of fine layouts. The best way to hide unwanted structural details in the ceiling is to simply "eliminate" that ceiling. Make it go away by painting it black! If you have an old ceiling like the one at my house with different layers and elevations, visible wiring, plumbing, and even ugly ductwork sticking down through it here and there, paint it all flat black. That directs the eye of the observer straight down to the layout, which now stands out with all its color and lighting and away from the distracting stuff on the ceiling.

Use flat black paint on all areas of the ceiling including wires, pipes, lighting fixtures, and anything else installed there. A track lighting fixture mounted to the ceiling waits for the remaining area to be rolled with flat black paint in Photo 9. Even the clunky old ductwork seems to blend

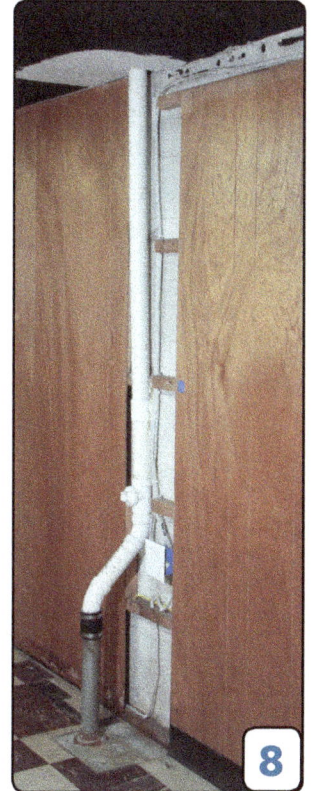

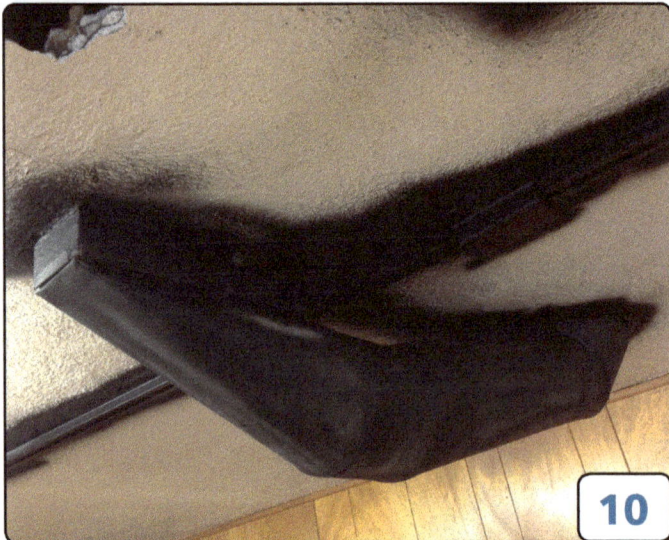

in better where everything is painted flat black (Photos 10 and 11). The same is true of the old and new copper tubes, conduit, and the new lighting fixtures that all seem to blend into the ceiling and go away (Photos 12 and 13).

Completed track and fluorescent lighting is installed in part of the finished ceiling (Photo 14). But wait…what about that paneling in the background? Nobody ever saw sky backdrops in brown colored wood grain now, have they?

We'll fix that in the next chapter.

CHAPTER 2 - Adding a Backdrop

In chapter one I talked about the things you should do before you even start with the first stick of wood on a new layout. Now begins the fun stuff. I'm starting my new layout, but after all the layouts I've built, this time I'm putting some thought into the design before I begin. My goal is to finish this one without saying, "Gee, if I had it to do over again, I shoulda...coulda...woulda...."

Take a look at the right-hand side of the track diagram on page ten, which depicts a part of the planned layout. I didn't want to just make loops of track like I've always done in the past, but trains do have to go somewhere and come back, right? This time I'm going to hide one end of the turnaround with a nice mountain...a big mountain...one with enough room to hide a helix somewhat inside the mountain that will let me go from one level of the layout to another. Using a mountain with a gorge cut into it at the front might even allow me to drop the bottom out of it and walk right in—handy to use for construction and occasional derailments. This plan started to give direction to the de-sign. All I have to do now is figure out what to do with those three trestles bridging Shallow River Bottoms. Oh well, I'll solve that later in the construction phase.

On the other end of the viewing area, I'm going to take advantage of the limited viewing space I have by punching a couple of holes through a wall so trains can go out of the room, turn around the furnace in the other part of the basement, and come back into the scenery room, so to speak. I'll show you my plans for that in a later chapter.

So many layouts I've visited have shared a common problem. Little consideration was given to the space needed for the people viewing the trains. That is a common problem because we O gauge hobbyists are always seeking more running space, and running space is almost always at a premium. We never seem to realize that we didn't allow for enough space to properly view the layout until it was too late.

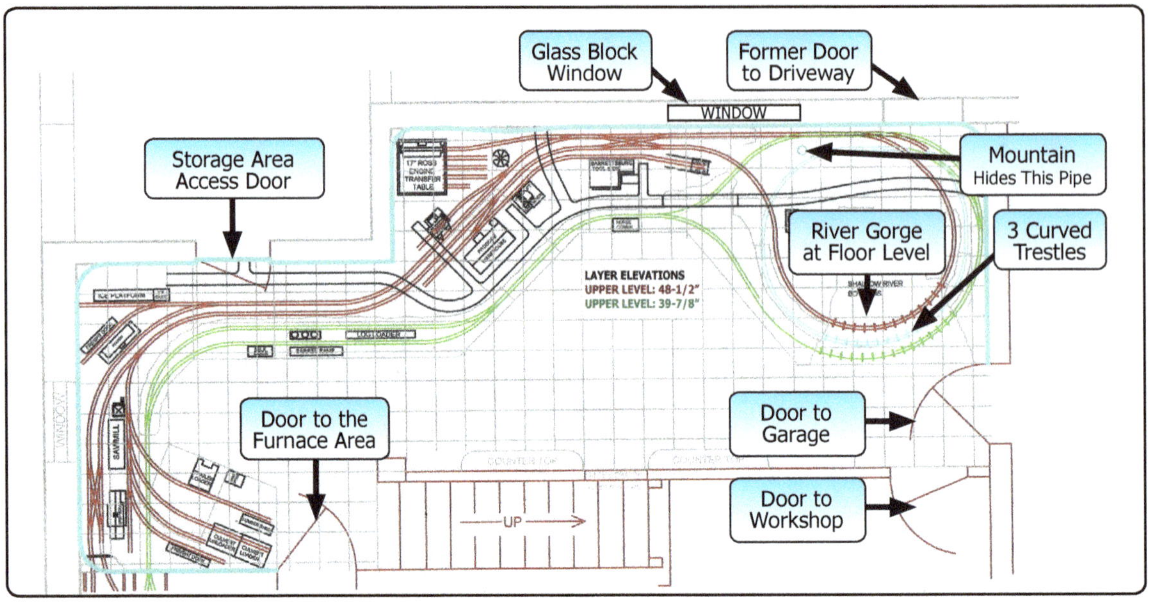
Glass Block Window
Former Door to Driveway
WINDOW
Storage Area Access Door
Mountain Hides This Pipe
River Gorge at Floor Level
3 Curved Trestles
LAYER ELEVATIONS
UPPER LEVEL: 48-1/2"
UPPER LEVEL: 39-7/8"
Door to Garage
Door to the Furnace Area
UP
Door to Workshop

We also tend to believe we can do a whole lot more with our available space than we actually can or should do. To help understand this before you start with actual construction, begin with an accurate sketch of your room using graph paper so you can realistically spot things by actual scale size — things like furnaces, water heaters, and closets. Most importantly, you can see the walking space, access space, and viewing space. Any time you can make any one of these last three spaces serve two or even all three of these categories, that is good planning.

On your own sketch, include all doors indicating which way they swing and where they lead. On my diagram, you see a door on the lower left that accesses the lower half of the basement. There is actually another door on the lower right end for access to the same area. Are two really needed? Well, no, but the walkway to the right goes to the garage door as well, so these doors stay.

But I did have yet another door along the upper wall at the far right. That is a pedestrian doorway leading outside the basement to the driveway and is totally redundant because the garage door is just on the other side of the wall at the right. Normal traffic pattern is to go to and from the garage to the car. A pedestrian door from the basement train room to the driveway outside just wasn't needed. That pedestrian door will be closed permanently, eliminating the pedestrian path to it. Now the layout space is starting to take shape.

It starts looking as though the layout must go up against the upper wall with a viewing area along the lower wall. Good! I've had lots of layouts with expansive tables needing pop-up holes and long poles to get to the trains. Not this time! I'm not getting any younger, so this layout will be along the upper wall, giving me good access without ducking under and crawling through.

But what about that pesky storage area at the upper left? I can't ignore that doorway no matter what. My design will allow me to hinge the upper level of the layout toward the back, drop down the lower level of the layout toward the front, and simply walk right through the layout into the storage closet. True, that plan presents a couple of design problems, but we'll work through those in later stages of the construction. That appealed to me so much that I actually designed three more walk-through or walk-in areas, which will allow me to comfortably reach virtually any and all parts of the layout. See? Old age, stiffness, and good planning will overcome youth and flexibility every time.

Now it was time to consider a scenic backdrop for the layout. So why do we need a scenery backdrop? Because it adds depth, beauty, and the feeling of endless space to an otherwise shallow layout area. Sure, being able to walk all the way around a layout is a good idea, but not in the limited space I have to work with. This room only totals about 300 square feet, and I would probably need at least another 200 square feet for walk around space if I wanted to have walking access to the back part of the layout as well. But I don't, so this scenery backdrop will visually expand the size of the room nicely. It simply makes the best use of the available space.

The box on page 14 shows and lists the tools and materials used for this phase of my room preparation and layout project. One of the most important tools is a set of combination countersink drill bits ranging in size from #6 to #12 screws. This particular set comes with an Allen wrench to adjust the length of the drill bit for the depth of the screws you will be using. If you break a bit, it can be easily replaced with another common drill bit of the proper size. These combo bits are indispensable for this scenic panel project. They will also be handy when we get into building the train table later.

Photo 1 shows a couple of other problems I had to deal with. The large glass block window didn't lend itself to any good scenery ideas, so I made the decision to eliminate it. The door to its right was already on the chopping block, so the window had to go. It couldn't really "go" anywhere, but it had to be covered up. If you have to deal with something like this, first make sure that you have eliminated any possible water leakage and that the window is secure. That's why I changed it to glass blocks when I first moved in. Also, block the inner face of the window with black foam core board, as seen in Photo 2. This material is a Styrofoam core between two sheets of heavy paper. I will eventually cover this blocked window with a scenic panel and I don't want solar heating to be going on between the panel and the glass block window. In addition, when viewed from the outside, the window seems to reveal only a darkened room on the other side. It just looks like any other boring darkened room to snoopy outsiders.

In Photo 3, I've added a horizontal wood support backing board at the middle of the window to help anchor the scenery panel to be added later. I've also done the same thing at two places across the abandoned pedestrian door just to the right. These support boards help form a backing for the Masonite panel to be added later. They also add some security to the closed off door. In addition, I took steps to secure the door shut and taped it to eliminate any possible drafts. I've also added a masking tape line to the wall all around the room showing where the bottom of the future scenic panel will meet the top of the future train table. Measure the nominal height for the scenic panel and cut the Masonite panels to that width. Sometimes you can even get a helpful employee at the lumberyard to cut all your Masonite sheets to the right width before hauling them home. If not, invest in a good carbide-tipped saw blade and a 7-1/4″ circular saw and do the cutting yourself. I've been blessed with some old wood paneling left on my walls by a previous owner, so attaching a 1/8″ thick tempered Masonite panel will require only some #6 x 1/2″ flat head Phillips wood screws. If you have gypsum board (drywall) to attach to, then use some #6 by 1″ fine thread drywall screws.

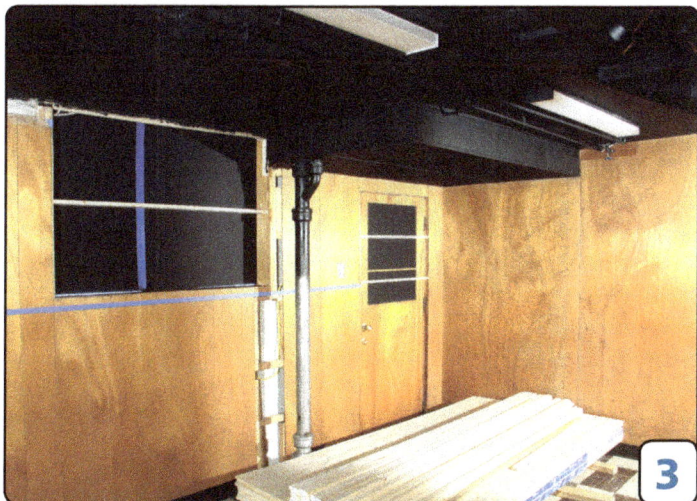

Photo 4 shows the first Masonite panel set in place, resting on a couple of scrap boards I've cut to a length that permits them to sort of jam up against the underside edge. That method held one end of the Masonite sheet in place while I anchored the other with a couple of wood screws.

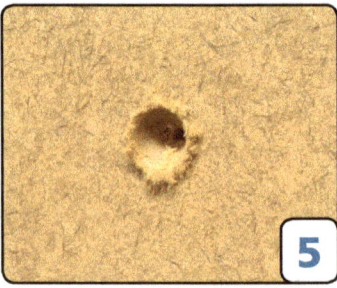

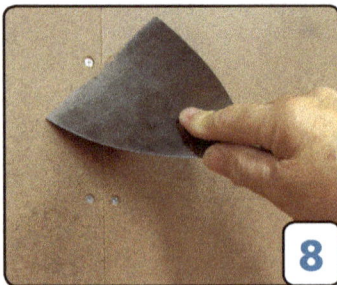

Once the screws are in and the joint has been scraped, equip a Dremel tool with a fiber cutting disk and cut a groove between the panels about half the thickness of the Masonite (about 1/16") deep all along the joint. Then with a clean, closely cut tip of a bottle of super thin CA glue, start at the top of the groove and control a steady drip of CA into the groove from the top to the bottom of the panel joint. That step will absolutely freeze the two panels together. Once the CA has taken its set, apply a thin coat of drywall joint compound over the joint, as shown in Photo 9. Sand its surface smooth when finished.

As you add Masonite panels, plan your panels and joints so most of a full sheet of Masonite ends up going completely through an interior corner as compared to ending in one. This practice is known as coving the corner and makes interior corners absolutely look like they vanished when you're done. Compare Photo 10 with Photo 3 and you will see what a coved corner does for you.

Once you are satisfied with the assembly, go over each of the screw heads on the Masonite with a thin coating of drywall joint compound and lightly sand all of them. The end result will be a completely smooth, ready-to-paint surface all around the backdrop.

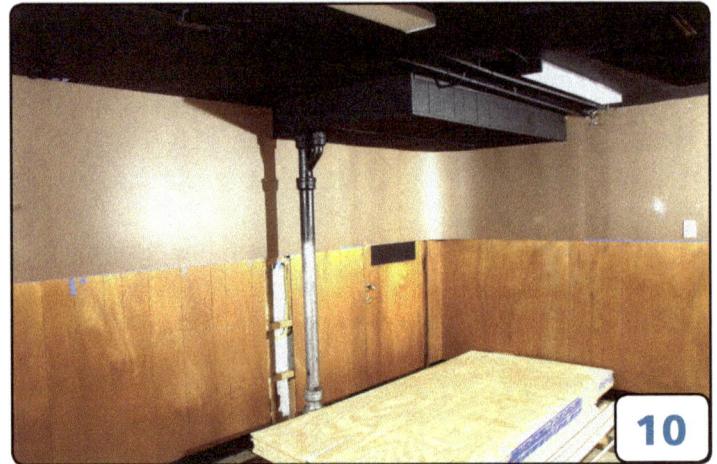

Drill deep enough for the screw head to set completely below the surface of the Masonite, as shown in Photos 5 and 6. Drive the screws with a small battery powered screwdriver with the release clutch set low enough to just get the screw in and to keep from overdriving the screw and stripping out the thin wood of the paneling behind the Masonite. After installing the screws, scrape the surface of the Masonite to remove any burrs from the countersink drill and also make sure the screw head is set deep enough. Using a small putty knife, pack some spackling compound into the screw holes, as shown in Photo 7. Don't be discouraged when the spackling compound settles as it dries. That dimple will be removed later with drywall joint compound.

Photo 8 shows a joint between two sheets of Masonite. Your goal now is to make these joints completely disappear. This is easier than you think if you follow these simple rules.

First, butt the edges of the Masonite panels tightly together. Then when drilling and attaching the sheets of Masonite, use twice as many screws, about every 3″ or 4″, along the edge joint as you would use within the sheet. Securing these panels against expansion and contraction is a real problem, but this time I will employ a trick I've learned from a commercial display builder.

Regardless of what else you may want to add to your scenic backdrop, you'll want to start by painting everything a sky blue color. There are probably a thousand colors representing blue sky. Keep in mind that the lighter the color, the more expansive the room will look. My first pick ended up being too light, so another coat of slightly bluer paint gave me what I wanted. Pick something out at a paint store and get a gallon of it in flat, cheap, latex paint. I think the gallon of Valspar 4000 I got at Lowe's was about $16. You will also need a 9″ roller and pan, a 2″ trim brush, some paper towels, and a wet sponge (keeps the floor clean). Cut first around the edges and then roll on the sky blue paint. You might need a couple of coats to cover the Masonite

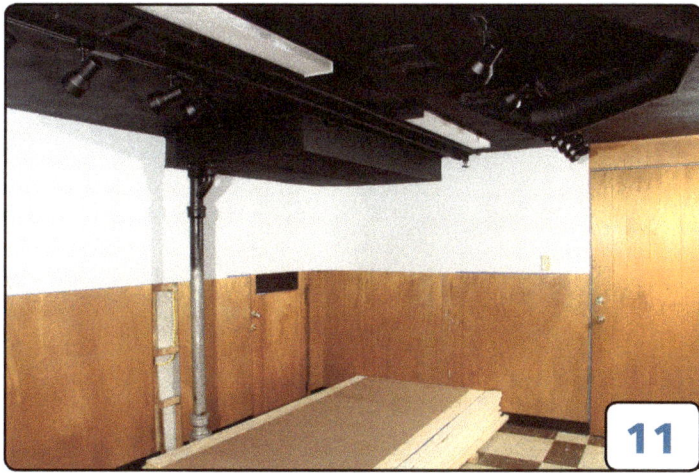

11

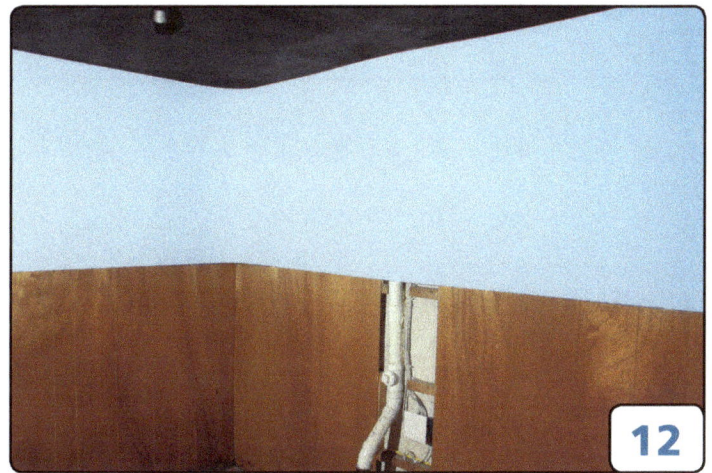

12

13

14

well. Look at Photo 11 and compare it to Photo 12. Also in Photo 12, see how well we hid the pipe bulging out of the wall. And for really dramatic results, look at how the small end of the room in Photo 13 vanished into what will be the expansive looking room in Photo 14.

It may take more than one coat of paint to get what you are looking for, but the end result will be worth every penny. Imagine how great your seamless sky will look above the future train table to be built below it. But there's still something missing. Where are the clouds?

Tools & Materials for Making Your Backdrop

- 3/8″ reversible drill
- #6 hex shank countersink drill bit
- Power screwdriver (preferably with adjustable release clutch)
- #6 x 1/2″ flat-head Phillips wood screws (if applying to paneled wall material)
- #6 x 1″ drywall screws (if applying to drywall material)
- 2″ and 5″ putty knives
- Spackling compound
- Drywall joint compound
- Sanding block
- Sandpaper (fine grit)
- Painter's blue masking tape
- Cyanoacrylate (CA) glue, super thin
- CA accelerator setting agent
- Paint roller pan
- 9″ paint roller handle
- 9″ roller sleeve (1/4″ nap for smooth surfaces)
- 2″ trim brush
- Flat latex paint (sky blue)

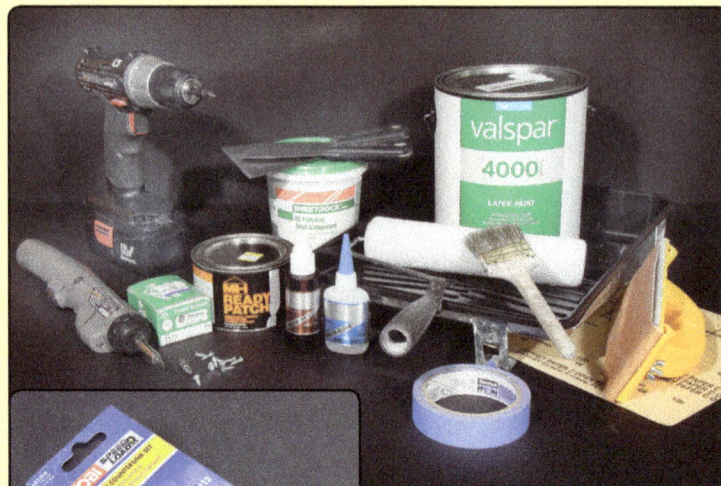

Basic Items Needed

Set of combination countersink drill bits

CHAPTER 3 - Credible Clouds

Creating believable clouds for a scenery backdrop has always been a chore for me. I am mechanically gifted but truly artistically challenged. That is to say, usually I can figure out a solution to most any mechanical problem, but when it comes to artistic solu-tions, I am just not in my element. Adding clouds to a scenery backdrop has been something I just can't do well enough for the results to be the least bit believable.

That being the case, for my previous layouts I've relied on preprinted scenery sheets such as those available in the Instant Horizons line from Walthers (www.walthers.com). These scenes have a printed blue sky complete with printed clouds. That's okay, but to my way of thinking, a printed blue sky is just not as believable as a painted blue sky. That is why I always have cut off and dis-carded the sky part of the backdrop sheet, spray glued the back of the remainder of the backdrop with 3M Super 77 spray glue, and applied it to a painted wall. To get the clouds, I've had to cut out each individual cloud from the printed blue sky,

spray glued it separately (yuk!), and stuck it on the painted blue sky. When it was done, I had what looked like...well, printed clouds stuck on blue sky, the classic lame mechanical solution to an artistic challenge.

I've tried making 3-D clouds out of all kinds of things, including cotton, furnace filters, fiberglass, and other materials, and sticking them on the blue sky. All that resulted in more lame solutions to the same artistic problem.

Then a friend introduced me to something called The Clouds, a series of stencils made by New London Industries, 8611 Norwich Avenue, San Antonio, Texas 78217. Finally, here was a mechanical solution to an artistic problem. Best of all, it was a solution that actually worked. These stencils along with several different cans of nothing more exotic than hardware store spray paint are shown in Photo 1. Holding these stencils up and spraying paint through them produced some of the best-looking clouds I've seen on train layout backdrops. And if a klutz like me can do it, anybody can.

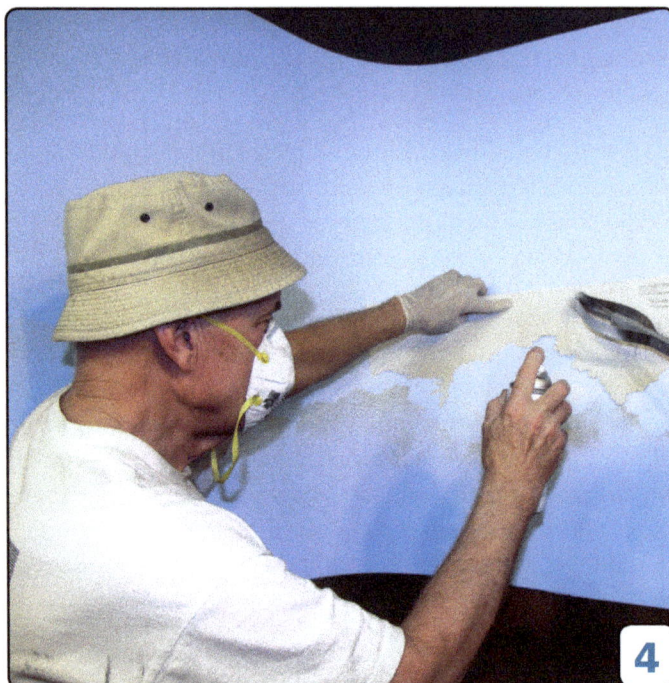

That doesn't happen automatically, of course. It takes practice, but the process does work. Buy some spray paint from your local hardware or home improvement store. Keep in mind that you want flat paint, not gloss. I found that paint labeled as primer is always flat and makes good "cloud" paint. The brand isn't important, but the color is. Get some pure white, some off white (very light cream color), and some very light gray color paint. I found that there are now artistic spray paints, such as the Valspar line, available at some big box stores, whose colors are flat and muted in intensity. These are excellent candidates for painting clouds.

Make yourself a test panel. Paint a piece of Masonite left over from the backdrop project covered in chapter two with the same sky blue paint used on that project. Using this as a practice piece, spray some of the flat white paint lightly onto the backdrop sample using one of the cloud stencils as a masking guide. Don't place the stencil directly on the backdrop sample as you do this because the cloud's resulting edge will be much too sharp. If you hold the stencil just 1/2″ or so away from the backdrop, the edge of the cloud will be just a little fuzzy like the edge of some real clouds. Practice this a few times, and you will see how you can get the sharply defined edges or soft edges you prefer.

Spend some time actually looking at real clouds. I know this seems like a silly piece of advice, but we never seem to spend time really studying clouds. If you spend some time actually looking at the real thing, you will notice that clouds come in several different types. Some are wistful things with very little defined shape, while others seem to have definite character with puffy shapes and "peaceful" plumps. Others have a threatening character with darker gray or even somewhat yellowish forms. Still others are downright edgy with darker threatening colors and an ominous character. My friend Bill Bramlage captured several different styles to show me how these stencils, along with the use of various different colors of spray paint, can capture all of these styles of clouds (Photo 2).

In general, clouds appear a little flat on the underside most of the time and also seem a little grayer in the middle. Another rule of thumb is that they appear to be along the edges darker on the bottom and whiter on the top. By shifting the same stencil over a little and using a different color of spray paint, you will see how you can duplicate these various styles of clouds and will learn how to apply the clouds you want to your customized backdrop.

You may want just some wistful, peaceful clouds of the type I wanted on my backdrop. In Photo 3, Bill shows how to hold the stencil out just a little from the backdrop and begin spraying the flat white color to outline the cloud. He will shift to a slightly darker color to do the middle of the cloud to achieve that white edge and somewhat darker body for the finished cloud.

With some stencils, you can do just the upper edge of the cloud (Photo 4). Don't be afraid to reuse the same stencil, shifted or rotated a bit, to continue some large cloud formations. Also experiment by using a different stencil over the top of a previous one to get the effect of clouds in front of other clouds.

Once you have used one stencil to form a cloud shape, switch to the next one to give the first cloud a little time to dry out before reusing that stencil right away. This will give each stencil time to dry out thoroughly as well as to sort of gently force you to use different stencils for different shapes to keep your overall cloud pattern more random.

Be sure to keep the paint can moving rapidly while you spray and also keep it quite a distance from the stencil to feather the edges of your clouds. Spray in slight, rapid strokes to keep the image looking less defined, too. There is a tendency to over control the finished cloud as you spray. You will see what I mean with just a little practice.

As you apply your clouds, keep in mind the height of future buildings or scenery features such as mountains or building fronts you might plan to use. Also remember that if you do some-thing you don't like, just get out the paint roller and the sky blue paint and simply roll out the entire cloud and then redo it.

If you want to have a storm front moving in behind your mountains, there is a natural tendency to do too much darkening on the cloud. It is easy to do! When that happens, just get out the stencils and spray some white back over the dark areas of the clouds to make them a little friendlier.

Photos 5 and 6 show the kind of clouds I wanted over most of my layout. Photo 7 depicts a dark storm front moving in behind the mountain that eventually will be built in one end of the layout. I may go back and lighten some of the darker clouds a little as the layout develops.

Resist the urge to fine-tune things until you have more of the layout built and more of the entire scene defined. You may find out that you don't have to do anything once you see the final form.

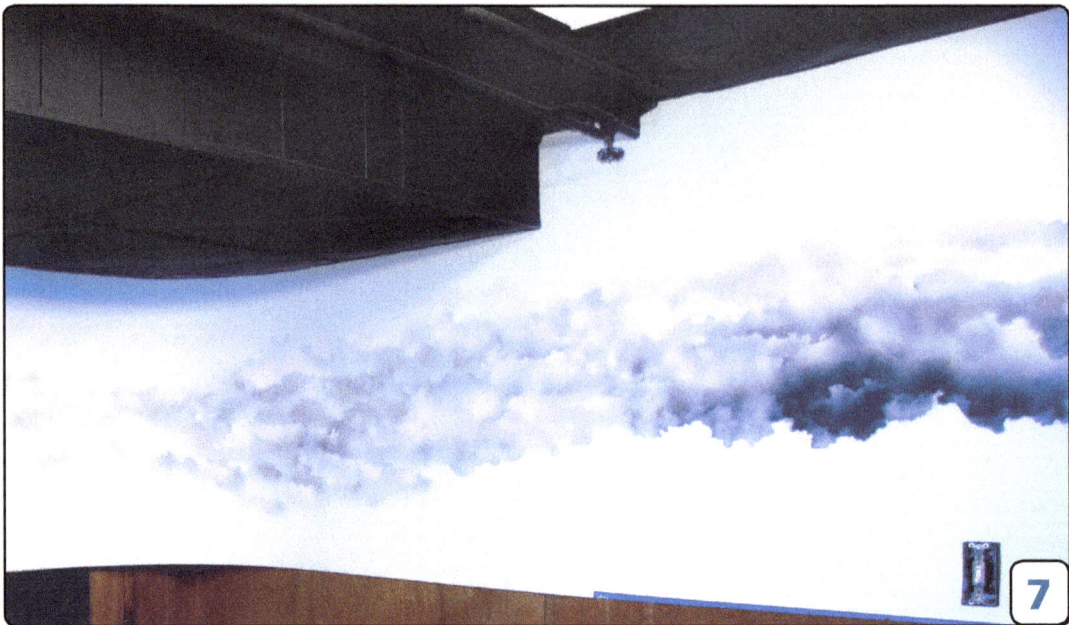

Don't get too carried away. My golden cloud rule is "less is more." You always can go in and add a small cloud here or there in the final outcome, but if you overpopulate the back-drop with too many clouds, it becomes very busy and less peaceful. New London Industries has other stencils, too. While I haven't used any of the others, they do look very interesting. You can go to Walthers website and look up New London Industries to see its full line of other stencil ideas.

I found these cloud stencils to be a great tool for a mechanical solution to achieve an artistic result. Even with a little of the frame-work showing in the photos, you can see that the clouds will have a dramatic effect on the layout. But I'm getting ahead of myself. The framework comes next 🚃

CHAPTER 4 - The Benchwork

There are many different types of model railroad benchwork, so what I will show here is the one kind that I have grown to know best. It isn't L-girder benchwork because I believe that while that type of benchwork is great for HO trains, it's not necessarily best for heavier O gauge applications.

For that reason, I've always believed in a simple table framework that more or less goes around the perimeter of the table on the outside edges as compared to leaving any part of the table hanging over the edge of the frame. That doesn't mean that the table surface is reduced to boring rectilinear shapes; it just means that more design thought goes into the framework shape than what might be considered usual.

I believe that the table surface needs to be no thicker than 1/2″ and that the surface needs to be supported by bracing (or table joists) that are nominally 16″ on center from one to the next. By keeping the joists closer together, the amount of vibration in the surface is greatly reduced. That means the trains will run quieter, which is a major consideration in O gauge.

I used to believe that a plywood surface of 1/2″ should then be covered by some sort of sound deadening material, such as Homasote, to further reduce the noise. There's nothing wrong with that, but in today's world, Homasote is getting harder and harder to find. If you can find it and desire to add an additional sound deadening surface, by all means go ahead and do so. I've found recently that it just isn't necessarily worth it for the money, material, and effort expended. I've seen quite a few good layouts that didn't use Homasote or any other second layer of sound deadening material and still had very little noise transfer. I've found that the best way to fight noise is with closely spaced table joists, such as the 16″ spacing that I now use.

Another fine way for reducing noise is the scenery itself. Ground cover, trees, highway paving material, cork roadbed for your track, layout structures, and stone ballast do more to keep a layout quiet than any other tricks you might consider. When I design a layout, I think in terms of 4′ x 8′ wooden frames supporting 4x8 sheets of plywood. Multiples of these frames simply continue to fill out the table until it gets to the fully desired table size. I first built these frames years and years ago from 2x4s, with 2x4 legs, until the price of 2x4s went sky high. Then I went to 1x4s with 2x2 legs and 1x2 braces. What I found was that the table was still strong enough to support any layout, and the cost was greatly reduced.

When I went shopping for 1x4s this time, I found that the price of good 1x4s was now off the charts, too. As an experiment, I decided to try 1x3s due to their greatly reduced cost. Surprise! The table is still as rigid as ever and very adequate for an O gauge train layout. An added benefit is that if you are installing grades from one layer of the layout to another, the distance between layers is somewhat less (due to the narrower 1x3s used in the frames), which makes for shorter and easier grades in your track plan.

As I mentioned above, a layout can be built to any shape by simply making as many standard 4′ x 8′ table frames as you need to fill the area, and then cut down the length and/or width of any frame needed to complete the outside edges of the layout space. This design technique quickly lends itself to a modular method of making and attaching frames. Make the first frame by cutting the frame members to the length needed and putting the frame members together with drywall screws (Photo 1). I use 2″ fine thread drywall screws to assemble the frame sides to the end boards and the interior joists.

Stanley makes plastic folding sawhorses that, when combined with a couple of sheets of your plywood for the table, provide a great workbench for building a train layout. In the photo, I'm putting together the first of many individual frames for the layout. Among the handy tools to have available are a couple of battery operated drills: one for drilling holes for the screws and another set up as a power screwdriver. It's possible to use one tool and to keep changing bits back and forth, but two makes the whole project much easier.

The drill bit you'll want to use for this project is shown in Photo 2 and is called a combination drill bit. It's the same one we used in chapter 2 to install the scenic panel material. You can get these bits from most any big box store. The combination bit drills the pilot hole and the countersink all at once. When you're driving screws right at the edge of soft pine 1x3s, pre-drilling the location for the screw eliminates any wood from splitting. Use a #6 bit as shown in the photo. It matches the #6 drywall screw size.

Another tool worth its weight in gold is a compound miter, like the one shown in Photo 3 below. This model #M2500RC3 purchased at Sears is a 10″ saw that is equipped with a laser beam to show exactly where the cut is going to be made. Current prices start for about $110. You will quickly find out how valuable it is when making cuts like some of the ones you see in the frame I am putting together.

Using a couple of the sheets of plywood as your worktable provides you with an excellent way to draw your cut plan right from the completed frame onto the plywood for its tabletop to be attached at a future date. While the finished frame is still clamped for the assembly process, simply draw around the perimeter for the cut plan on the plywood. Use a jigsaw, like the one shown in Photo 4, to cut the plywood top pieces for the frame.

Photo 5 shows my first completed frame sitting on the floor next to a bunch of 2x2 table legs. The nominal height for my table is 40″, but I cut a bunch of 8′ long 2x2s in half, making them 4′ long. The exact height isn't important just yet because I will cut off each leg to the exact height of the table frame once the frame is attached.

Use four or so legs to first get the table frame up to the approximate height you want your table to be. Clamp the legs into the corners of the frame. Once that is done, adjust the height of the frame on one of the back legs until you get that leg right at the nominal height you have selected for your table frame. Drill two holes through the frame member and into the leg. Drive the two 2″ screws through the frame member and into the leg.

Next, go to the opposite back corner of the frame and, using either a 3′ or a 5′ carpenter's level, adjust the frame on that second leg until the level tells you it is indeed level from the first leg to the second leg. Clamp the second leg into place and then attach the leg with two more 2″ screws.

Repeat this process from the back legs to the front legs and clamp each leg in place and then attach with two more screws making the frame exactly level in all directions. Repeat that process for all four legs and then take a look at the finished frame. If you think a leg is needed in the middle of the front or back frame member, go ahead and add that leg accordingly. When you are done, cut off the tops of all legs that protrude above the frame.

Make up a bunch of leg braces all at once by cutting through three or four 1x2s at the same time with the miter saw. I made one master brace about 20″ long with 45-degree cuts on both ends. Using this brace as a master pattern, I drew on the face of an 8′ 1x2. Doing it this way and reversing the pattern brace each time will get about five braces per 8′ 1x2. Cut out the braces and stack them for future use as needed. Keep in mind the saw will take out more than the pencil line, but the length of each brace is not that critical.

Everywhere you need a leg brace, begin by clamping the brace into the inside face of the frame member and attaching with one 1-1/4″ drywall screw through the side of the frame and into the side of the brace. Put the other end of the brace up against the 2x2 leg, drill through the end of the mitered brace into the leg, and attach with a 2″ drywall screw. Continue this process using two braces for each leg (Photo 6).

Once the first frame is in place, build the second frame and add it to the first frame (Photos 7 and 8). Begin by clamping the face of the second frame's end or side board right onto the face of the first frame, as shown in Photos 9 and 10. Attach by drilling through the two frames and screwing them together using some 1-1/4″ screws. From that joint, go down to the end of the second frame, level it up, and attach needed legs accordingly (Photo 11).

Photo 12 below shows my upper level and lower level frames all attached and in place for the far end of the layout that is beyond the closet door on the right.

Sometimes one leg can be used for more than one frame, such as in Photo 13. On my layout, the front level is lower than the back level. That means that the back of the lower level frames can all be attached to the legs already in place for the taller frames.

In Photo 14, the framework is continuing from the other side of the closet door and is working its way down to the other end of the basement.

Photo 15 shows a bag of plastic C-shaped clamps available from home improvement stores. These clamps come in various sizes (the ones shown are 1/2″). A wonderful use for these clamps is to attach them to the underside edges of the table frame members with only one screw at one end of the clamp. The other end of the clamp will now flex down easily, allowing you to add and neatly route wires when you get to that stage of your layout construction. The time to add these clamps is now, before you add the plywood for the tabletop. Photo 16 shows the clamps in place, even though I've added the tabletop over the frame since they were put on.

Another great benefit in using these plastic clamps is that any one of them can be replaced with a larger one if the number of wires exceeds your initial expectations. I bought some 3/4″, 1″, and 1-1/4″ clamps just in case that happens. A word to the wise: I bought the clamps shown in the photo from Home Depot at a cost of about 8 cents per clamp. I found the same exact sized plastic clamp in a national branded hardware store, but the price there was a whopping 44 cents per clamp. It pays to shop around!

Note in Photo 17 that sometimes you need to do some preliminary work on the lower levels before you add the second level framework. As you see in Photo 18 with the new framework added, getting to some of the track work would certainly be much more difficult. Always keep this in mind as it is very easy to get carried away with framework construction only to realize that you now need to disassemble a part of your frame to first do some track work that may not be easily accessed later.

Also note that I have painted the legs black and the tabletop and frame members brown as I go. The reason for that is to keep moisture (humidity) from getting into the finished framework and warping the wood. If you paint as you go, you won't cover up key pieces of the frame without painting it first. The brown is just my universal color for earth, which might later become exposed for some reason. Better for it to be earth brown than lumberyard yellow!

As you may have noticed in some of the photos, there are large gaping holes in the framework here and there. Those will be for my hinged panels that will allow me to access the hard to get to parts of the finished layout.

For those areas of your benchwork, keep reading!

CHAPTER 5 - Making Hinged Sections

1a

1b

Hinged sections on my layout are movable parts of the train table's surface that can easily be lifted up or dropped down, allowing you to gain access to interior parts of the layout or even to pass completely through it, if necessary. Photos 1a and 1b show a lift up and a drop down door allowing passage through the layout into a storage closet.

When done right, these sections, complete with track, layout structures, scenery, and wiring, can be repeatedly hinged open and then returned to their original exact location every time. Some of them may not even be used when the layout is completely finished, but they sure do come in handy during construction and landscaping, making those tasks much easier. I used to hinge only the track bridges, but that has obvious limitations. When I found out that it is indeed very easy to hinge whole sections of the layout, I learned how versatile this trick becomes when solving problems building layouts in confined spaces. In O gauge, confined spaces mean almost all spaces.

HINGE POINT MUST BE ABOVE THE TOP OF THE RAILS

Lift-Up Sections

Any portion of the layout table that opens by lifting up poses a singular problem. If there is track on the panel to be lifted up, the hinging point (hinge pin) must be just at or above the tops of the rails to keep the track from bending back against itself, as shown in the illustration. I've not been successful finding a cheap, ready made hinge that solves that requirement, so I devised a way to modify a simple hardware store 3″ leaf hinge that will do the trick (Photo 2).

2

You will need a bench mounted vise, a small hammer, and some hands on practice to do this. Turn the hinge upside down with the hinge pin side down (Photo 3). Using a sharp pointed felt tip marker, draw a line between the two mounting holes closest to the hinge pin as shown in the photo. Mount one end of the hinge in a vise with the line you drew aligned with the top of the jaws (Photo 4).

Using a hammer, slowly bend the portion of the hinge sticking up above the vise back against the top of the vise jaws (Photo 5). Make the bend right on the drawn line very sharp right on the top of the vise. Use the hammer to sharpen the bend precisely at that point. Be sure that the hinge pin ends up on the top of the bend, not underneath it.

Remove the bent side of the hinge from the vise and remount the remaining end of the hinge into the vise (Photo 6). Repeat the process (Photo 7). You should end up with a finished hinge shaped just like what you see in Photo 8.

You'll need two or three hinges identical to this for every lift up panel you plan to have on your layout. The finished height of the hinge pin is what's important in this process. In my case, I use cork roadbed and GarGraves or Ross track. Using a 3″ leaf hinge, the finished height of the hinge pins will end up just above the tops of any future track rails, allowing the panel to lift up and back without binding the ends of the track against themselves.

If you use any track and roadbed combination that makes the tops of your rails higher than what I used, be sure your hinge is the next size up from the example shown here. The end result of bending the hinge will need to put the hinge pin high enough to keep it at or above the height of the track and roadbed combination you use. Photo 9 shows what the hinged side of the lift up panel looks like.

Photo 10 shows an opening in the table that will accommodate a lift up panel I plan to make. Carefully measure the opening and then make a plywood panel to fit into it (Photo 11). Make the finished panel exactly 1/8″ narrower than the opening and plan on mounting it with a 1/16″ gap at the rear of the opening. Mount some scrap pieces of 1x2 on the top surface of the opening and trial fit the plywood panel into the opening, but don't install it yet (Photo 12). Just check the fit. Make sure you have a clear 1/8″ gap on the opening side of the panel with the other edge, the future hinged edge, flush against the opening.

On the underside of the panel, mount some lightweight, narrow 1x2 framing to keep the panel totally flat (Photo 13). Be sure the framing of the layout is flush with the hinged edge of the panel and 1/8″ in from the swinging edge of the panel. You will need that gap to allow the finished frame to swing up without rubbing the edge of the train table when the panel opens.

Return the finished lift up panel into the layout table opening, leaving the scrap wood still mounted on top of the panel. Be sure to keep the panel flush against the hinged side of the opening and add some temporary screws to the ends of the scrap wood to keep it flush with the tabletop.

Now is a good time to note future locations of track, scenery, and structures to help determine the locations of hinges you are about to install. Keep in mind that only the hinge pin portion of the odd shaped hinges you made will show above the rails in finished scenery so any roadways that make a grade crossing on the finished layout will also be at the height of the rails. Locating such roads right on the edge of the opening is a great way to disguise the hinges of the lift up panel where possible. That's obviously not the only way to hide the hinges; something so simple as a strategically placed bush will also do the trick.

The hinges you made are for swinging the finished panel up and down only. They might not be structurally able to support the finished weight of the panel when it is at rest in the opening. For this, you need to install some supports along the underside of the frame, both on the hinged side and on the swinging side of the panel.

With the scrap wood still installed on the top side of the panel, locate a load rest under the hinged side of the lift up panel (Photo 14). Note that when positioning the load rest, be sure to allow a slight gap, for example the thickness of the cardboard flap from a box of screws, between the bottom of the hinged panel frame and the load rest. This is necessary to prevent the hinges from binding when opening and closing the panel. Photo 15 shows the finished result.

When installing the load rest under the swinging side of the panel, attach some thin felt pads to the surface of the rest bar and position the load rest bar up against the bottom of the frame of the lift up panel (Photos 16 and 17).

When you have determined that the location of the hinges won't conflict with any track or scenery on the finished layout plan, install the hinges with the pin portion of the hinge exactly above the crack between the table and the lift up panel. Install the hinge leaf on the door side first. Then install the leaf of the hinge on the table making sure that the side of the hinge on the table is not pulling the panel down as you install it. If it is, put a shim under the hinge leaf on the table.

Now you can remove the scrap wood from the top of the panel and gingerly test the panel by slowly swinging it up and down a few times. Note how quietly the door closes on the felt pads. If you encounter any binding on the hinges, remove the screws on the table side of the hinges, slip a piece of thin cardboard between the hinge and the table, and then reattach. That will likely clear up any binding.

Then install something to keep the lift up panel open so you can work with it open and out of the way. I used a simple chain and hook method including a turnbuckle so I could adjust the chain for a specific opening (Photo 18).

Drop-Door Sections

If your layout has more than one level, you may need drop doors or even a combination of lift up and drop doors. To make a hinged drop door, start by carefully measuring the same way as done for a lift up section. Since any framework under a drop down panel would pose a host of problems, don't use a thin section of plywood to fill the opening like for the lift up section. Instead, I like to use Aspen shelving wood, available from home improvement centers. Aspen is a smooth white wood that is glued edge to edge in such a way as to virtually eliminate any warping.

As before, make the finished panel exactly 1/8″ narrower than the opening with a 1/16″ gap at the back of the opening. Mount some scrap pieces of 1x2 onto the top surface of the Aspen panel and trial fit it into the opening (Photo 19). Make sure you have a clear 1/8″ gap on the swinging side of the panel with the future hinged edge flush against the opening. Fasten the scrap wood ends to the tabletop keeping the hinged edge flush with the opening and the 1/8″ gap on the swinging side of the panel.

As anyone who knows me will likely tell you, I believe that piano hinges are a wonderful thing. They solve all kinds of problems. They are available from hardware stores in various lengths up to 3′ or 4′ long and can be cut with a hacksaw to any length needed. Photo 20 shows a cut hinge being installed onto the underside of the swinging panel and the layout table frame opening. The nice thing about a piano hinge is that it is structurally strong enough to support the drop down panel without any further framing needed.

To keep the swinging side of the drop door latched up, a simple dead bolt, like for screen doors, will do. But if you plan on using the drop door frequently, you'll need something more elaborate. Photo 21 shows what is called a transom catch. Many hardware stores still carry them, but if you can't find these catches near you, go to www.houseofantiquehardware.com. There you will find examples of all kinds of transom catches complete with striker plates. The finish isn't important since you will not see the catches when everything is closed. Buy the cheapest ones that will do the trick.

I used these on my drop doors with an added operating mechanism I've devised to make opening and closing the doors very dependable and easy. Photo 22 shows two transom catches installed on the underside of the drop door, complete with my cable system joining them together so both can be operated simultaneously with the movement of the opening lever. Two transom catches per door are necessary however deep or shallow the door might be to ensure that the whole panel will remain flat when closed and encountering the weight of the trains above them.

The cable is standard hardware store cable of 1/16″ or .063″ diameter mounted through some 5/32″ diameter holes drilled into the transom catch pull levers. The cable is quite easily soldered with rosin core solder used for electrical connections to ensure that the cable connections will stay connected. No additional flux is needed beyond what is already in the rosin core solder.

Photo 23 shows plastic wheels that guide the cables mounted into the board with threaded bolts that match the diameters of the holes in the wheels. Drill the holes into the board with a diameter slightly smaller than the bolt threads and secure the bolt with CA glue once it is screwed in. The wheels are standard replacement wheels for sliding screen doors, also available at hardware stores. The metal bar, wooden knob, return spring, and washers can also be found at the hardware store. Once the cable is routed and secured with solder, also secure the cable with T-25 staples acting as wire guides. It's a very simple but elegant solution.

Photo 24 shows the striker plates for the two transom catches mounted in the table frame. Take care of this before installing any track. Install the striker plates flat onto the wooden frame of the table opening. Locate it by drawing a line on the underside of the transom catch right where the bolt of the catch will contact the frame wood of the table. This will serve as a guide where you will mount the striker plates.

If you have left enough gap between the drop door and the frame, it won't be necessary to recess the striker plates into the wood of the frame. If not, you'll need to clear out a space for the thickness of the striker plates using a wood router or a router attachment for a motor tool. If a striker plate isn't flat on the transom catch you have, flatten it out on the top of a vise or steel plate using a hammer.

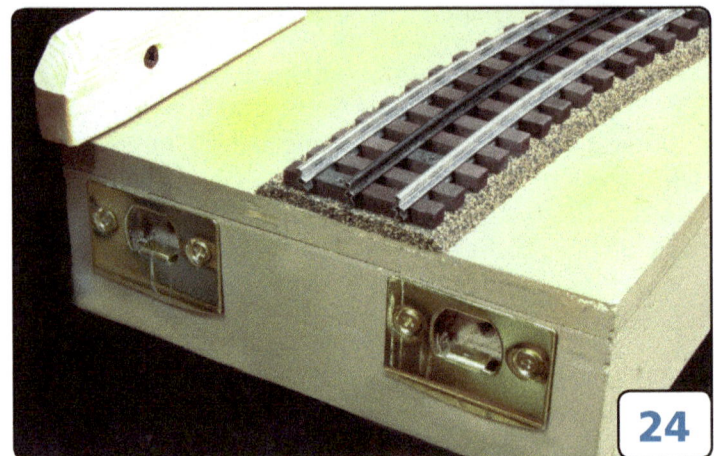

Shim the actual location of the transom catches under the underside of the drop door to allow the catch bolt to extend into where the striker plate will be. Mark the exact location where the catch bolt will contact the table fame. Trace the location needed for the striker plates to be for the catch bolt to contact the striker plate correctly. When you have traced the opening of the striker plate on the table's frame, drill a relief hole into the wood of the frame with a 7/8″ spade bit to allow the catch bolt to extend through the striker plate. Mount the striker plates on the frame of the table and shim the transom catches until there will be an even, flat surface between the top of the door and the tabletop.

Check your final assembly to ensure the drop door closes and latches back to the exact same location every time. Shim or adjust where necessary to make the drop door come back to the same level as the table surface. Finally, install a stop block to prevent the drop door from coming up past the top of the train table when closing.

Keep in mind that transom catches were never designed to close like a door. In fact, you must hold the opening lever open while you lift the drop door up to the closed position and then let it latch. You cannot close it like a door by simply lifting it up and forcing it to latch.

Once you have installed all your drop down and lift up sections, paint them and let them thoroughly season to the humidity of your train layout location and then check again for fit. It is important to let the installation conform to the humidity levels it will be in for a while before doing any further work on the layout. 🚃

CHAPTER 6 - Laying Roadbed and Track

We are truly blessed in O gauge with having several different brands of track and roadbed to choose from for building our layouts. Each brand has its strong and not-so-strong points, and the final selection really is a matter of personal preference. For the layout I'm building, my choice is to use GarGraves track, Ross Custom Switches, and Ross preformed sectional track. These two brands of track and switches fit together seamlessly and are easy to use.

GarGraves flexible track is cheaper per foot over long distances, but the formed curves may not be the best thing to use when you go over hinged or movable sections of benchwork. When forming curves with GarGraves track, the rails making up the curves remain under some spring tension after forming and being attached to the roadbed and

tend to spring back toward straight if they are anywhere in the curve to accommodate a hinged panel joint. The same is not true of preformed curves in Ross sectional track. For this reason, I switch back and forth from GarGraves to Ross track if I see that a curve will fall on a needed track cut.

As a rule, I lay my track on Midwest Products cork roadbed. This roadbed is split lengthwise so, when properly positioned, each half joins right on the centerline of the track. The outer edges of the cork roadbed strip are cut on an angle to represent the ballast shoulders of the track. For us 3-railers, this is ideal because it allows us to scribe a centerline where we want the track to go and then lay the cork roadbed halves against that line.

First you'll want to transfer your track plan from your drawing to the tabletop using single pencil lines where you want track to go (Photo 1). Now locate the general locations of accessories and trackside structures (Photo 2). Even if you have made a detailed plan on paper, there's no better reality check than positioning them for the real thing. You'll almost always see minor or even major location changes that you'll want to make before you put down any roadbed and track. Some rail cutting might even need to be done on certain rails or switches to accommodate your track plan. This is the time to prove out the feasibility of your track plan before you start laying roadbed and cutting up track and switches.

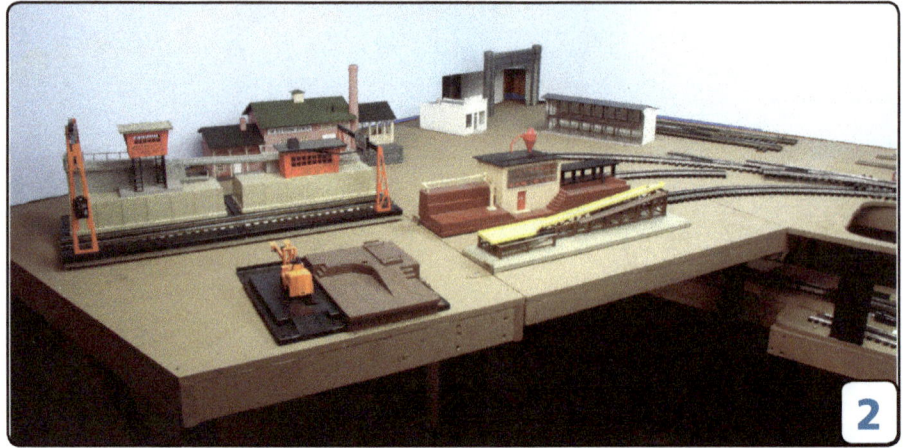

Once you are certain that you can make a viable layout track plan after making the necessary cuts and adjustments to switches plus scenery and structures, then and only then should you proceed with laying the cork roadbed. When you are sure that you're ready, separate the cork halves along the split line (Photo 3). Turn the cork halves around so all the slanted edges are upside down and away from you.

Place them on a covering of newspaper to protect your work surface from any glue overspray.

Using a can of 3M Super 77 spray glue, coat the exposed underside of the cork halves until the cork strips appear to be evenly coated with the glue (Photo 4). The effect you want to achieve is like spray painting a large piece of material using long even strokes.

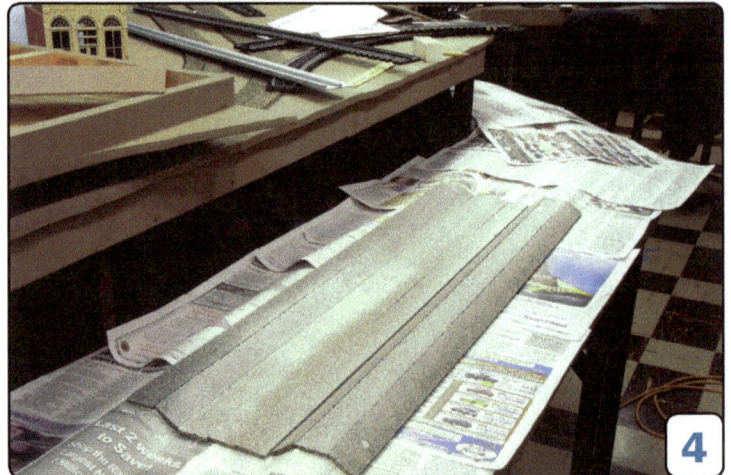

Lay the cork strips against the pencil line right over any hinged section joints and staple them in place (Photo 5). I use an Arrow T-33 staple gun that shoots curved-top staples through the cork, leaving a curved top to grab and pull out after the glue has set.

Cork used as a roadbed covers up a world of sins. You will always have slightly uneven tabletop material between one plywood layer and the next and possibly a slightly uneven layer at hinged panel joints (Photo 6). Not to worry! Cork can be easily leveled with a plane on an uneven hump at the joint line. In Photo 7, I am using a carpenter's jackplane to do this. If such a tool is unavailable, you can also use a Stanley surform file.

Track is laid using #4 flat head wood screws and also a combination drill bit and countersink (Photo 8). Note that ties have been spaced so the benchwork joint line goes right between the track ties. The ties on either side of the joint will get two holes each since this is a hard point where the rails must be kept perfectly in line on both sides of the cut.

When laying track through curves, pre-bend the Gar-Graves track sections to approximate the shape of the curve (Photo 9).

On the curves, note that the ends of the track section will no longer be even (Photo 10).

Cut off the two extended rails using a motor tool and fiber cutting discs (Photo 11). When the track section is placed down on the cork, drill and attach a screw about every 4″ or so through the curve. I alternate sides of the center rail for each screw.

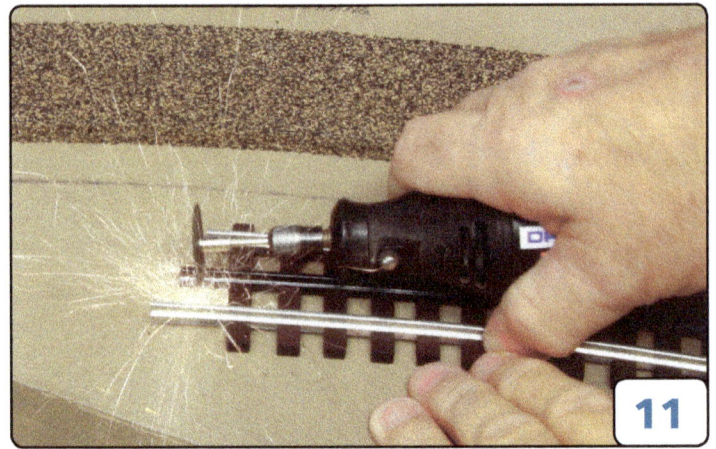

When you get to the uneven end of the track, resist the urge to cut the ends of the rail off evenly. Using a block of wood and a small hammer, tap each of the three rails back through the ties so that they totally close the previous track joint (Photo 12). Then cut off the ends to make a nice square track cut.

You may also note that the curve is not totally smooth throughout its length. This is easily corrected by noting where the slight kink in the track is, driving track screws at roughly the beginning and the end of the kinked area, and then removing any screws between the two you just put in. Then gently tap on the edges of the ties right at the middle between the two screws you just added. Use a piece of scrap wood along with a small hammer (Photo 13). You will be amazed at how smoothly and perfectly you can make the curve.

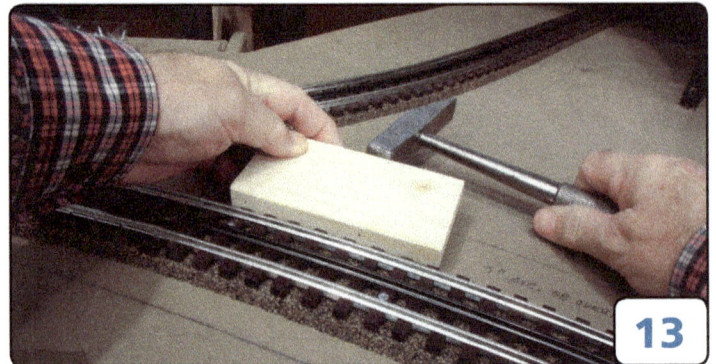

When all the track has been laid, smoothed out, and closed track joints completed, this is the time to open the track at the benchwork joints previously covered. Look closely at Photo 14, and you will see that you will end up with a slanted cut line in the rail, slanted either one way or the other depending on how you hold the motor tool and cutting disc. For a raised panel, if you are cutting on the hinged side of the panel, cut so that the slant will lean toward the hinged section when it is lifted. On the opposite edge of the panel, cut so that the track cut will lean away from the panel. Using this method will prevent the track from binding against the table side of the track when raising and lowering the hinged section.

Don't be bashful about cutting switches. Just make sure the frog of the switch or any moving rails on the switch don't end up on the cut line when you are positioning track and switches (Photo 15). Also, don't forget to pad any switch machine or switch track ties by adding some cork where it is needed (Photo 16). I plan to add a switch lantern to the opposite side of the switch machine later, so the ties that stick out on that side are also padded.

Here's a nice touch. On real railroads, mainline tracks are almost always maintained better than sidings. Why should things not be this way on your railroad, too? When you have a track switch leading off the main line to an old spur siding, don't use any cork roadbed where that siding track will be (Photo 17). Just screw that siding track directly to the table. The result when the ballast is added will be a distinct height difference between the mainline tracks and the siding. Sure, that means the switch may need to be bent sideways a little, but that is how it looks on the real railroads. It will show a subtle grade change as the siding track settles into a lower roadbed. Also, you can make that siding track look all kinked and misshapen from heat and the lack of maintenance by intentionally kinking up the siding track a little. The end effect is marvelous.

Be sure when you are laying track and switches to make the track joint as closed up as possible before you go to the next section of track (Photo 18). Eliminating little gaps will result in a much smoother main line and a notice-able difference in a lack of noise as your train rolls through the area. Also note how easily the screw head goes away with a touch of flat black paint. If the actual height of the rail at the joint is slightly different, use a flat file on the high rail surface. That makes for a smooth-running train as well.

Check things as you go when laying track over butted end joints. Photos 19 and 20 show how important this becomes on hinged drop sections. Also, make sure that you have waited some period of time between building your benchwork and laying track when dealing with movable sections of bench-work. The wood needs to cure out at residential temperature and humidity before you proceed with laying track.

Now I need to figure out how my trains are going to go through the wall into my furnace room, make it around the furnace, and then get back into the viewing room. I also need to figure out how I'm going to do that while still leaving the furnace available for maintenance when needed. That may be a tall order, but I that I'll show you how to do that in the next chapter. 🚃

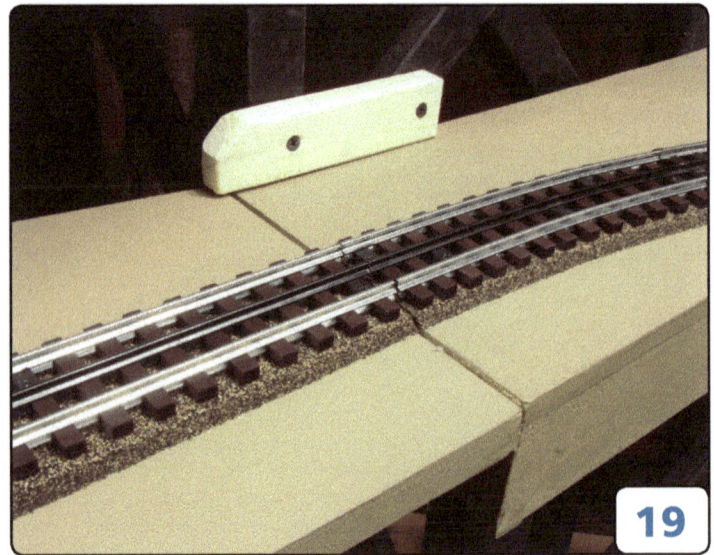

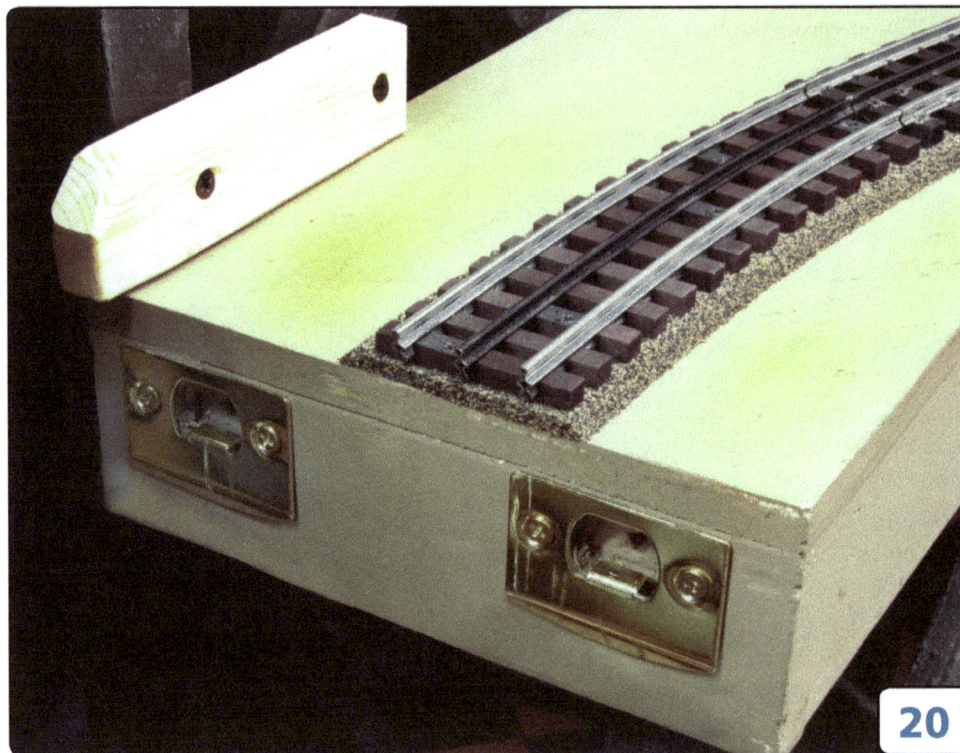

Track & Materials Jim Used on the Layout

- GarGraves Trackage Corporation - www.gargraves.com
- Ross Sectional Track - rossswitches.com
- Midwest Cork Products - midwestproducts.com
- 3M Super 77 spray glue
- Arrow T-33 gun and staples
- #4 flat head 1" wood screws

CHAPTER 7 - Run Around the Furnace

I know you've planned at least one railroad pike in your life and bemoaned the amount of space your home's furnace or central air system takes up right where you want to build your layout. There it is, an immovable roadblock filling your otherwise valuable layout space.

In my house, the furnace is on the opposite side of a block wall running along one side of the layout room. That meant making that end of the layout room nothing but a turnaround area so I could send trains in the opposite direction. If I want to use O72 turns, this means losing at least 3-1/2' to 4' of valuable layout space just to turn the trains. This space could otherwise be used for yards, operating equipment, and lots of good scenery. So how else could I turn the trains around? How about just punching through the wall and turning them somewhere in the next room?

Over in the furnace room, on the other side of the block wall, space is lavishly wasted on the furnace, the air filter, the central AC unit, and various vent pipes making their way to the exterior basement wall. That space can't really be used for any other purpose aside from these systems. Or can it?

Photo 1 shows the layout side of the block wall. Photo 2 shows the furnace room side of that same wall along with a couple of nice big holes I made right through the wall using a "wet" concrete saw. What a mess! If you have to do this, be prepared for an exhausting job when you rent one of these saws or hire someone who does this sort of work for a living, if you can. One hole is at the height of the lower level train circuit on my future layout, and the other is at the upper train level height.

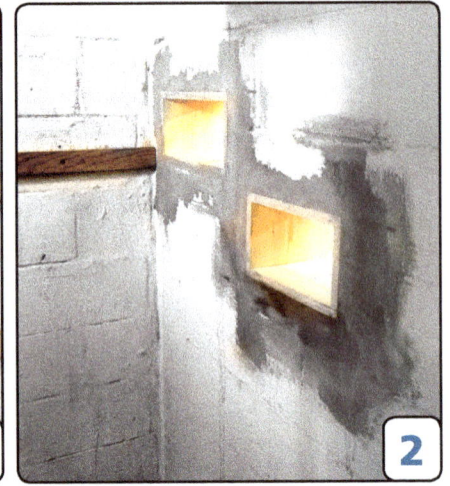

I made the holes much larger than needed. There is no such thing as fine tuning those holes once they are made. Make them much bigger than you think you'll need. I made two wooden frames at the right opening size for the trains and then shimmed these wooden frame boxes into the rough holes through the wall. I filled the gaps, some were huge and ugly, with concrete patching compound. A fresh coat of paint on the walls hides all the ugly mistakes (Photo 3). In chapter 1 you can see the furnace area of my basement before I started this project.

My general plan was to make as many hinged shelves along the wall as I needed to support the upper and lower levels of track as they entered the room and ran along the back wall of the basement right behind the furnace. The plan was for all of these shelves to hinge back out of the way when any furnace maintenance was needed.

Most exterior basement walls are poured concrete or concrete block. To smoothly and accurately hinge shelf pieces to the walls, you need to attach 2x2 wooden furring strips along the wall at the right height for the track shelf. Your wall will undoubtedly be uneven, so plan to attach the 2x2 furring strip to the wall with large steel spacer washers placed as needed between the board and the wall where you plan to drill holes for the concrete screws. That way the 2x2 won't conform to the uneven wall when installed.

Tapcon makes a nice flat head, countersunk 3/16″ diameter by 2-1/2″ long self tapping concrete screw. These come packaged with a concrete drill bit in each box. If possible, get access to a hammer drill to make this job much easier. It doesn't have to be a huge one, just something large enough so it has a slight hammering action as you drill into the concrete wall.

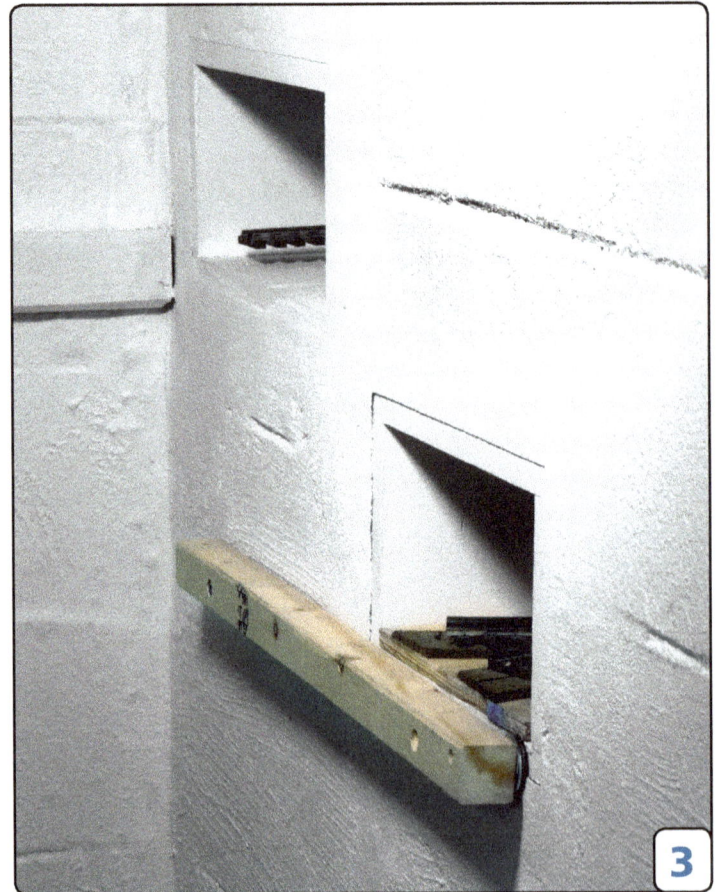

You may opt to attach a 1x4 to the wall first and then attach the 2x2 to the 1x4. The reasoning here is that the 1x4 is much easier to attach to the concrete than the 2x2. The 2x2 may then be easily and accurately adjusted on the face of the 1x4 with simple 2-1/4″ drywall screws. If you opt to do this, use shorter Tapcon screws for the 1x4 to be attached to the wall. Only 1-1/2″ long screws will be needed even if you have a few shim washers. The end result is that the 2x2 must be evenly flat on the wall so a piano hinge can be attached to it.

Photo 4 shows an odd shaped 1/2″ plywood surface with 1x2 framing being built. This will be the first of many folding surfaces to be installed that will hinge onto the 2x2 furring strips. Photo 5 shows the finished shelf painted black and hinged onto the furring strip with a 1-1/2″ piano hinge, which is shown along the underside of the 2x2 furring strip and the underside of the odd shaped shelf.

Piano hinges come in 48″ lengths at your hardware store and can be cut to any length with a fine tooth hacksaw. The beauty of a piano hinge is that the longer it is, the stronger it is. If you place one along any board, it will hinge that board in any direction you need but will hold the board within a few thousandths of its mounted position all along the hinge. That's great for keeping track lined up perfectly.

Photo 6 shows the same shelf swung up in position and being supported by a couple of temporary legs. Just to the right of the shelf in the train room, there is a wye track peeking through the hole in the wall, and some furring strips are already installed and painted along the back wall.

Photo 7 shows three more shelves: two hinged along the back wall, and one hinged along the wall with the upper hole.

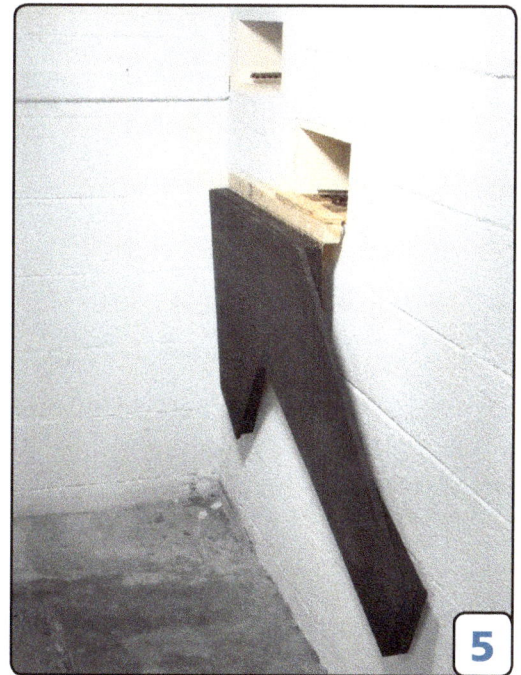

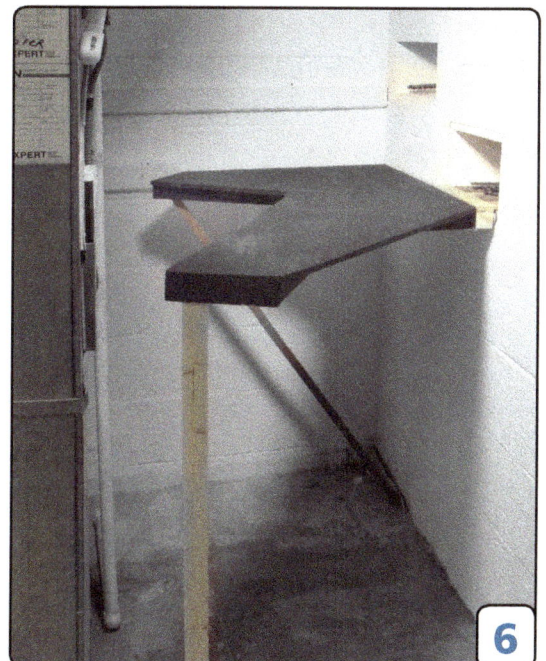

Photo 8 shows one of these panels hinged down and in place and resting on a leg, which is hinged onto the underside of the folding shelf with a small butt hinge. Photo 9 depicts both upper shelves hinged down and in place. Note the placement of the piano hinges so that any upper shelf must hinge up, and lower shelves must hinge down.

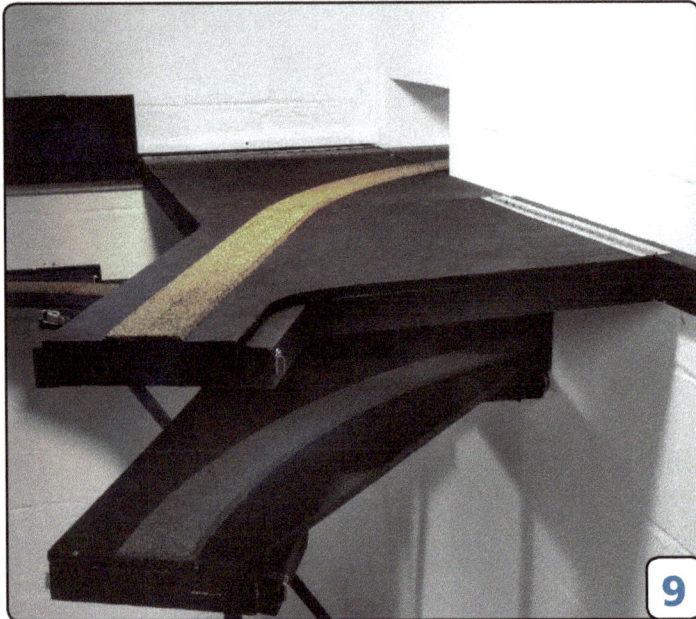

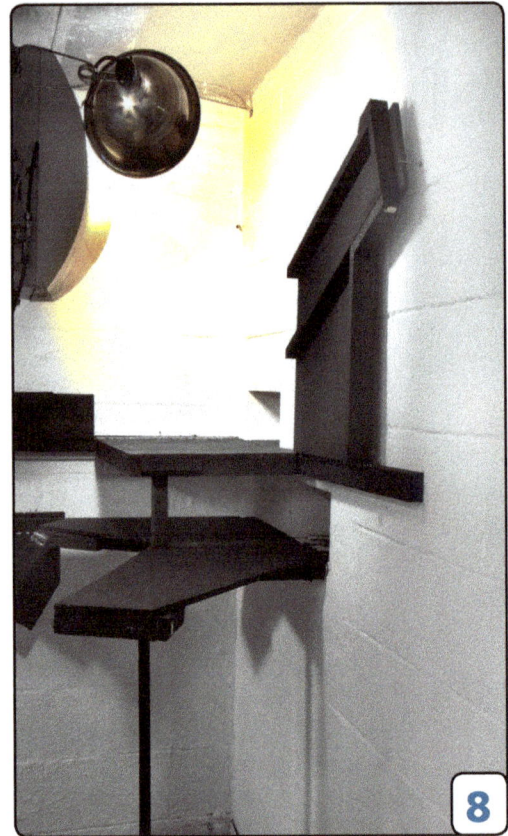

Along the back wall are the two track levels. I had a little problem with the vent for the water heater, which made me add another hinged piece to allow the upper shelf to hinge up and clear under the vent pipe (Photo 10).

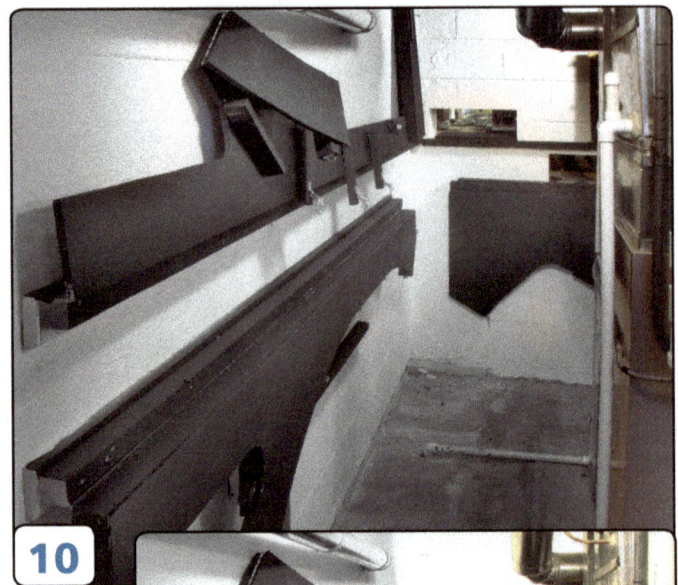

The lower track level has two sets of legs hinged up and clinging to the bottom of the shelf when it is folded down against the wall. This is a relatively simple process of making the legs as an assembly and then hinging the finished leg assembly to the underside of the lower shelf with piano hinges cut to fit the width of the leg set. Photo 11 shows this clearly. Here, the lower shelf is hinged up with both leg assemblies hinged down to support the running shelf.

There is an added advantage to doing things this way. The upper shelf can now hinge down, and simple 1x2 support legs can be hinged to the underside of the upper shelf, allowing it to rest on the now solid lower shelf (Photo 12). Anytime I needed to hinge a simple 1x2 brace, I used a small 1″ butt hinge. Note that the addition of simple hardware store suitcase snaps can be added everywhere needed to securely latch the whole assembly together. It is quite remarkable how solid the whole assembly becomes when these snaps are closed.

Photo 13 shows the key assembly to the whole project. The removable turnaround section is a full half circle of track that, in my case, can be as small as an O72 curve. My furnace and ducts fit nicely and snugly within that track circle. The assembly needs to be two separate levels of track, which means that I cut plywood sections for both layers.

Since plywood comes only in 4′ widths, I needed to make the half circle in two separate sections of a quarter circle each. I have found over the years that absolutely everything made will fit inside of an O72 running board that is 6-3/8″ wide. That means that the track centerline is on a 36″ radius, and the inner and outer edges of the circular plywood will Since plywood comes only in 4′ widths, I needed to make the half circle in two separate sections of a quarter circle each. I have found over the years that absolutely everything made will fit inside of an O72 running board that is 6-3/8″ wide. That means that the track centerline is on a 36″ radius, and the inner and outer edges of the circular plywood will end. Three additional support pieces are attached and evenly spaced between each end of the quarter circle.

Each of the two quarter circles are supported by six 1x2 legs. They have to be straight and free of defects since their stability is very important. There are two places evenly spaced between the legs where full height legs are not needed, but the upper and lower levels must still be connected to make the assembly rigid. The length of these connectors, as well as the length of the legs, depends on the application and layout elevation. A 1x2 cross brace between each pair of legs about halfway up will stabilize the leg sets. I connected the two finished curve assemblies together to make a full half curve by connecting a piece of plywood between the legs at two locations on each side near the top of the assembly at the double leg set.

I have allowed for the height of all the 1x2 legs and 1x2 platform connectors to be able to support a simple and effective guard wall in the event of any derailment. That nifty 1/8″x 2-3/8″ high Masonite strip makes a very rigid wall, which keeps all those articulated engines and 21″ passenger cars off the floor. The Masonite strips can be easily connected to the insides of the 1x2s using #4 x 3/4″ flat head screws

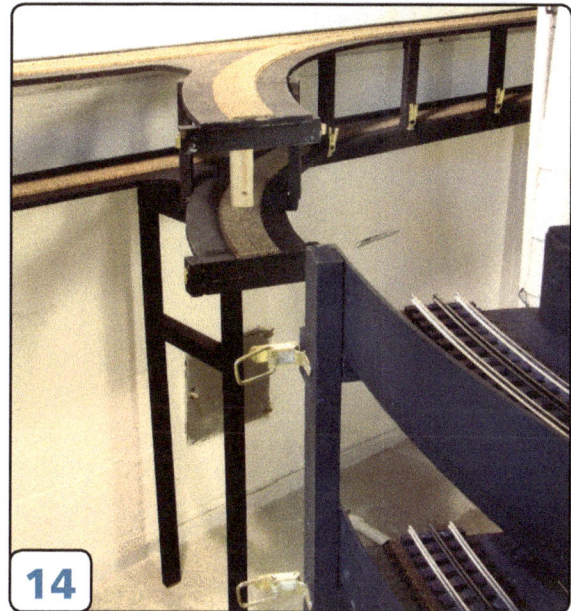

fastened by going from the inside of the walls through to the 1x2s. I used my hex shank countersink drill bit to allow the screw to set smoothly in the wall.

There is also a 1x2 landing attached to the ends of the semicircle at each track level. These will serve as the support base for each of the four hinged track shelves where they will mate up to the turnaround assembly (Photo 14).

The finished turnaround assembly with roadbed and track is shown in Photo 15.

The suitcase snap hardware snugly and securely connects the double deck turnaround to the track running boards that hinge on the walls (Photo 16).

The final result is a very firm and secure turnaround on both levels that can be removed or hinged back out of the way to allow for routine maintenance on the furnace, air conditioner, or humidifier in just minutes.

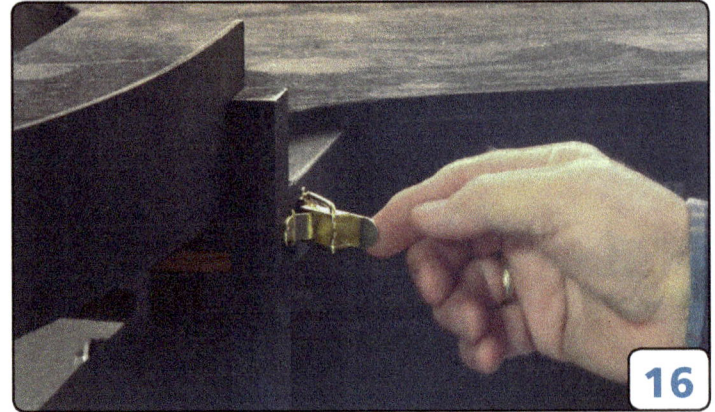

So let's take the grand tour! In Photo 17 a mixed freight train travels between two rows of buildings that mask the hole in the wall. The train immediately passes through the hole in the wall and travels down the back wall behind the furnace (Photo 18). The train starts around the turnaround and heads back to the same hole in the wall en route to the layout on the other side (Photos 19 and 20).

Chapter 7

Building A Layout by Jim Barrett

In Photo 21 the freight reenters the layout and proceeds on its way through the industrial area. Photo 22 shows why it was in such a hurry. The train was being pursued by "the cat that ate the industrial area" played by Tigger, my house cat who loves to chase trains through holes in basement walls.

Using this furnace turnaround allows me to go from cursing the furnace area to embracing it as a functional part of my layout. But what about the other end of the layout? We're going to need to turn the train there, too. Employing another little scenery trick, I will not only turn the trains but also let them move from one level to another.

Watch a video of this "Run Around the Furnace" Project ogaugerr.com/jim/

CHAPTER 8 - A Removable River Gorge

I have shown you how I found a way to turn trains around by going through a wall into the next room and thereby saving valuable layout space. To turn the trains on the other end of the layout, I'll show you another trick I've come up with to solve the space problem, as well as to create a way for trains to travel from one level to another.

At first I thought I'd just make a big mountain on the other end of the layout so all the tracks making the turn-around would simply go inside of it and come out at the back going the other way. With influence from some great layout builders, such as Bob Bartizek in southern Ohio and Bill Thompson in southern California, I decided to improve on the basic hidden turnaround in a mountain idea and actually add a helix to go from the lower level of the layout to the upper level. That means you must have one O72 or greater turnaround for each level plus another O72 or greater climbing grade to connect the two levels.

Bob had a wonderful trestle on his layout, and Bill had a great way of using three trestles and a deep river gorge all in the same area. I liked that, but I wanted my gorge to be huge. In keeping with my design goal of never having to duck under or climb over any part of the layout to get to all the areas I would have to get to, I had to come up with a trick of my own to incorporate all of that plus include a hidden helix to allow trains to change levels.

Here's my solution. It is so easy! I can think of any number of uses for it near the ends of any layout. In Photo 1, hinged sections can gain you access to many areas both over and under the layout surfaces. But for what I wanted to do, hinged sections just couldn't be large enough to be practical.

In Photo 2, what I did was to build the layout with a gaping hole right on the front edge of the end of the layout where the trains needed to turn around. The upper level cork roadbed is making its turn except for in the gaping hole area, and the lower level is making its sweeping turn through the gaping hole but at a much greater radius than used on the upper level. At the far right of the lower level turn you will see a switch right near the right wall. That is where the helix grade will begin climbing from right to left inside the mountain at the back of the layout. It will come out of the mountain through a future tunnel portal that eventually will be on the left side of the photo. Then, dramatically, it will continue its climb, crossing a future trestle between the two upper and lower level trestles, now represented by the gaping hole in the layout. On the right side of the photo in the back, it climbs on up and joins onto the upper level through another switch, not visible in the back of the photo.

The trouble is that this solution hides not only one but two switches inside the mountain along with other tricks like a grade track on a curve. These things are problematic. How is all this going to be easily accessible without ducking under or climbing over to get to potential problems?

How about a nice removable valley on rollers complete with breathtaking trestles! In Photo 3, I'm using a trick that dressmakers use but on a scale befitting O gauge train layouts. Using a wonderful product called foam core board, some masking tape, and a utility knife, I made a perfect fitting pattern, or template, for my future roll around module.

Foam core board comes in many colors and sizes and is available from art supply stores. I have found it to be a layout maker's best friend, not only for this project but for many more uses. I like to use the computer and digital design tools, but sometimes, with all the odd angles this valley will turn out to have, nothing works better than a full size pattern cut to fit exactly. This basic keystone shaped design for the roll around module will lend itself well to making it fit snugly and exactly with the gaping hole in the layout.

Photo 4 shows the template on a piece of 1/2″ B/C grade plywood, where I will trace the cut lines onto the plywood. I will make two of these odd shapes: one for the floor of the valley and one for the bottom of the roll around module.

Photo 5 shows the 1x3 frame being built onto the bottom level of the roll around module.

Photo 6 shows the support legs being attached at all the critical places with drywall screws through the 1x3 frame into the 1x3 connector legs.

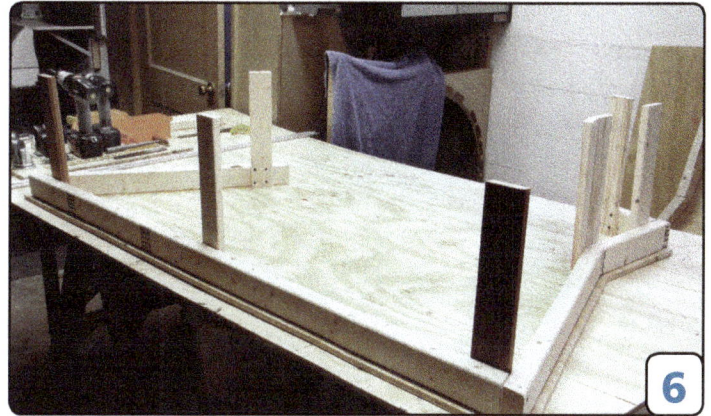

In Photo 7, the mirrored image assembly for the valley floor is being trial fitted onto the legs. Before making this assembly, I decided to first attach the wheels onto the underside of the bottom of the module since weight and size were both becoming an issue.

Photo 8 shows the wheels being attached. The wheels are a critical part, so don't skimp on the size, weight, or cost. I ordered these wheels from a W.W. Grainger industrial catalog. They are capable of handling several hundred pounds on each wheel; the beefier the wheel, the smoother the function. This intricate module, no matter how heavy, must be able to roll around very smoothly and easily without putting undue stress on the future delicate trestles and scenery that will be built on the module. In my case, I used a 3″ hardened, rubber wheel swivel caster on a ball bearing mounting plate. A group of four should handle the load nicely. I mounted the plates with lag bolts to the plywood of the bottom of the module. Make sure when you do this that no part of the swiveling wheel will ever stick out beyond the edges of the module when finished.

In Photo 9, the valley floor deck has been added along with plywood sides to fill the gap on each side of the layout. The plywood sides were added by attaching scrap plywood high enough to fill the gap directly to the ends and edges of both decks of the module. I attached a scale drawing of the future trestle bent for one of the tracks to get a feel for the dramatic effect of the future trestle. Wow!

Notice I have attached a clamp to the side to more firmly locate the roll around module for remaining work.

The tall, flimsy side walls will need to be reinforced to stiffen them up. Don't begin doing this until you have already secured the side walls to the layout with some temporary screws. One or two locations on each side will be enough. These screws will need to remain in place from now until the construction is finished. Remember a fragile set of trestles will fill this valley, and the trestles won't be able to put up with flexing side walls of this module while rolling it in and out of its home in the layout. Photo 10 shows the use of some 2x4s and some 1x2 braces capped off with a small amount of plywood layout or track bed floor, which will stay with the valley module when it is rolled away. The brighter and cleaner plywood shows what is attached to the module as compared to what is attached to the layout table.

Note in Photo 11 that the whole deep canyon wall will eventually pull out with the module, including some amount of terrain at the top of the layout. By designing this into the roll around module, removal of the module will let me gain direct access to all areas under the layout's upper deck because the side walls of the valley are part of the roll-out module.

Photo 12 shows the left side matched up between the side of the module and the side of the layout table. The cut line in the three levels of cork roadbed show exactly what will come out with the module when it is removed.

In Photo 13 you can see the beefed up side of the module wall at all three levels. When the 2x4s and 1x2 bracing are complete, I could easily roll the whole module around by just holding onto the track levels at two points.

Photo 14 shows the nearly complete roll around module snugly locked into the layout at its match points. The area behind the module will be more canyon area with scenery on the sides and on the valley floor. I plan to make the valley floor in the canyon hinge down and out to allow me to go all the way to the back of the layout if anything needs attention back there. The other reason for a removable roll out section is that it will make finishing scenery at the back of the layout much easier to get to.

Photo 15 shows how easy it is to gain access to the back. I am preparing to roll the future valley and trestles out of the layout.

In Photo 16, I can easily roll the module out.

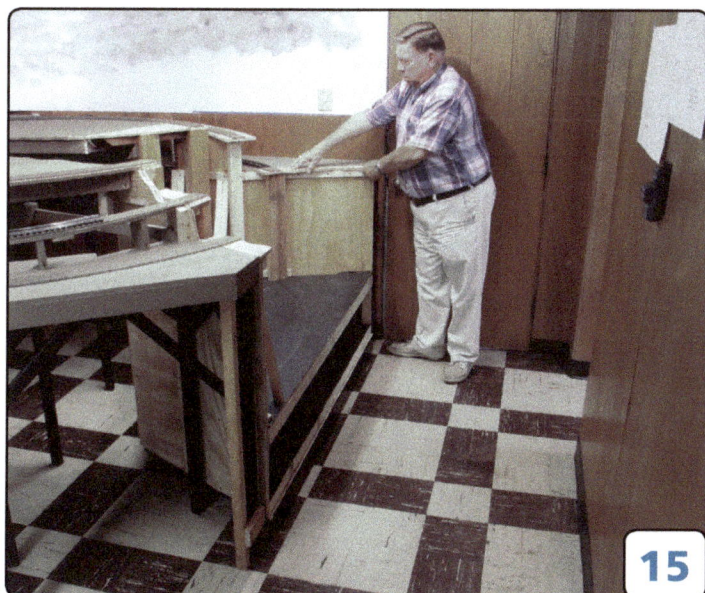

Note in Photo 17 how strong the end panels need to be once you see them rolled away from the layout that they fit into. Compare it to the right side of Photo 14. If need be, the module can also be rolled to another part of the room or even into another room, assuming doorway space permits it.

Hmm...that means that when it becomes trestle construction time, I can actually roll the whole module right over to my workbench and access the trestle from both sides while I sit and build. The more I think of ways to hinge and roll parts of this layout around, the better I like it! 🚃

CHAPTER 9 - Foamcore: Your Layout Building Buddy

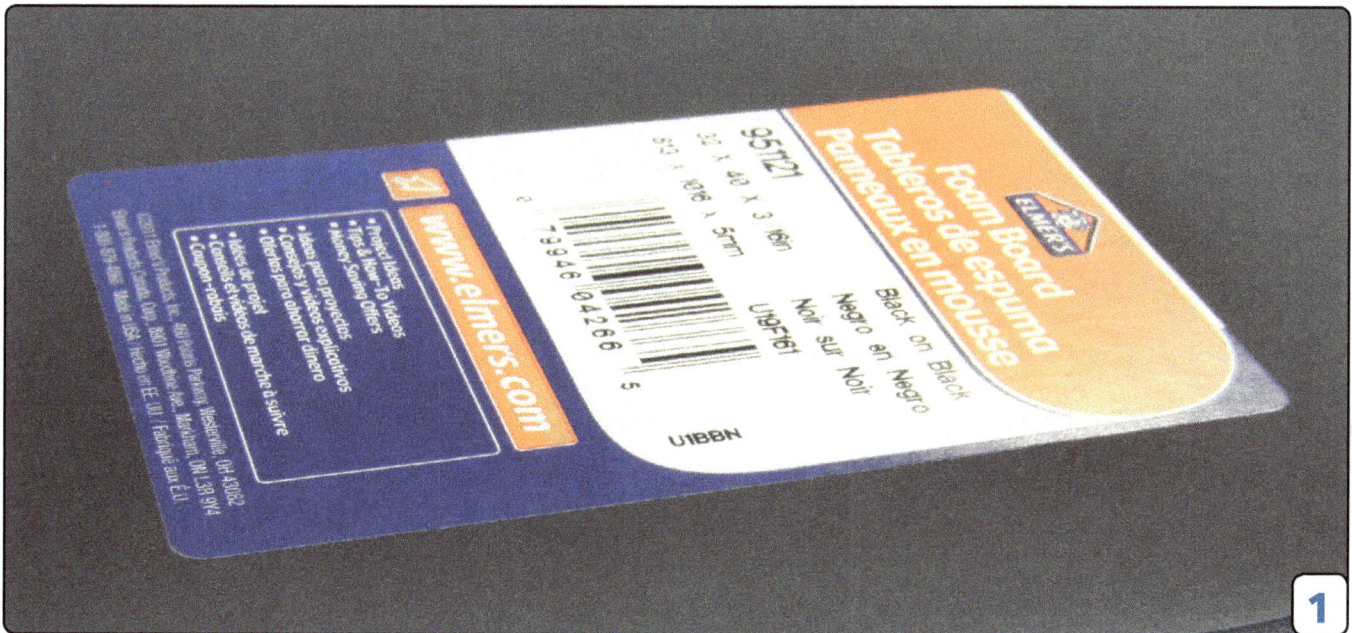

Foam core board or foam board is a sheet stock material that can be used for all sorts of things on your layout. It consists of an interior material of semi-firm sponge foam that is laminated between sheets of cad stock. The construction method of laminating layers is good because it keeps warping to a minimum. Photo 1 shows the edge of a sheet of 3/16" thick foam board.

These boards come primarily in either black or white. Other colors are available in art stores, but these are the two most readily available. It is important to note that black foam core board comes with black surfaces and either black or white interior cores. Always get the sheets that are black throughout because the edges of the board are often visible in our applications as well as the surfaces.

Thicknesses range from 1/8" to much larger, but for our purposes the most common thickness is 3/16". The foam board shown was 32"x 40", but a little digging on the Internet shows sizes up to 4'x 8' and thicknesses up to l".

Foam core board is available from art, hobby, and office supply stores as well as on-line if there are no stores handy to you. Just run a Google search for the product, and you will get a quick education. Sheets up to 3/ 16" thick will cut freely and cleanly with a sharp knife. Foam board can be glued face-to-face, allowing you to build up thickness for scenery purposes. I use 3M Super 77 spray glue, which is a form of rubber cement, or Elmer's white glue for gluing edges. The one glue to *not* use on foam board is CA glue. The process of spraying the fixing agent on the CA glue sometimes causes the CA to heat up, delaminating the paperboard surfaces from the core.

Photos 2 and 3 show one great use for foam core board, which is an exact template I covered in chapter eight. The template shown was easily made by taping smaller pieces of foam board together. In this case, I used some chair backs to hold the foam core board at the right height as I worked.

You can draw right on the surface of foam core board with a pencil, even if you are using the black foam core board. The pencil lead shows up as a gray line on the black paperboard surface of the foam board. I used a beam compass of a pencil and a center point mounted to a yardstick for large arcs to score a radius on the foam core board. The foam board is then cut using a knife to make a template for drawing arcs on plywood. That is the way I made running boards for track that will be mounted at different elevations.

On my former layout I had places where hinged scenery panels would allow access to hidden places actually inside the layout scenery. They formed a place where I could store things I needed to get to easily and frequently.

In Photo 4 the cardboard lattice scenery panel hinges up to show a small caddy of handy materials frequently needed for the layout (Photo 5). The caddy is made from custom cut white foam core board glued on the edge with Elmer's glue. The caddy is rugged and doubles as a backing for the hinged scenery panel.

Using that idea, I also made some large removable sections of scenery to provide access to trains that ran under the hill behind the scenery (Photos 6 and 7). Once again, all I had were foam core board baffles, a foam core board floor, and end panels glued together. Those pieces were covered with my cardboard lattice method of scenery construction and then covered with plaster cloth to create the surfaces. The cardboard strips were glued with hot glue to the foam board edges and then interwoven by applying a spot of hot glue at the crossings.

Perhaps the best use for foam core board is for making lightweight, firm scenery layers for such things as building up gravel parking lots, rail yard grounds, and other applications.

In Photo 8 I have a relatively small area to build a freight yard in. The pencil lines on the table surface indicate future track centerlines.

Photo 9 shows the cork roadbed for the tracks being installed along the pencil lines. These sidings will go over one of my hinged scenery panels covered in chapter six. These hinged panels need to be as light as possible, so using foam core board to build up these surfaces instead of just adding lots of gravel will keep down the weight of the hinged panel.

In Photo 10 I've laid out trackside operating accessories and other trackside structures to determine what might be the best location for each. Most Lionel trackside operating accessories work using either a vibrating mechanism or a motor mechanism.

Once their locations have been determined, I create vibration dams out of strips of cork roadbed, dampening out the vibrations to the tabletop (Photo 11). This trick makes the accessory work much better as well as much quieter.

The nice thing about the cork roadbed and foam core board is they are both the same thickness of 3/16". That allows for the use of the foam core board to fill in perfectly beside the cork. Additional foam core board can then be used on top to build up the surface scenery. Photo 12 shows the additional layers of foam core board that allow the parking lot for the truck to put the truck bed at just the right height for the dock of the forklift accessory.

In Photo 13 I've used two layers of foam core board: one 3/16" and one 1/4" to get the surface up so it will be just short of the base of the milk car platform. The addition of some gravel to the top of this surface will make it just about right. That layer of gravel will go right over to the edge of the outside rails of the yard track, which is often seen in real rail yards. A final 3/16" layer of foam core board for the road will let me place gravel for the yard right up to the road's edge. The surface of the road can then be painted to complete the black-topped surface of the road.

If the edge of the road pavement is too close to the top of the rail for the track, another great quality of foam core board is you can press down the edge of the board to get it to fall just at or below the edge of the rail. Once the foam core board is depressed using the edge of a putty knife for example, it will stay at that height. That will let wheels sit firmly on the metal of the track.

Photo 14 shows another way to use the depressible quality of foam core board. Using just your fingertips, you can create tire wear tracks in the pavement by simply pressing down where the wheels have caused the natural depressions in the pavement. They will show up even if a light gravel surface is added to the top of the foam core board.

Making grade crossings is also very easy (Photo 15). On many secondary paved roads used in rail yards, such a crossing usually amounted to nothing more than additional blacktop material being packed in between the rails with a slot cut out for the wheel flanges. If you use operating cars, such as a log dump car, simply depress the ends of the blacktop filler strips you place in between the rails to keep the sliding shoe from picking the ends of the filler blacktop. Be sure that the foam core board material being used to represent blacktop between the rails also permits the pickup rollers to sit firmly on the top of the center rail. If they don't, depress the foam core board inserts to make sure they stay below the center rail. Pickup rollers are often worn in the middle, right where they have rolled along the rail. That means the center rail must stick up just slightly higher than the roadway surface to keep the pickup roller from lifting off the rail as it rolls over a grade crossing.

Even if you need to add grade crossings through the curve on a curved track, you can still make this happen with foam core board. Using a soft lead pencil, place the edge of the pencil lead on the tops of all three rails and coat the tops of the rails with pencil lead. Then hold a piece of foam core board down on the top of the rails and move it slightly, just enough to get some of the lead onto the surface of the foam core board. Lift it off, and you'll see the marks showing the exact location of the rails. Cut along those pencil lines using a knife, and this will result in a precise cut line for the pavement butting up to the edges of the outside rails as well as lines for the inserts to be cut and filled in between the center and outside rails.

There are many other creative uses for foam core board. It can be used to make interior floors and roofs for trackside buildings. It can also be used as a backing for printed building flats, which will be added to backdrops (Photo 16). Laminating the printed building onto the foam core board and then carefully cutting along the edges of the building will add depth and dimension to the building.

As my layout progresses, I'll show you even more ways to make use of foam core board in building a layout. For now, go have some fun!

CHAPTER 10 - The Big Valley

Back in chapter 8 we constructed a removable roll-around section of the layout, which is where I will build three trestles for three curves of track (Photo 1). If you'll recall, I wanted to make these three curved trestles removable to gain access to the river gorge behind them as well as to be able to work on the back part of the layout in that end of the room. In the photo, the separation line between the fixed part of the layout and the removable part shows up as two different surface colors. The light-colored wood will be part of the removable module, and the darker brown part will be the fixed layout. The pencil lines on the flat black part of the bot-tom of the valley represent where the track center lines of the three curves will be.

A train trestle has many parts. A trestle "bent" is the name applied to each vertical trestle support assembly. Those penciled track lines indicate where the foundations for each trestle bent will be placed. The trestle bents on my layout will be 4″ apart, representing 20 spacing (on center) between each trestle bent (1/4″ per foot). My valley floor will also feature a stream coming from the waterfall I plan on modeling at the back of the gorge. This means that the railroad engineers would have had to plan for the valley floor to be somewhat unstable since spring rains might cause the river to flood the valley floor on occasion. For this reason, I'm going to model concrete footers at the base of each trestle bent. They will be represented by pieces of basswood cut to 3/8″ widths by 3/8″ depth and painted with concrete color paint. The beams making up my trestle bents will be made of 1/4″ square basswood (12″x 12″ in scale) which means that the concrete foundation will be about 6″ wider than the beam footers of my trestle bents. That will make a nice stable base for my railroad's trestles.

Chapter 10   *Building A Layout* by Jim Barrett

In Photo 2 I have spaced the footers at exactly 4″ apart along the track centerline. The angle of the footers can easily be eyeballed to make them evenly spaced. A touch of CA glue along the base of each footer holds it down in place. Note that I have used some risers under a few of the concrete footers at each end of the trestle as it nears the edges of the canyon to allow for the slope of the sides of the gorge (which we will add later).

If you will have more than one trestle side by side as I have, be sure not to make the risers identical for each track since Mother Nature would never make each part of the wall slope in exactly the same way.

Note also in the back of Photo 2 that I have added two 1x3s to the table legs on what will be both sides of the canyon walls (to be added later).

My goal when this project is finished is to be able to go from a finished scenicked canyon, train trestles, river, and canyon floor to a free and unencumbered walk-in space all the way to the back of the layout where the trestles, the river, and the waterfall will be located. That will mean that those two stringers I just added will eventually have two piano hinges attached where I will locate my river floor. The piano hinges will allow that river floor to split and fall away, thereby allowing me to gain that access.

Note that I have also left out a few concrete foundations in the middle of the valley since a river or large stream will be flowing through there. That means that somewhere up the trestle bents, footings for a bridge will have to be added at each trestle to span that gap later on.

In Photo 3 I have added the plywood for the river bed and painted it and the floor around the concrete foundations a brown color. Keep in mind that the canyon floor is a roll-away floor and the river floor is attached to the fixed part of the layout. For that reason, the rollaway canyon floor must fit neatly and as close as possible just under the river floor.

Before painting the river floor, I sketched on the plywood where I wanted my river to be and then cut the floor in two along the left edge of the river. Both halves of the river were then attached to the piano hinges on each stringer. I covered the piano hinges and the edges of the drop-away river floor with an overlapping plywood piece cut out with a jigsaw to show where the bottom edge of the canyon's walls will come down and be attached. Now the front edge of both river floor halves rests on the removable trestle canyon floor. When the trestle module is removed, the river floor falls away neatly, allowing me to walk to the rear of the layout right through where the river used to be.

There are all kinds of ways to make terrain including screen wire mesh, the paper wad method, and numerous others as well. I like the one I use, which is to cut up 3/4" strips of corrugated card-board and lace them together. This method enables you to change each part of the terrain as you go or to cut the strips and alter things at any time dur-ing the construction. In Photo 3 I have started by attaching the vertical card-board strips with a hot-glue gun and low-temperature hot glue. I begin by attaching them all at the top, as shown on the left side of the photo.

In Photo 4 a trestle wooden barrier has been added to hold back the ballast at the end of each track before it cross-es over the edge to the future trestle. I built this simple crib out of basswood parts stained a wood color and cemented with CA glue on top of the small concrete footer. That as-sembly was cemented to the wooden riser at each location.

The vertical cardboard strips beginning the top edge of the canyon wall were hot-glued to the undersides of the footers. Photos 3 and 4 show these vertical strips running down to the edge to the next concrete footer. Horizontal cardboard strips lace in and out, over and under, the vertical strips, as shown in the photo. In Photo 5 you can see the top edges of the cardboard strips hot-glued to the layout ply-wood surface next to the track roadbed. Also note that the wooden crib intended to hold back the ballast should be ex-tended up to the underside of the track in order to hold back the ballast properly. I used a scrap piece of track as shown to get the height of the wooden crib right.

Photo 6 shows how the terrain wall is coming along. Note how the concrete foundations for each trestle bent al-ready look like they are resting on the edges of the future terrain wall. As you go along with the cardboard webbing, you can push or pull the webbing in or out to customize the terrain to your liking. Then hot glue the joints of the card board strips using a clothespin at each location until the glue cools off and takes a set. It only takes a few seconds for the hot glue to cool. If you don't like what you've done to this point, just cut the strips in a few locations and change the whole effect. That's the nice thing about this scenery-mak-ing method. It is very easy to alter and reset.

The best and most common tools for this project are pictured in Photo 6. A pair of scissors, some model-ing knives, maybe a flat blade screwdriver or two, some clothespins, a couple of spring clamps, and a hot-glue gun and glue sticks should be all you need. I got most of these from a nearby hobby shop.

My project is a little tricky since I need to make some of the scenery (all the canyon walls of the roll-around mod-ule) first and then match that part of the canyon up to the rear part of the canyon so the module continues to easily separate and roll away. In addition, the joint line between the movable scenery and the fixed scenery needs to match well enough so that the modeled illusion isn't betrayed by ill-fitting scenery.

CHAPTER 11 - Make a Right-of-Way Clearance Gauge

One of the first things we have to decide on before we start designing and building a model railroad is what track radius we're going to pick for the main line. Most locomotives made by the manufacturers will run on O54 curves (a 27″ radius curve marked at the center rail of the track). But many of the best, most highly detailed steam locomotives need a minimum of O72 curves. It is a good rule of thumb to follow a guideline of using nothing less than O72 curves, at least on the main lines of your layout. Even if you don't currently own any locomotives requiring O72 curves, it's entirely likely that you will someday.

Scale engines needing O72 curves will still tend to have either the nose or the cab of the locomotive hang over the outside of the curves due to the fact that even at O72 it is still a very sharp curve compared to the real thing. But even if you own an O72 only locomotive, it may not be the worst case locomotive as far as how much its nose hangs over the curve. Take a look at the scale model of the Union Pacific Big Boy shown in Photo 1. That locomotive hangs over the outside by a full 3″ measured from the center rail of the curve. That bad boy can easily take out a misplaced tree!

Just because you may not actually own a UP Big Boy doesn't mean that you won't someday. Even worse, you might invite your friends over for a running session, and one of them may want to run his prized Big Boy on your brand new, beautiful layout. Don't say it won't happen...it almost always does. I built layouts for a living, and not one customer who initially told me he would never need an O72 layout made it to the end of the construction project before he had indeed bought one.

But even if you already have a nice UP Big Boy or similarly large locomotive, who wants to lug it around all over your layout during its construction to see what clearances you'll need for tunnels, buildings, and scenery? What you need is a worst case right-of-way clearance gauge.

Here's a simple project that will result in a gauge that will always tell you where and when anything you are about to place on your layout will work. Photo 2 shows just how far a worst case UP Big Boy hangs over on an O72 curve. If you hold a pencil at the most extreme edge of the front of the locomotive's boiler, the distance from the centerline of the rail to that point is 3″.

While we're at it, don't forget that there is another dimension you need to know. How far does a long passenger car hang over the inside of the curve? For my worst case example, I used a 21″ passenger car made fairly recently by K-Line. In Photo 3, I positioned a pencil in the middle side of one of those passenger cars and made a mark on the inside of the O72 curve. Photo 4 shows that distance to be 2-1/4″ measured from the center rail to the mark. Also shown in that photo is the 3″ overhang on the outside of the curve for the UP Big Boy.

To make my gauge, I cut two pieces of 1/4″ square balsa sticks, making each of them 5-1/4″ long. I marked both pieces with a pencil line 2-1/4″ in from one end of the cut. That mark indicates where the sticks should be positioned over the center rail of the track. Photo 5 shows a spare passenger truck I dug out from my parts drawer. I positioned the two balsa pieces on the truck with the pencil marks right at the center mounting screw. Adding a small dab of gap filling CA glue will hold them in place on the truck.

In Photo 6, I've added two small balsa frame pieces between the long balsa sticks to make the assembly more rigid. Gap filling CA glue was used once again to hold the

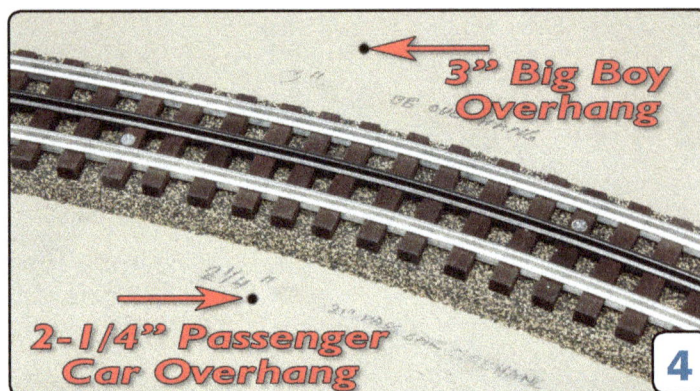

3″ Big Boy Overhang

2-1/4″ Passenger Car Overhang

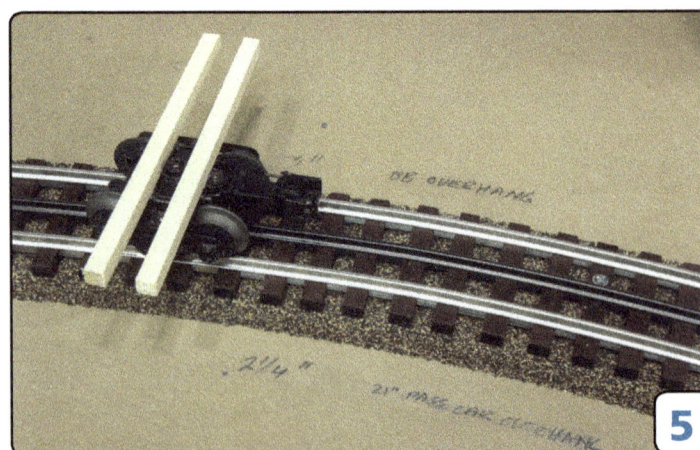

small pieces between the long pieces. To keep me from mistakenly tossing this gauge assembly aside someday, I gave it a nice coat of orange maintenance-of-way paint to remind me that this is now a true piece of my railroad's MOW equipment.

There are lots of ways to use this little gauge. In Photo 7, I used it to mark on the tabletop where those long steam engine noses will hang over through the outside of the curve. In addition, I marked the inside of the curves to show how much room a long passenger car needs as it goes through the curve. This will come in handy at scenery building time!

Photo 8 shows a polyurethane foam stone tunnel portal from Scenic Express. Note how our rolling gauge shows what needs to be done to the tunnel portal since it will be located right in the middle of an O72 curve. Both sides of the portal need to be enlarged to fit our worst case clearance gauge. In addition, the portal is far too tall for the application needed on my layout.

The nice thing about these Scenic Express polyurethane foam tunnel portals is that they are easily carved with a modeler's knife and filed with standard files to be custom fitted to your needs. Photo 9 shows the same tunnel portal shortened and opened up to allow our nice little rolling gauge to easily fit through it. Mismatched stone lines can be hidden with a little work using the tip of a file. A bit of touch up with gray paint will hide all the modifications I needed to make.

But before I do that, I'll prove out my modification with both the Big Boy steam engine and the long passenger car (Photos 10 and 11). It may not look totally prototypical, but sometimes you have to take a few liberties with the space you have to work with. Besides, it only lasts for a short while until your train gets back to the wide-open spaces, right?

Photos 12 and 13 show two other tunnel portals I've modified. It looks like the one in Photo 13 needs a bit more work to open up the left side, but that will be easy to do with a knife and a file. After the opening has been widened with a knife, file the stone joint lines with the edge of a half round file. When that is done, a little touch up with a matching gray paint, and we'll be ready to add the insides of the tunnel. I have a neat trick for the often missing insides of a tunnel that can be viewed through the portal, and we'll cover that in a later chapter of this book.

Photo 14 illustrates that I'll have to be careful when I add the scenery transition between the two levels of the layout near this curve. I can't get any closer than our rolling gauge shows on the bottom layer. In Photo 15, our gauge shows that the placement of this building can't be any closer than shown or the passenger car will be far too close to the building when it negotiates this curve.

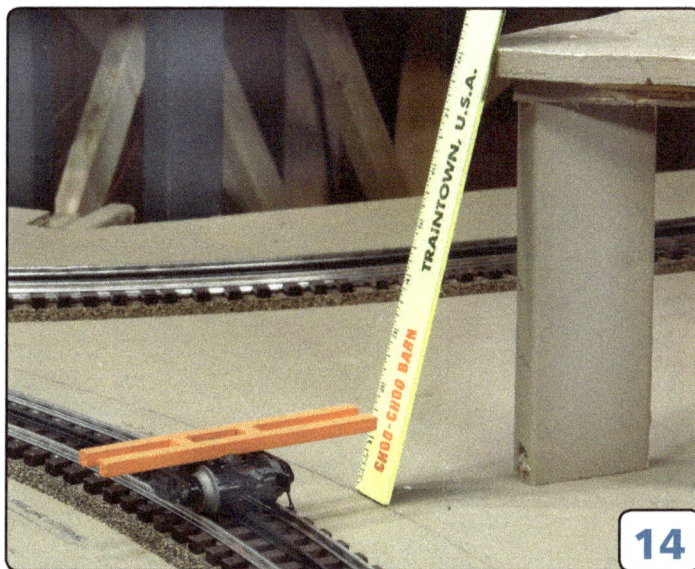

Here's another good use for our rolling gauge. At the O72 wye in Photo 16, I have a neat little Weaver switch tower that was looking for a home. The junction of these two tracks would be an excellent place for this building. But because my UP Big Boy could approach the wye from either side, I needed to check it with the long legs of our gauge from one side, turn it around, and check it from the other side as well. The gauge immediately showed that the final placement of the switch tower needs to be much farther back from the junction of the wye than I first thought.

If your layout will be made with only O54 or O42 curves, get out what you suspect will be your own worst case big steam engine and your worst case long passenger car and use the same method I've outlined here to build your own gauge. Don't forget that in some cases large or long steam engines might have cabs that hang out farther over the curve than any part of the boiler does. Check both ends of the locomotive. Also check the locomotive going both forward and in reverse. Many engines will have their most extreme corners hang out farther in reverse than they do when going forward.

If you use molded tunnel portals and scenery pieces such as those offered by Scenic Express, this little rolling gauge will save you a lot of tunnel and scenic feature rework. Best of all, it may save you a whole lot of embarrassment when you make that first trial run with your friends standing around to admire your work.

CHAPTER 12 - Dress Up Your Tunnel Entrances

Tunnels are an engineering marvel on the real railroads. In amazing achievements, builders blasted their way through sheer rock, came out on the other side, and capped off the entrances with stonework portals. That's why tunnels on our model railroads are so important to model correctly. In Photo 1 you see some dramatic tunnel entrances with stonework portals, such as these from Scenic Express. The details of the portals have already been taken care of for us with highly realistic model portals such as these.

What about the illusion of the tunnel itself and behind the portals? Nothing destroys the effect worse for me than to look into a model railroad tunnel and see plywood and empty air inside. What we need is an easy way to simulate the blasted rock that would normally show just inside the tunnel entrance.

To accomplish this, we need some sort of wall inside the tunnel portal, if for no other reason than to hide the effect of any light sources behind the tunnel entrance. It's supposed to be dark in there, right? We need some walls, but not walls that are just plain black. They don't have to go very deep into the tunnel or even very high. A couple of feet beyond the entrance, the tunnel lining can look like anything it wants to because we can't see that far into the tunnel.

Let's try this. Using some black foam core board, cut some base walls a foot or so long and about an inch or so higher than the tunnel opening. If your tunnel is on a curve, mark the location for the interior walls with a clearance gauge (Photo 2). Be sure to make this interior wall location about another 1/4″ farther away from the track than where the initial line is drawn. This is needed to allow room for the imitation rock material we will apply to this wall later.

Insert your foam core board for the wall into the tunnel opening (Photo 3). You'll have to turn it on a slight angle to get it through the opening. You want the wall slightly taller than the opening so that you won't be able to see the top of the interior tunnel wall from outside the tunnel.

If your tunnel is on a curve, you might have to buckle the foam core board slightly like what you see in Photo 4 to allow it to follow the curve inside the tunnel. Push the foam core wall back about 1/4″ or more behind the inside of the tunnel portal and glue it into place using a hot glue gun (Photo 5).

Wow! Even with just the black foam core walls in place, look at the dramatic difference (Photo 6).

But the real dramatic effect takes place next. I discovered long ago that a simple way to simulate interior rock walls was with nothing more elaborate than oven strength aluminum foil...and some paint. The brand of paint isn't important to achieve the effect you want. I've used enamels, lacquers, and acrylic paints; amazingly enough, they all stick to the surface of aluminum foil nicely. If you want to simply use Krylon spray paint, I've used Smoke Gray #K01608 or Platinum Primer #K01314. Unfortunately though, using commercially available spray paint severely limits the colors you can use. They also severely limit your wallet as well.

Before you go out and buy commercial spray paints, please consider this. If you haven't noticed it lately, the price of spray paints in general and model paints in particular have gone sky high recently. The Krylon Platinum Primer is now all the way up to $16 or $17! The availability of certain model railroad colors has shrunk or in some cases even disappeared as well. I've seen as much as a 500 percent to 600 percent increase in the price of bottled model paints compared to just a few short years ago.

On the other hand, prices of simple airbrush spray painting systems have gone the other direction. Their prices are down dramatically. One of the most familiar brands, Paasche, now packages its H model single-action airbrush complete with a handy little tankless portable compressor, adjustable pressure valve and pressure gauge, air hose, and mixing and dispensing bottles. You can find the complete set on Amazon.com for less than $130. At today's prices, it sure won't take very many cans of commercial spray paint to go past that price. The little air compressor that comes with this set, complete with a handle, is only about 6″ high by 7″ wide and 10″ long.

This set will let you spray any paint or ink in any color and take it right with you to the application site. Since most any paint you will probably use will be either acrylic or latex, the airbrush cleans easily with water, some pipe cleaners, Q-tips, and some paper towels.

At that price and for all the work you might need to do on a complete layout, it makes airbrushing spray paints very affordable. With this kind of system, now even common house paints such as Valspar latex interior wall paint can be thinned with water and sprayed through your airbrush. You can go to the paint department at any home improvement

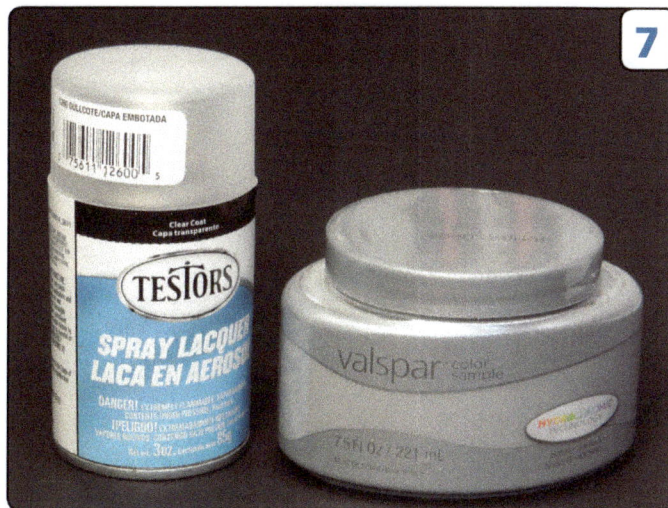

store or equivalent and get a professionally tinted sample size bottle of any mixed latex paint color for only about $2 to $3 each. What I selected was one of Valspar's satin base latex gray colors, Valspar #0760-D-20150131104430, from the sample paint cards at the store.

The store will custom mix the paint in the little sample size bottle, shake it up, and sell it to you (Photo 7). At home I mix that sample latex paint with water at a 50/50 ratio. That will let you spray it though an airbrush with fantastic results. I found that I can even vary the intensity of the actual color by mixing in a few drops of black ink to achieve any effect I want. That changes the shade of gray I get for darker interior colors, like inner tunnel rock, or lighter exterior applications, such as mountain rock and so forth.

The Valspar paint sample is shown along with a small spray can of Testors Dullcote. I still prefer to use Dullcote to overspray any finished paint color, getting it as flat as possible to look more like the rock seen in nature. Dullcote used to be readily available in bottles and thinned with lacquer thinner for your airbrush, but sadly, that too has now nearly vanished.

Okay, back to the project. Photo 8 shows the progression of aluminum foil from roll to finished interior rock. Cut off a piece of foil to more than cover the foam core wall that you have installed in the tunnel and then gently crush it up and gently pull it out to get the effect shown on the middle piece of foil in the photo. Don't "smooth out" the foil; just gently pull it back apart a little.

Spray the foil, but with very light applications. If you use an airbrush, you can adjust the air pressure up a little to get the paint to dry more as it goes from the airbrush to the foil. As you see in the photo, the paint may still have a slight satin look rather than the flat finish you'll want for rock. Once you overspray this coat with Dullcote, the finished result looks exactly like interior rock walls. Amazingly, the paint also doesn't flake or peel off the foil.

Once you have trimmed the dried, finished foil sample to an area a little larger than the wall piece it is to cover, turn it over back side up and spray it lightly with 3M Super 77 spray glue (Photo 9).

Then curl it gently and carefully apply it to the interior wall (Photo 10).

You'll just want to loosely tamp the finished foil covering in place, leaving it crinkled (Photo 11). Avoid the urge to spread it out smoothly on the foam core board. Smoothly spreading it out on the wall will cause it to lose the rock appearance you are trying to achieve.

Once you've gotten to this point, add the track ballast of your choice to the track and to the sides of the ties all the way over to the wall (Photo 12). I like to use actual granite ballast from Scenic Express, correctly sized to O gauge track. Look at how much more dramatic this entrance is to the earlier photos. Now is also the time to add any airbrush finishing touches for interior staining; smoke stains above the tunnel portal entrance; and trim such as rocks, small branches, twigs, and trash.

Finally, make sure to close up and cap off any distracting light sources. Room light coming from inside the tunnel tends to destroy the dramatic effect. Once it is dark inside as it should be, light from the locomotive's headlight coming through the tunnel and shining on the interior rock walls adds lots of tunnel drama, too. In addition, keeping your tunnel dark will prevent being able to see where the rock wall ends inside the tunnel.

Dressing up tunnel entrances is a small trick with a big effect. It adds depth and believability to a model railroad. Tunnel entrance work needs to be done early on in the scenery building phase. Attending to them later on is almost always a big inconvenience. By then such work can easily interfere with other finished scenery.

If you do decide to go ahead and purchase an airbrush, which I highly recommend, be sure to keep it handy. We're going to have lots of fun with airbrushes. As we continue our layout construction, we'll make good use of your newly found artistic talents in future projects we undertake in building your layout.

CHAPTER 13 - Tunnels & Tricks with Mirrors

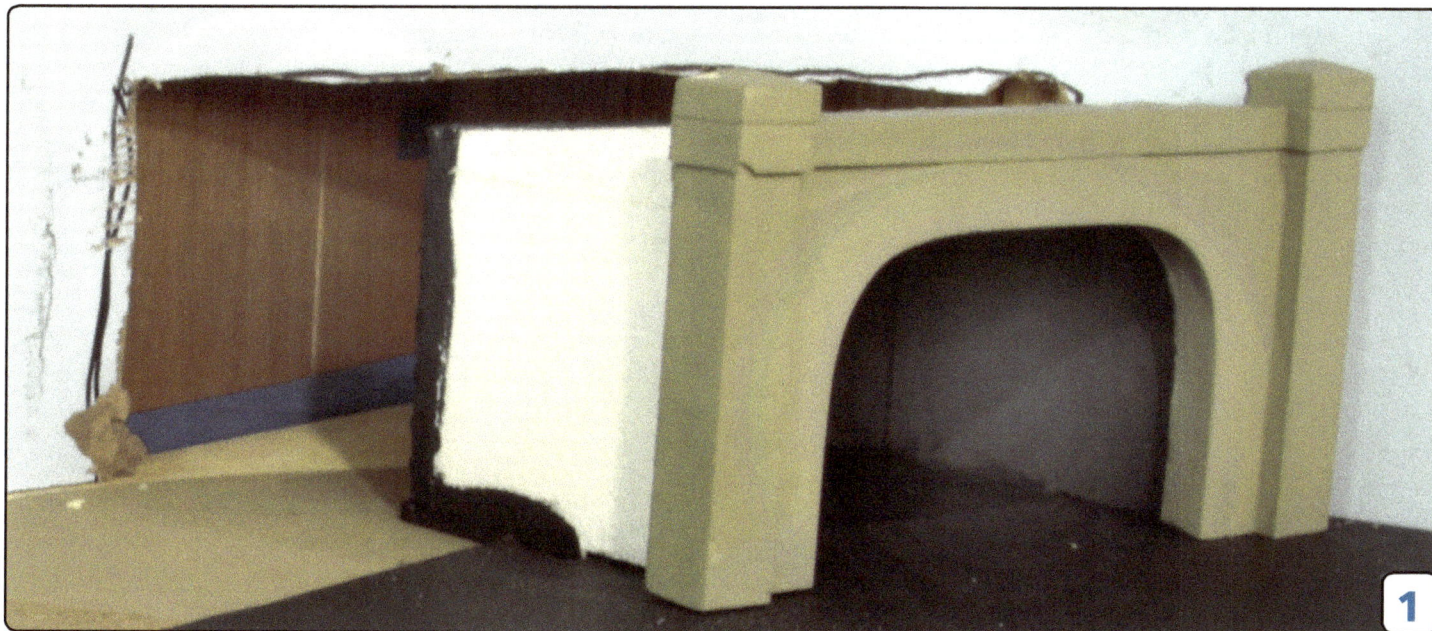

Good O gauge train layouts used to be all about trains, some mountain scenery, a few simple houses and other buildings, and that was about it. But these days, we have a vast and wonderful world of accurately modeled vehicles from almost any era to choose from. If you're like me, you've probably spent a lifetime going to train shows and train stores, acquiring all kinds of great vehicles to use on the layout, just to find that your appetite for classic period vehicles has far exceeded the roadways you've planned for your current (or even next) layout.

I planned this layout to have a prominently featured "common sense" highway, as well as the railroad itself so that I would have a place to show off a reasonable number of my O gauge vehicle collection. When it comes right down to it, a highway running roughly parallel to the railroad track is one of the most common features of American transportation. The historical fact is, many of America's prominent two lane highways originated as work roads for the railroad construction crews to build the railroad track. That makes having a nice highway alongside your model railroad very natural.

But here's the problem. When we design and build our model railroads, we need every square inch of real estate for the track, especially when we get to the corners of

the train room since the train needs to turn and go the other way. That leaves precious little, or no room for highways, right? Time to get creative!

Hmmm... Corners of train rooms are a natural place for mountains, right? They give reason for the train track to "dodge" the mountain with a sharp curve. Then it would follow that it would also be a "natural" for the highway to go through the mountain with a tunnel of its own. That would be a "common sense" scenery method for the highway to exit the layout. The trouble is, once the highway goes into the tunnel, it is immediately greeted by the wall in a most unnatural way just a couple of inches beyond the tunnel.

Several years ago my friend Gayl Rotsching showed me an interesting solution to just such a problem. He had a highway tunnel on his layout that seemed to go on forever. Remember in chapter 2 when I showed you how to make corners of a room go away by forming thin masonite backdrops into a curve into the corner? Take a look at Photo 1. As you can see if you look closely, I've cut in to that formed masonite corner (shown painted blue). I used a Dremel tool with a rotary cutting blade to remove the bottom of the curved panel to regain access to the actual corner of the room showing up behind the curved backdrop.

The same photo also shows a tunnel portal I kitbashed from an existing O gauge railroad tunnel portal. Obviously, your situation will not need the exact same dimensions that mine did, but I cut down an existing train tunnel portal to a somewhat smaller highway tunnel size.

For reference purposes, my two lane highway will scale out to be 19 ft. wide (9-1/2 ft. per lane). As layout roads go, this is a pretty generous amount of width for a roadway. Yours may vary as your needs dictate, but a two lane road at 4-3/4" width (19 scale ft.) will nicely accommodate two of most O gauge sized vehicles side by side. If you are planning the type of layout similar to this one that goes around the train room wall, there will be just enough room for a couple of tracks, a highway, and some roadside buildings.

Also sitting partially into the removed corner in photo 1 behind my tunnel portal is a shadow box made from easily sliced 5/8" to 3/4" thick white styrofoam insulation panels. A good source for this material is home improvement stores. It is sold as insulation panels installed between furring strips behind wood paneling. They come in inexpensive packs of 5 or 6 sheets 13-5/8" wide by 48" long. They slice accurately and easily using an Xacto # 26 long knife blade (also called a whittling blade) and a straight edge. Assemble the material using LOW TEMP glue sticks in a low temperature hot glue hobby gun. If you use a high temp setting on any hot glue gun, you will end up with a mess.

Make your styrofoam "shadow box" big enough to fit behind the tunnel portal opening by about 1/2" in on the sides and top. Hot glue the top edges of the two sides to the ends of the top piece. Be sure to keep it squared up to the tunnel portal as you let the hot glue joints cool down. After your three sided styrofoam box has cooled down, attach the finished styrofoam shadow box to the tunnel portal equally on the sides and top using hot glue. Once this has cooled, paint the insides of everything flat black.

The key ingredient for this project is a clean, clear unblemished glass mirror panel. Once again, its exact size will vary depending on your own needs. If you go to any Hobby Lobby store, they sell various sizes of good quality mirror glass for use in hobby projects. Get one that is slightly larger, but not too much larger than you need to fit onto the back of the styrofoam.

If you need to alter the size of a mirror, they can be cut down using a glass cutter tool which can be purchased at local hardware stores. A word of warning, if you are not familiar with cutting glass, it is a system of etching a line into the glass (mirror), placing the glass mirror panel across a threshold right where the etched lined is, and sharply cracking the glass right along the line. It is not dangerous, but you may need to practice to get the hang of cracking the glass smoothly right along the etched line. If you are in doubt about doing this, take the mirror to be cut to a local hardware store. They can do it for you.

The finished mirror panel needs to fit flat on to the back of the styrofoam shadow box shown on the back of the tunnel portal in photo 1. It too can be easily attached using the hot glue gun. Once it has been attached, paint the outer edges of the hot glue joint flat black to prevent any light from getting in.

Photo 2 shows another mountain I am also recycling from my former layout. It was a corner mountain which, with a little butchering with a hack saw blade for the tunnel portal, will also work nicely for this installation. Look how nicely that blue sky curved panel hides the room corner! I just love that trick!

The close up of the opening in photo 3 shows that I'll have a good three or four inches of depth available to me for the tunnel shadow box. That means that I will be able to turn my tunnel opening ever so slightly, so that the layout viewer will easily see to the inside of the opening. Don't turn it totally square to him though, or he'll just be looking at himself looking into the tunnel!

Photo 4 shows how a trial fitting worked out. It looks good! Sure, we've got a lot of rough gaps here and there, but that is what scenery materials like lichen is good for. Another trick to employ is to make the tunnel slightly canted up at the rear. In the mirror, this will appear that the road goes up hill as it goes out of the tunnel. Its real value is that it discourages nosey layout observers from trying to see themselves when they look in the tunnel too far.

In my case, I am able to turn the roadway lightly as it goes into the tunnel, making the reflected image appear go slightly off to the right as it goes out of the tunnel. In photo 5, I have glued my slightly raised roadway thickness down to the table base. I have also gently pushed the roadway surface up to and flat against the mirror in the back of the shadow box.

The finished illusion is shown above in photo 6. The road, the cars on the road, and indeed the whole world looks to be going through the mountain, and out the other side! If you look closely, it appears that there is a train on the other side of the tunnel going away from you when you look through the tunnel. In fact, it is the mirror reflecting a train just beyond the photo's right edge on the layout on THIS side of the mountain. Remember as you look into that tunnel that it is actually only three inches deep!

CHAPTER 14 - Working on Main Street

The main streets of America are indeed the backbone of nearly all small towns in the country. Interestingly enough, railroads can also trace their history right back to these very same small town main streets (Photo 1). In fact, many small towns originated from nothing more than the railroad construction camps where work crews and supplies were headquartered while building the railroad.

All over the country, you can see the connection between what became American highways and the railroad tracks that often parallel them. As the forward surveyors and engineers made wilderness camps along the way, they laid out the route of the railroad toward their location. As construction gangs approached, they eventually passed through the camp and pressed on to the next site.

The previous camp often became a train station, and the train station became the railroad's headquarters and the freight hub for developing commerce in the area. And so the small towns of our nation were born around them.

Connecting these stations across the landscape involved not only the railroad tracks but also the leftover construction trails that often paralleled the tracks. These construction roads later became natural roadbeds for highways, so it is natural for your train layout to have a highway and streets roughly paralleling the tracks.

This concept lends itself well to around-the-room layouts like mine. Besides, what a wonderful excuse for displaying all my O scale vehicles! There now are so many different makers of appropriate vehicles that the cars and trucks you collect can be used to help set the time period of your layout and the equipment you run on your trains.

Large train layouts can support big cities. Small and medium size layouts generally need small towns, particularly in our scale. When I began planning my layout, train table space was at a premium, of course, so my basic vision was to create what would appear to be a double track main with a highway running alongside. A double track main can actually be a giant loop that turns around on itself at the ends of the layout. Scenery can disguise the fact that the track just folds back upon itself so it looks like a double track main line.

When planning a main street business district, there are some key businesses that were key to a town's success. They included the train station, police station, drug store, grocery store, gas station, movie theater, clothing store, hardware store, bank, and restaurant. This list doesn't imply that your main street needs to incorporate all these businesses; it is meant to be just a list of primary businesses to pick from as space permits.

Among the more important considerations to keep in mind when planning your own town's Main Street are infrastructure items such as pavements, sidewalks, grade crossings, and roadbed—all of which have varying thicknesses.

You already know that I love to make use of 1/8″ black foam core board. It is a great product to use for scenery in so many ways. My complete Main Street will lie between the building at the far end of Photo 2 and the corner of the wall shown in the foreground.

I want to make use of some beautifully detailed plaster cast buildings I obtained many years ago while on a trip out west. They are shown in Photo 3. I've also added Weaver's beautiful brass water tower at the corner of the room. It will make a nice separator between Main Street and the rest of my layout world, and it detracts nicely from the unwanted "corner effect" of the sky.

But I also want to use some parts of OGR Ameri-Towne structures as well. One basic problem is that the bases of my plaster cast structures are over 1/4″ thick, making their threshold height (the height at the bottom of the entrance doors) much higher than the thresholds of the Ameri-Towne buildings. That means the AmeriTowne structures must start out a full 1/4″ higher than the plaster buildings to remain in scale proportion to them.

Using two layers of 1/8″ foam core board to vary the height of buildings from one brand to another is very easy. But there is another consideration that is also very important. Since my Main Street is also going to make a grade crossing over the double track main line, I need to make the grade crossing believable and in proportion to the track height as well. With my Main Street's pavement still coming up 1/8″ lower than the rail height, the street height must rise up to meet the rail height.

Photo 4 shows a number of things in one shot. It shows a base layer of foam core board plus another layer of foam core board representing the street level on top. It also shows the cork roadbed of the track, then the ties, then the rail height. I've intentionally left the ballast off some of the ties to illustrate the height differences. The surface of the street comes out nearly even with the tops of the ties—just about another 1/8″ too low to bring the street up to the rail height.

That means the final piece of foam core board for the street must rise up so the bottom of the pavement thickness will rest on top of the track's ties. If you look closely at Photo 5, that's what I've done where the road crosses the track. Simply gluing the underside of the foam core board onto the wood ties with Elmer's white glue does the trick perfectly. The scrap wood in the background held the foam

core board down firmly to the ties while the glue dried. I've got another method for filling in the spaces between the rails while leaving a gap for the wheel flanges, which I'll cover in a later chapter on details.

The road pavement must now drop all the way from rail height down to the train table surface and off to the right in Photo 6. The use of foam core board now makes this a smooth and even slope by simply gluing the starting edge of the roadway to the ties of the track. Then over some reasonable distance determined by the amount of drop needed in the pavement, you simply glue the other end of the pavement piece directly to the table.

Once both ends of the pavement piece of foam core board have dried firmly to the ties on one end and to the table on the other, inject some bathroom tub and tile caulk directly into the gap between the pavement piece and the tabletop. The caulk will cure in a few hours to provide firm bedding for your road pavement that will neither expand nor contract over time. You can fill in and smooth out the slope between the edges of the pavement and the tabletop with some spackling compound the following day.

Photo 7 shows more base layer and pavement layer being added to the hinged tabletop piece.

Photo 8 shows this process continuing down what will become more of my Main Street. I intend to use the plastic sidewalk pieces of the AmeriTowne kit under my buildings, but I can't do that to the rounded roof building to the right of the photo. The sidewalk will make the plaster base of that building sit up too high. I'll have to cut a hole into the two foam core board layers, using a utility knife, for that building to sit down into the two layers of foam core covering. That will make that building come out just about right in its height proportion. A similar building "socket" is already finished just to the right of the building in the photo. Believe it or not, that is a fairly easy job to do with foam core board.

Also note that the hinges for the tabletop are gradually beginning to disappear into the pavement. The nice gray blacktop appearance on my Main Street pavement piece is due to the application of a single coat of Woodland Scenics Road System Top Coat #ST1453 Asphalt. Thankfully, it is one of those products that works perfectly as advertised. If you want concrete instead, then use #ST1454 Concrete. Either is easily applied with a simple 1″ to 1-1/2″ trim brush. When dry, you can streak "wear marks" into the surface with nothing more elaborate than your fingers. Good stuff!

The sidewalk pieces that we at OGR offer in the AmeriTowne kits are also available from us separately in pairs. The nice thing about them is that they measure out to be a little over 1/16″ thick, making them scale out to be about 4″ to 5″ high. That's perfect for curbs in O scale. I painted them with the concrete paint. You may need to trim them in length or make some curved ends with a little cutting and sanding. Paint them when you are finished, glue them down with Elmer's white glue, and you're in business for curbs and sidewalks.

I'm showing you Photo 9 just for fun. It's a real photograph in a brochure of a main street in the small town of Orleans, Indiana. I grew up near there and was always fascinated by that corner building. I found the plaster cast building shown in Photo 10. I plan to add the Styrofoam cone top to the building and make it look like the roof of the real building in Orleans. It will be a challenge that I hope to reveal to you at a later date. Stay tuned! This photo also shows progress in filling in the slope in the road pavement going up to the grade crossing as well as beginning to lay out the locations of a police station with a jail on the second floor and also the town's movie theater.

Also note the crossbuck. I had to modify the base of the MTH crossing flasher by turning the base 90 degrees to make it fit beside the road. Photo 11 shows that by digging into the foam core layers, I can sink the ugly base of the crossing flasher down and out of sight into the "earth."

With the addition of Woodland Scenics Street Accessories #A2764, the devil is in the details. What a difference rust colored paint on the sides of the rails makes! I left the rust off the rails below the crossing flasher to illustrate what a dramatic difference that little detail makes. Add a little gravel, as shown in Photo 12, and now look at the difference that made in the base of the crossing flasher and the realism of the scene.

The real difference comes with the addition of ballast added to the tracks, as shown in Photo 13. Now just a little brown earth shows through between the tracks, which can be littered with weeds, junk, rusty fish plates, derelict pieces of old rail sections, spikes, and other details of your choice.

There is enough real estate to add four more main street buildings, too! Nearly all of small town America is made up of two-story, not three-story buildings, which is why we came out with our two-story AmeriTowne building kits. Three-story buildings were more often a function of larger cities back in the first part of the 20th century.

Those common small town two-story buildings are almost all located side by side. It was a common architectural practice back then to actually use the walls of two adjacent freestanding buildings for the walls of another one built between them simply by adding a front and back. How they got away with that I'll never know, but I've actually seen many instances of that construction practice still existing in small-town buildings.

If you wish to imitate that early 20th century small-town main street appearance, it is not necessary for you to actually buy four AmeriTowne building kits. Just buy one full kit and then buy three additional building fronts of your choice.

Take a look at my workshop in Photo 14. Since I also want some parallel parking like my own small town had, I have laid out my four building fronts and two sidewalls on the work desk, with one sidewall at each end. But I have intentionally cut the depth of the sidewalls off by about one third. That will give me the parallel parking space I need along the street in front. Also notice that I will intentionally set the limestone front of the bank building slightly out in

front of the other three buildings. That was also a common practice intended to make the bank buildings appear a little more imposing than the brick fascia of each of the neighboring buildings. Photo 15 shows the bank building front positioned slightly forward by adding 1/8″ thicknesses of plastic to the back sides of the edges. I used a very thin strip of styrene (1/32″ thick by 1/4″ wide) to seam the fronts together firmly.

To firm this all up into one assembly of building fronts, I have added a piece of foam core board cut to fit snugly between the end walls of the whole assembly. The foam core interior base is glued to the plastic fronts and ends with nothing more technical than a bead of low temperature hot glue.

Photo 16 shows the nice dramatic effect of the bank's offset building front up close.

Photo 17 shows the addition of interior walls made from individually cut foam core panels.

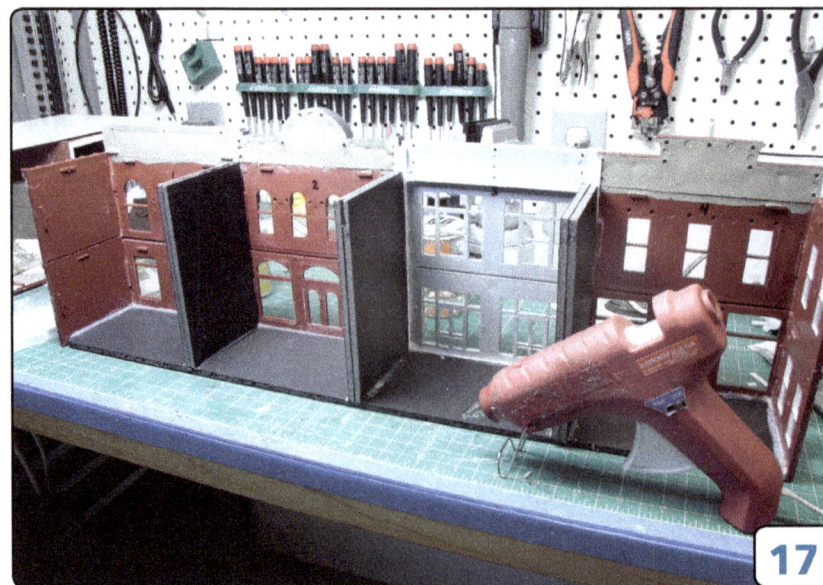

With the addition of foam core roof panels and back walls, the finished dramatic effect is shown in Photo 18. The whole finished assembly of building fronts sits on top of the sidewalks attached earlier. The assembly is light and easy to move around and will be permanently attached to the hinged base panel, allowing the whole town section to swing up and out of the way to gain access to the closet behind the town.

Photo 19 shows the addition of gravel between my Main Street and the tracks plus the addition of parking meters, fireplugs, trash cans, manhole covers, and a bench or two from the Street Accessories detail kit from Woodland Scenics. Now all I need are some people, a train every couple of minutes, and a sound module of honking horns to be right at home in good ol' Mitchell or Orleans, Indiana!

Now go have fun making your own version of a main street.

CHAPTER 15 - What's In A Backdrop?

In chapter 2, I covered making a Masonite backing panel for the train room and painting it blue to represent sky. Then in subsequent issues, I added clouds, framework and table surfaces, along with some mountains and track. Since then I've been adding town buildings as well as train yard structures and trees. Now I have a pretty clear image of where things currently are, or will be, on my layout and what I might want to add to the painted backdrop behind the foreground to add to the illusion.

It is quite possible to simply be satisfied to let the sky drop down all the way to the layout surface with nothing more than the trees and the buildings to break up the line at the base of the wall. But when you do that, you miss out on the chance to add amazing depth and scope to the scene, which is all important when you model O gauge in any space, much less a limited space like what I have for my layout.

If you add scene panels to the back wall of the layout, you are actually creating a comfortable place for the observer to be happy to look off the end of the layout and not be disturbed by the ugly reality of the "edge of the world," so to speak. Scene panels let your observer continue to be entertained by the illusion of the small world that has been created (Photo 1).

There are any number of manufacturers that produce scene panels, which is to say that the ones I'm showing you here are nothing more than what I've had experience with in the past. It certainly does not mean that they are the only ones nor even the ones I recommend over others.

To get an idea of what a backdrop scene panel can do for a small area of the layout, look closely at Photos 2 and 3. Notice that the only difference between the two photos, with the exception of some small differences in placement, is the addition of a rolling backdrop scene on the back wall to add depth to the scene. Realize that the addition of some strategically placed trees, bushes, and other ground details at a later date will add even more to the illusion. Fill in some cinders, loose coal, and ballast cover to the tracks and the base of the surrounding coal structures, and you can use your imagination to see how even more important the scene panel becomes.

2

3

I like to use Walthers Instant Horizons scene panels, one of which is shown in Photo 4. There are a series of 17 different scene panels, each nominally 24″ high by 36″ long. These scenes are claimed to be scaled to HO (1:87), but that really is only a function of what you put in front of the scenes. Scale isn't too important when you are creating the illusion of distant mountains or prairies. Also shown in the photo is an aerosol can of 3M Super 77 spray adhesive. That is what I use to attach the scene panel to the painted blue wall.

Some of the scenes in the Instant Horizons series are cleverly designed and painted to allow the ends of one scene panel to match up with the ends of several other scenes in the set. This provides the freedom to design your own finished wall mural by combining different scenes edge to edge in a manner that best suits your layout's geography and structures. When it comes to mountains, deserts, and rolling hillsides, there are more than just one or even two scenes in each type of landscape. This will let you stretch out any type of landscape or even blend from one to the other to suit your layout's length. In fact, packed inside each scene panel box is a sheet with all the various scenes depicted in miniature. Each miniature color scene print on this planning sheet is 2-1/2″ tall by 4″ long, which is about 1/9th the actual scene size. Adding up the total linear distance of your train room

4

5

wall and dividing it by 9 will tell you how many scene panels you need to make your continuous wall mural around your train room. You can then lay out your scenes in a mix-and-match fashion to determine what you want. Keep in mind that some actual layout scene items like freestanding mountain modules and other scenery items such as structures will use up some of that space, so plan accordingly.

The problem with this or any other printed backdrop scene panel system is that they all have a printed blue sky. There will almost never be a time when you can match up the printed blue sky on one print with the printed blue sky on another print and not come up with an ugly line. That is why I went to such great lengths to make a seamless Masonite wall and paint it for my own blue sky. Photo 5 shows one of my rolling countryside scenes after I have nearly finished cutting off the printed blue sky with an X-Acto #7 knife. It really isn't hard once you get the hang of it, and carefully whacking off that printed sky is really worth it!

In Photo 6 I have turned the scene panel over and laid it on the surface of some scrap paper. I'm literally painting the back side of the panel with the 3M Super 77. Just use long even strokes the same as if you were painting it. Let the finished glue surface dry just a little until it is slightly tacky.

In Photo 7 I've located the panel right on the only exterior corner that I have in the train room. Notice that I've located the scene panel with the dip in a valley between two mountains right on the exterior wall corner. Wherever possible, place the panel on the corner with either a low point or a high point in the scene on the corner. It looks more believable that way.

Have a piece of scrap plastic or foam core board handy before you start this procedure. Make sure that it has at least one straight edge and use it to smooth out the printed scene panel onto the backdrop. Be careful to start the panel on the corner, but also be careful to start the scene evenly along the bottom of the wall where the train table meets the backdrop. If you goof this up, don't panic. You should still smooth out the scene panel as much as possible and cover up any goofs in the paper later with added brush, weeds, trees, or other terrain distractions. The first rule of scenery is that it can cover up a multitude of goof ups. You still need some dimensional scenery texture in front of the scene panel even if the match line is perfect, or the scene will be too boring.

Wow! What a difference a scene panel backdrop makes. The next four photos show how far I've come. Photo 8 shows the ugly, odd shaped, narrow basement with a closet door in the middle of everything on the back wall that no one would think has enough room for a beautiful train

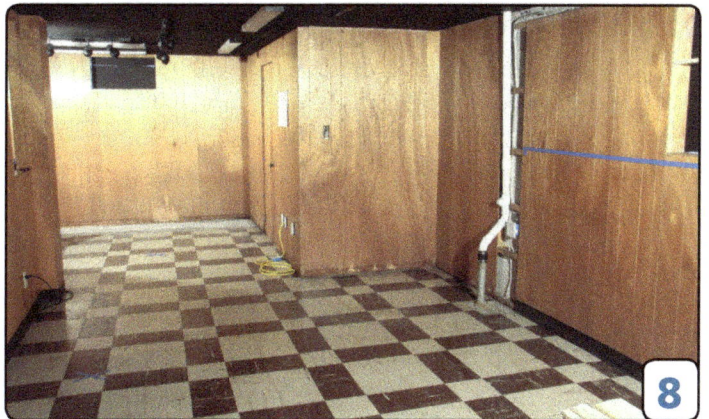

layout. Now look at Photo 9 and see what a difference there is with just the curved Masonite backdrop panel pushed into the corner and painted blue.

Photo 10 shows the layout table added with the track and the structures in place.

Now look at Photo 11 with the simple, subtle scene panel added. It literally is hard to believe that the ugly interior corner is the same "non" corner shown. This demonstrates a good lesson in scenery. It doesn't require a dramatic tall mountainous scene panel in the background to provide a great effect. Just a subtle short scene panel adds so much more depth to the layout.

Remember that closet door on the back wall in the middle of everything? That is the same wall that makes up the background behind Barrettsburg. Carefully placed backdrop scene panels with an occasional flat, three dimensional tree glued right on them can add a ton of depth.

Photo 12 has a three-story house high on a hill, all within less than 3/4″ between the train room wall and the back of the building on the right of the scene.

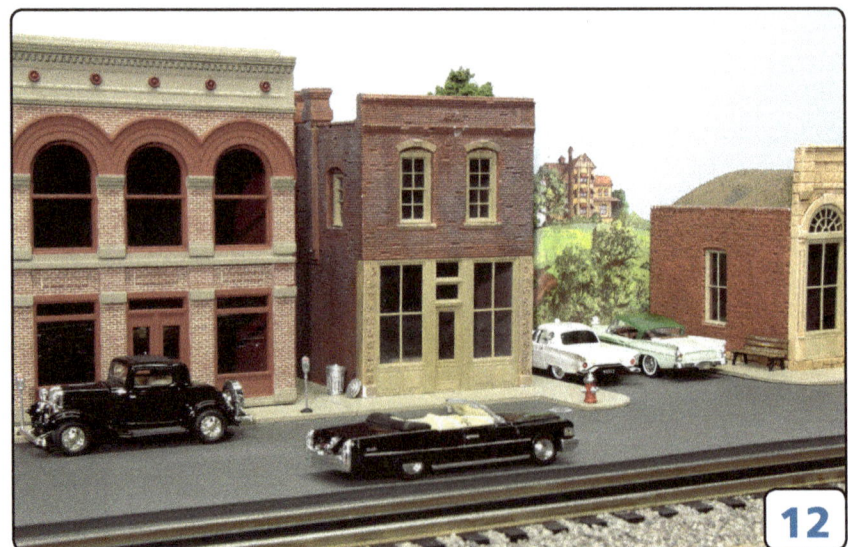

In Photo 13 the building on the left is not as deep as the one on the right, which allowed me to get generous and place a real layout tree (less than 3/4″ thick) right on the back wall and still keep it mostly behind the little main street building. In addition to all of that, the Studebaker, the Thunderbird, and all the buildings on the left of the two cars swing up past the tree, which stays on the wall, and over the top of the building to the right. I love scenery; it hides all kinds of tricks!

Photo 14 below shows the powerful difference a scene panel makes. In the tiny space of no more than 1/2″ between the back of the town's corner bar and the wall, we now have a nice mountain or so, trees, and gray scene panel mountains leading into the real mountain we located in the back corner of the layout using a tunnel mirror. The bar building in the immediate foreground also serves the purpose of letting me combine heavily mismatching scene panels or parts of scene panels behind the building. The mountain on the left and above the bar is in no way connected to the tall tree on the printed background at the right of the building. But you don't see that because the building is in the way.

And here's one of my favorite visual tricks. The building on the right side of Photo 15 is quite large. In fact, it is actually right smack up against the blue sky wall behind it. Sometimes you just can't get around this kind of problem during layout design and construction. I flat ran out of inches—even fractions of an inch. It didn't look too bad, but when I added the little bit of scene panel behind it, the whole illusion turned to junk. It just looked dumb for the corner of the building to be right up against the rolling countryside behind it. But just the addition of a tall scrawny tree shoved right up in the corner where the wall and the building meet gave just enough separation to the building from the backdrop scene to make everything work out. The tree doesn't even have to come up to the top of the building, just up above where the printed backdrop is. The blue sky will always seem farther away than it really is.

So what is a scene panel worth? You tell me. Scene panel backdrops add vast comfortable spaces to your layout, no matter what the actual dimensions happen to be. It's the same thing as free real estate. And who couldn't use a little bit of that on an O gauge layout?

CHAPTER 16 - Grade Crossings on Curves

When you make grade crossings (where a road crosses the tracks) on a train layout, it is always best to make them on straight sections of track (Photo 1). If you're using GarGraves or Ross track, the height of the center rail above the ties is always .215″, or just a little over 7/32″. That makes constructing grade crossings pretty easy due to one nice simple fact. If you use 3/16″ thick foam core board for the road filler material between the rails, the actual thickness measures out to be just about .180″. The rail stands up .215″, so the rail will stick out above the road filler material by .045″, or just a hair above 1/32″.

That little 1/32″ will help ensure that the locomotive's center rail pickup roller maintains good electrical contact with the center rail while it goes over the road. Even if the roller is slightly worn, as long as the roller doesn't have a gap deeper than 1/32″, it will still pass over the grade crossing and stay in full contact with the rail.

The width of the foam core board filler material between the center rail and the outside rail must leave a wheel flange slot at least .170″ (just under 3/16″) to pass wheel flanges through the grade crossing smoothly. Both modern style fast angle wheels and postwar style wheels will pass easily through a slot of that width. Don't forget to bend down the ends of the foam core board to allow a slight ramp for operating car slide shoes to jump up and ride smoothly over the grade crossing. But reality being what it is, it sometimes just isn't possible to make a grade crossing on straight tracks.

My layout has just such a problem. Due to space restrictions, I ended up with a two lane road that must cross right over a double curve main line as it runs through town (Photo 2).

Photo 3 shows how I made the road come up to the outside rails of the grade crossing by gluing down the foam core board to the tops of the ties on the curves.

In Photo 4, I've finished off the surface of the road with Woodland Scenics #ST1453 Asphalt Top Coat paint. This is wonderful stuff that makes modeling road surfaces easy.

Photo 5 shows something very interesting and very important about what happens to fast angle wheel sets when they go through a curve. If you look closely, you can actually see that the wheel set rides up on the outside of the curve until the outer wheel flange catches the outside rail. Because of the angle on the wheels, that actually adds to the realism, too. It will cause the railcar to lean over just a tiny bit as it goes through the curve simulating banking of the track, also called superelevation. As you can see, the result is the inside wheel actually pulls away from the rail leaving a gap between the wheel flange and the inside rail. That gap becomes very important when you make a grade crossing on curved track because you have to allow for a wider gap on the inside of the curve than you do on the outside of the curve.

My tests showed that the wheel flange gap on the inside rail on a curved track needs to be every bit of .185″ wide, a little more than 3/16″, while the outer rail needs only a gap of about .130″, or 1/8″ wide. Anything less on the inside of the curve will result in some wheel flanges catching on the road material, jumping out of the flange slot, and derailing the train.

The foam core board that fills up the area between the center rail and the wheel flange gap also needs to bend a little to form a curve as it follows along on the track curve. I have found that if you cut foam core board wide enough to fill the whole gap between the center rail and the wheel slot, it then does not want to bend enough to follow the curve of the track without buckling up on the surface. That just isn't going to work.

The cure is to cut the strip of foam core board narrow enough to allow it to bend easily to follow the track curve and then glue it down so that you can control the wheel flange gap as you go. Sure, that will end up leaving a gap between the center rail and the foam core board, but don't worry about it. I have a cure for that, as you will see.

When you cut the foam core board filler strips, make them only 5/16″ wide (Photo 6). That is narrow enough to gently bend the foam core board filler strip to follow the curve of the track without buckling up on the surface. When you cut them to length, make them an inch or so too long for the width of the grade crossing itself. On one end of each strip, cut a bevel (Photo 7) so it ends up looking like the ones shown in Photo 8. Then notice how much past the width of the grade crossing the strip needs to go, and cut the strip to the length needed to allow the remaining end to be beveled.

In Photo 9, I've done a trial run using some steel T pins (Woodland Scenics #ST1432 Foam Nails) to force the foam core board strip into a curve to follow the curve of the track. When you push the T pin through the foam core board and into the track tie, the material follows the curve of the track very nicely without buckling up on the surface.

Make a gap spacing tool out of material that is 3/16″ thick. I used a stick of plastic that I found to be 3/16″ thick. Then put down a bead of Elmer's glue on the ties near the center rail of the inside of the curve (Photo 10).

Using your gap tool to space the foam core board away from the outer rail, push in a T pin through the foam core board and into the wooden tie (Photo 11). I found that I could do that on every other tie. Later I found that it was just as easy to do it on every tie, making sure that the gap remained the same all the way along.

When I finished my double track main line, it looked like what you see in Photo 12. In the inset, you can see the unwanted ugly gap that results on both sides of the center rail. This was necessary due to the need for the foam core board strips to be narrow enough to bend smoothly and follow the curve of the track. When the glue has dried, carefully remove all the T pins.

Photo 13 shows Woodland Scenics Smooth-It #ST1452. This is what you will use to fill the gap on both sides of the center rail. Mix it half-and-half with water, pushing it in the gap between the foam core board and the center rail. If it is too thick, add just a drop of water and stir to a thinner consistency. Smooth off the top of the Smooth-It paste so that the filler comes out the exact same height as the top surface of the foam core board.

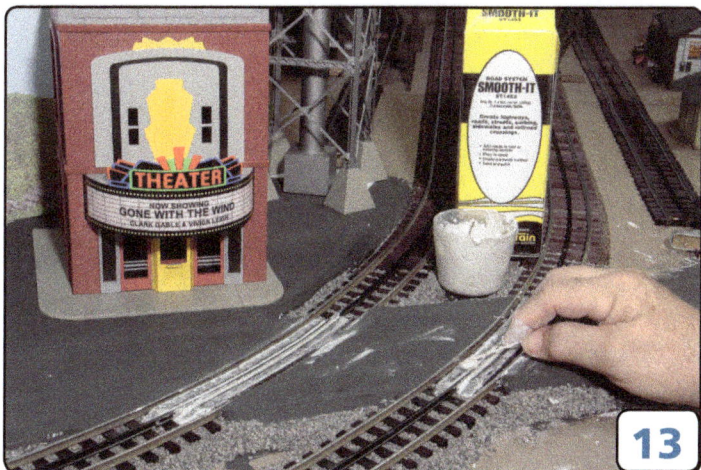

I used a coffee stir stick to fill in the gap and a chisel blade hobby knife as a small putty knife to smooth off the top surface (Photo 14). Keep the edge of the knife tight against the center rail as you sweep away the excess paste. Be sure to trim off the excess paste on the ends with a knife or the rounded end of the wooden stir stick.

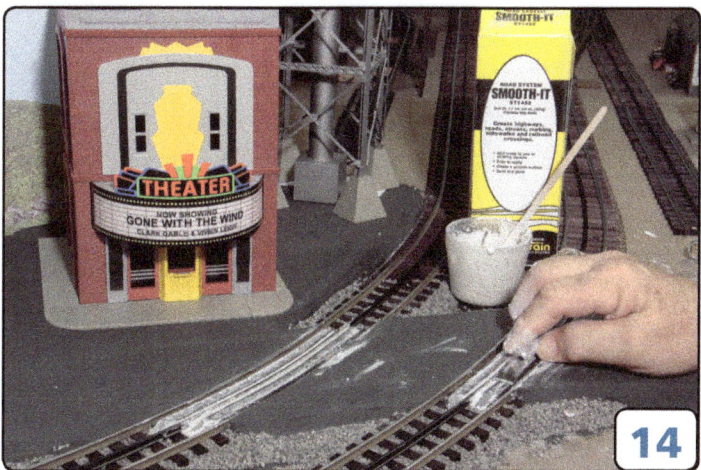

When the paste filler has hardened, sand the surface smooth with a sanding stick designed to fit in small spaces (Photo 15). Sand it so that the filler material is at the same level as the top of the foam core board filler. Also be sure that you have that center rail still sticking out that all important 1/32″ above the top of the pavement height.

To finish this project, paint the surface of your grade crossing using some more of the asphalt top coat (Photos 16 and 17). Be sure to wipe the paint off the top of the center rail and the wheel rails with your finger to keep the rails clean for good electrical contact.

When the paint dries, it should look like the grade crossing in Photo 18.

Add some white striping for the road edges (1/16″ wide Chartpak Tape #BG6210M or 1/8″ wide #BG12510M found online and in art supply stores). The finished result is shown in Photos 19 and 20. Grade crossings that look good and perform well are an important touch on a train layout. It's another part of the illusion that makes the whole scene a lot more believable.

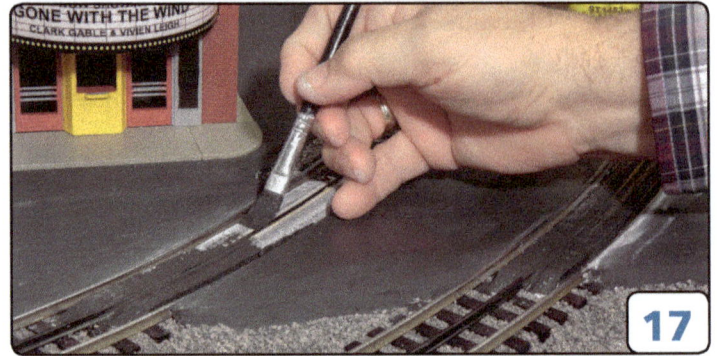

CHAPTER 17 - It's In The Details

There are a lot of qualities that separate a great train layout from a good or even average layout. In this chapter, we're going to go over the one thing I've seen time and time again that really makes the difference for most of us. Sure, workmanship is important. So is good planning. But the most overlooked one involves the great finishing details that go into making a layout look real.

And that's a shame because that is the one thing we all have time for. Often, when a layout is "done" (if there ever is such a thing), we are lost in imagination while we actually run it. When that gets old, we might drift away from the project to other things. But that is the best time to think about all the wonderful details you can add! Now is the time we can stop, take a long hard look, and begin the art of personalizing the layout and making it unique to you. This, I believe, is the never ending fun of the hobby. As a particular scene gets old to us, we can sit back and think of the things that we might add to change the whole scene that appears right in front of us. Here are some examples.

Take a look at the sanding tower in Photo 1. The importance of the detail that I want you to take notice of is the fact that there was always some spilled sand at the base of a sanding tower. The operator might get a little careless with the sand filler pipe (or filler hose, as the case may be). Maybe some sand would spill out and down the sand dome on the engine's boiler, landing on the ground by the base of the sanding tower. Just adding a little sand to the ground by the track where the operator of the sanding tower got a little careless is a wonderful detail that really adds to this scene. Also note that layout owner Bob Bartizek took the time to add a little rust to the steel structure of the sanding tower. Details! Wonderful realistic details!

Photo 2a shows a wonderful little device that can be added wherever you want to arrest the movement of a railcar. Even though it is shown at the end of a siding, it can be used anywhere. The prototype item is called a "skate." It is a portable device that a brakeman places on top of the rails. The railcar is then shoved over the small hump on the tongue of the wheel skate so that the wheels rest in the curved portion of the skate. The weight of the car keeps it in place, either for unloading operations or for some other reason. Bowser sells these devices, which are made by Selley. This is a great detail to add to a scene like an operating log dump car left at a sawmill or a lumber loader awaiting the dumping operation. It can also be added to a lonesome boxcar awaiting unloading at a freight dock. Things like this add interest and conversation for layout visitors, prompting them to ask questions and become more familiar with the hobby. Details such as these also make O gauge layouts really stand out.

Photo 2b is a different type of device. These are Nolan wheel stops and they were made to be more permanent. The prototypes shown here were called Model CS50. If you Google Mr. Detail Parts, you can find them. The O gauge models are made by Shapeways, in plastic. They are a 3D printed product, meaning that they are one of those technological marvels that come from original drawings but "print" in physical form to any scale desired. The real ones were meant to be mechanically installed on the rails at the end of a stub siding, as shown in the photo. Look what a marvelous detail they are when added to a siding track in a coal loading yard on Bob Bartizek's layout.

Photo 2c shows some Hayes wheel stops mounted at the end of a siding on my own layout. These little working models are made of metal by Tomar Industries. Their part number is O-803, and they come in a package of four. The O gauge models work amazingly well. At first, I thought soldering them to the rail would be a great idea, but the soldering gun tip will melt the entire casting in an instant if too much heat is applied. I switched over to using CA glue, and that process worked like a champ. A pair of them will even stop a locomotive instantly if it hits them. Using little details like these is so much better and more realistic than using clunky O gauge bumper stops. They also take up less space and they work better as well.

Photo 3 is a water filler standpipe, which we all have seen in the past. They are offered by Bowser, MTH, and others. The wonderful detail is the drain! Bob Bartizek made this from fine mesh screen wire and Evergreen plastic parts. The curbs are from round plastic rod, cut to fit, and the basin is a piece of .020 sheet plastic with the square mesh of screen wire added. Add a little rust paint to the screen mesh, and you've got a wonderful drain for your filler spout standpipe.

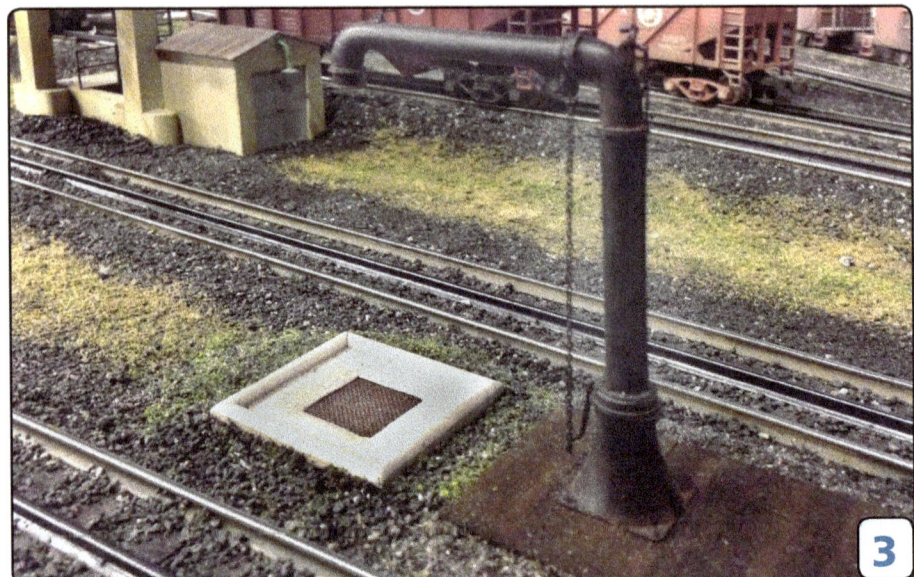

Photos 4a and 4b show a couple of wonderful details. The object in the photo is a Caboose Industries #208S ground throw, which can be added to any Ross Custom Switches or GarGraves track turnout. The problem has always been that it is somewhat difficult to determine at a glance which way the switch is thrown. By just adding either red or green paint to the switch lever, one can tell at a glance if the switch is thrown for straight or turnout position by simply looking at the exposed color!

But the big detail Bob Bartizek came up with takes care of the problem with mechanical switch stands if you have a remote control panel that needs to show the yard master which way even the mechanical switches are thrown. The electric switch machines will leave their own indicator light to show the position of the switch. What Bob did was to mount a nearly invisible sub-mini electric lever switch right at the end of the switch throwbar. The physical movement of the track switch throwbar will engage the lever of the electric lever switch, allowing you to electrically activate anything of your choosing by simply throwing the switch bar on the Caboose Industries ground throw. What a great mechanical idea disguised by the optical addition of the painted switch lever! It actually steers your eye to the switch lever to the point that the electrical lever switch is nearly invisible.

Here's a guy in Photo 5 who just wants to get warm between jobs in the yard on a cold day. He has "diverted" a little coal from a steam tender or a coal hopper with his trusty shovel. He has also procured a couple of steel drums, one of which looks like he is going to get a fire going in it to give him someplace to warm his hands. Or maybe he can use that coal in the stove inside his work shack. He is sitting on some ties made from leftover balsa or bass wood and then stained with something like black shoe polish to look like some spare creosote ties. The fellow is an Arttista figure, and the coal shovel and drums are available from Bowser or Selley.

Photo 6 is even easier. That is a left-over guard rail from a switch. They are already formed and make excellent junk beside the yard tracks, particularly near a switch. Just paint them up in a rust color, and they become a wonderful detail. A detail like this is a perfect example of what might be regarded as junk in one layout builder's eye but a nice scenic touch in another's.

In Photo 7 above are some more leftover ties and a couple of yard workers who are taking a break. Bob makes a point to always select figures in static poses. That way, he says, it doesn't look wrong when you look over at them later and they still haven't moved. They're still talking or resting!

Photo 8 is a plastic luggage cart like what you may find in a Walthers station kit or as an individual part from Selley (again sold by Bowser). The wonderful luggage is from a Woodland Scenics blister pack of luggage pieces, and these items come perfectly painted, looking already this good when placed on a luggage cart. Woodland Scenics is a great place to find highly detailed and painted scenic layout details.

Don't forget to Google places like Matchbox Models of Yesteryear (Photo 9). The Pennsylvania Railroad Ford pickup truck, complete with rail wheels and detailed truck bed parts, came just like you see it. You may have difficulty finding this exact truck since they are made in somewhat limited runs, but Matchbox is a great source to find detailed vehicles that will fit your layout.

A fast freight goes swooping by the West Valley station on Bob Bartizek's layout, which is definitely an eye-catching scene here in Photo 10. But it all goes unnoticed by the two pigeons perched on the peaked roof of the train station. Arttista makes the painted pigeons, which can be supplemented by some less expensive plastic ones made by Model Tech Studios in unpainted form. But, as Bob points out, you have the Arttista ones that can be used as perfect models of pigeon colors. A little time, some paints from Hobby Lobby, and you can add pigeons to your layout at will, time permitting. Such tiny details as this are great for close-up places where you know your layout visitor's eye is sure to catch them.

Photo 11 shows what you can do if you have an odd shaped, funny little corner on your layout that is otherwise unused. The track for the gondola is right on the edge of the layout (not visible at the bottom of the photo). The addition of some fencing from Rusty Stumps (part D2502, shown here) and various junk piles from Model Tech O scale Junk Piles make a nice little siding industry where junk is waiting to be tossed into a waiting gondola car some day. The simple addition of a sign on the fence makes it the scrap yard of an unseen industry. Don't forget to add some tufts of weeds to complete the scene. What a great detail to put on an otherwise unused corner of your layout!

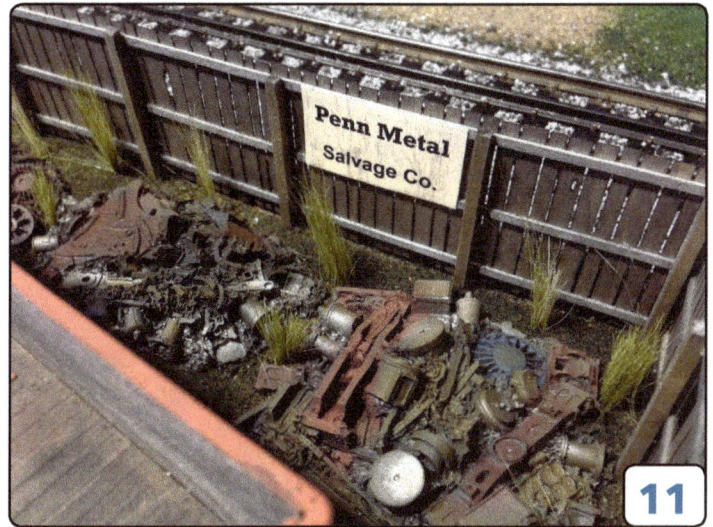

Photo 12 shows little piles of details on a freight dock, like sacks of flour or barrels of just about anything waiting to be put on board a boxcar. The addition of a couple of resting guys sitting around on the goods adds a wonderful little detail to an otherwise boring freight dock.

Here's a nice little cattle pen detail on Bob Bartizek's layout (Photo 13). He scratch-built this from balsa parts and stained them all with shoe polish. I think this can even be added to the loading ramps on the Lionel horse corral to make that accessory look much more scale in appearance and very believable. I think I'll add a modification like this to my operating horse corral when the time comes. That's the best part about the detailing process. As a layout builder, I can have a working model of the cattle or horse corral, but I can add this to it anytime, as time permits. Such detail additions as this keep the layout from growing old.

All along Bob's trestle are concrete foundations like these added to the bottom of the trestle bents. It turns out, these concrete foundations are actually leftover 2x4s that held up the trestle track until the mountains and gorges were actually built many years after the layout was up and running! Once Bob knew where the valley floor was going to be, he simply made trestle bents to fit perfectly between some point above the now-visible valley floor and the track above. He then sawed off the 2x4 supports, did a little filing here or there, and painted the resulting 2x4 stump to be the concrete foundation for the trestle (Photo 14). Nice touch!

These are just a few of the things I've documented, but there is certainly no end to the possibilities. The only thing limiting you is your own imagination.

CHAPTER 18 - Appearance Upgrades for Old Favorites

E ver notice how our favorite postwar accessories, which used to look absolutely perfect to us back then, now appear to be out-of-scale toys? It isn't because they got old. It's because we got old. As we evolved from children to adults, we became more sophisticated. What used to look perfect to us as kids begins to fail over time because your eye becomes more knowledgeable and wants to see the finer details of what you are looking at.

The same is true of your ears, too. That's why we now need to hear more realistic sounds coming from our trains than we did when we were kids. As we "kids" become more adult, we need to see and hear things in greater detail to get that same thrill we did when we were youngsters.

I think it's due to imagination. When we were young, we exercised our imaginations in abounding quantity. But something happens to us when we grow older. To have that same imaginative strength, we need a little more help in the sight and sound department than what we did as kids. That's why our train locomotives went from "toys" to elaborate-

ly detailed sight and sound machines. With that in mind, there's nothing to keep you from taking timeworn classic toys like Lionel's many trackside postwar operating accessories and making them look much more realistic with a little detail painting and modifications.

Photos 1 and 2 show two views of the classic Lionel No. 362 Barrel Ramp in its original form. It was a fairly smooth operating accessory introduced in 1952 and it was offered through 1957. You'll notice that it consists of obviously plain light brown plastic fencing on a gray base. Within the fencing is a yellow metal ramp powered by a gray vibrator magnet under the lower end and a long flat gray spring underneath the upper end. If you were lucky enough to also have the No. 3562 operating barrel car to unload barrels, it came with the black metal extension piece shown in Photo 4 to clip onto the barrel ramp. That allowed the barrels to smoothly roll off the barrel car to the barrel loader. It was a great toy, but not very realistic looking by our adult standards.

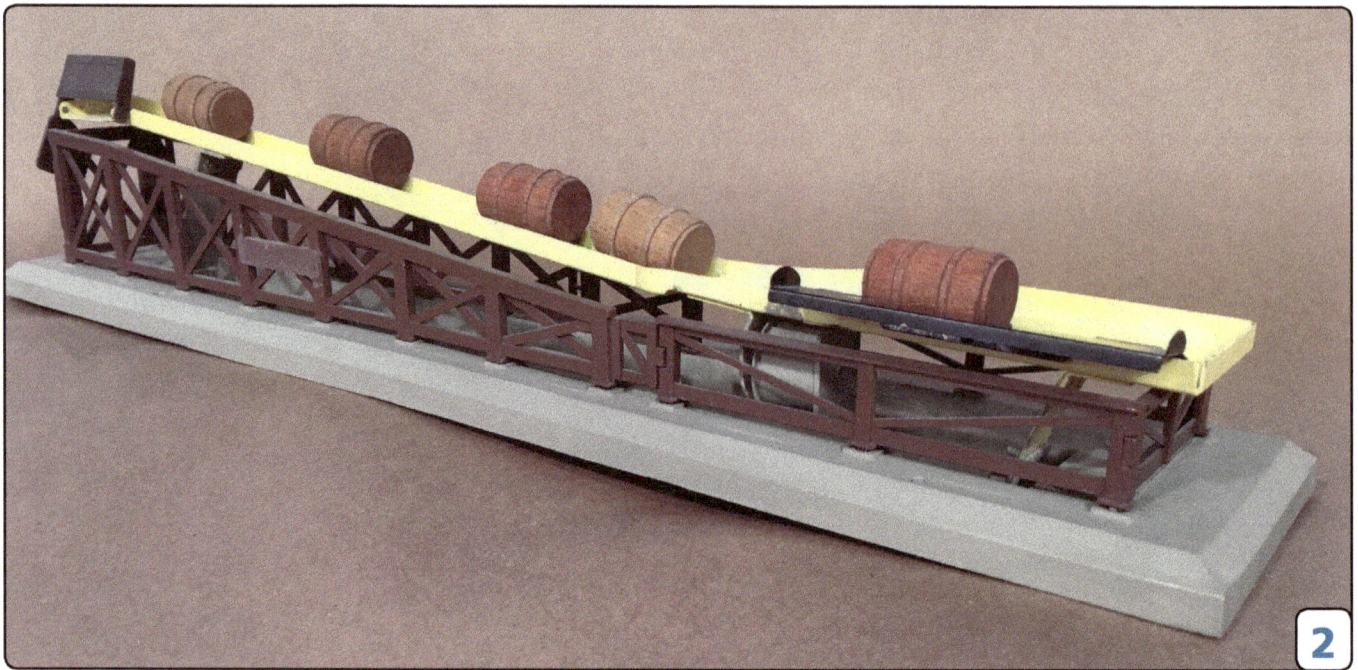

Now take a look at how Bob Bartizek made that toy look more realistic in Photos 3 and 4. There's the same old No. 362 Barrel Ramp, but it never looked this good in its straight out of box state. This one has been decked out in much more realistic flat colors. Gone is the toy-like yellow metal ramp. Now it is a much more believable flat black. The fencing went from a very plastic-looking light brown to something more like creosoted lumber. And things you don't want to see, like the easily noticed gray metal mechanical parts under the ramp, are now painted out in flat black and seem to disappear. The base looks much more like concrete with a coat of dull concrete paint.

Photo 5 shows what was once my original postwar Lionel No. 464 Saw Mill made from 1956 to 1960. It was a great accessory that appeared to saw logs into boards. But it looked like what it was: plastic. I found some super thin 1/32″ balsa sheet and stained it with some woodworker's oil based stain to get the rough brown look. I also measured it off and scored it with a simple black ballpoint pen. When I cut the balsa sheeting to fit the surfaces of the accessory, I grooved the ends of the joints between the boards with a jeweler's file. That one simple trick alone made the planks of the accessory really seem to jump out. I cut the balsa sheet stock to fit the surfaces of the sawmill base and 2 applied them with contact cement. Now, what was once simply ugly gray plastic is now a much more believable brown wooden structure. The corners of such a structure need to be protected, so some Evergreen Plastics angle channel was applied to cover up the wooden corners. It was painted gray to closely approximate the gray plastic. It all looks like painted metal now.

With these and other operating accessory examples, be careful not to cover any of the original plastic surfaces that the accessory needs for smooth operation (notice the original gray plastic in Photo 5 under the board that comes sliding out of the sawmill).

It has always bothered me that the output side of the sawmill had no awning to shade the workers like the one on the input side did where the logs went in. Using some corrugated plastic sheet (Evergreen Plastics #4530), a bit of plastic rod, and some plastic strips (all from Evergreen Plastics), I installed what looks like the corrugated metal roof you now see on this end. I painted all three corrugated roofs silver and added some rust colored paint wash over the top of all three to look like the first hints of rust forming on the metal. Once it was finished, it came out looking so good that it made me wonder why it hadn't been done by Lionel originally.

Now we need some workers! All five of these fellows are from Arttista. The one guiding boards off the end used to be shoveling something until I snatched his shovel and replaced it with a pole made from brass rod stock that I had painted brown. He now has a slight pay upgrade, guiding finished boards off the ramp onto the wooden loading dock. At least this fellow now has a place under his new roof to get in out of the hot sun once in a while!

Also note that the formerly white plastic jib crane is now repainted to look like a metal jib crane mounted in a concrete swivel pad. The broom pusher on the wooden sidewalk (Photos 5 and 6) and the other two men guiding the logs in Photo 7 are also Arttista figures.

The corrugated roof of the mill itself actually has an ugly slot formed in it that enables the operator to insert the boards back in. Adding a simple sign in front of that unsightly roof slot totally conceals it from the layout visitor without losing the function of the slot for reloading the boards. I removed the original office window with all the red Lionel wording on it and replaced it with a clear plastic replacement window trimmed with some more of the plastic angle from Evergreen Plastics. I'll probably trim it out in dark brown, like the door that is below it, and tape off the clear window with some windowpane detail.

The space between the window and the metal plate behind it left just enough room for an Arttista foreman figure and foreman's desk. That just seemed like a natural. I'll mount a graphic of the inside of a shop office onto the metal panel. Little things like that, and adding a human element with Arttista workers, add a ton of realism to the model.

The shiny white plastic clapboard siding on the original got a coat of flat antique white paint to make it look a lot more like how I remember lumberyard buildings looking like when I was a kid. All the trim got painted a nice contrasting dark brown.

In Photo 6 on the previous page, the natural wood on the base carries through to the input loading ramp as well. The antique white siding color ties in to the rest of the structure, as does the metal corner protectors and the dark brown wood trim paint. The steps and door stoop were painted a concrete color to add to the illusion.

Keep in mind that flat paints (such as those previously made by Poly S) can now be found under a variety of names from places like Hobby Lobby or other craft stores. While we're on this photo, take a look at the right side in the gravel near the roadway. Do you see that little light brown thing near the edge of the blacktop road? That is all that's left of the ugly hinge we made back in chapter 5 to create a lift up panel. You can see it more clearly in Photo 8. Scenery is extremely functional in covering up a bunch of layout construction problems. I might even further conceal the hinge with a bunch of weeds or loose trash.

Grouping more than one accessory can also be important in creating a believable scene. Lionel's No. 464 Saw Mill can easily be grouped in with the Lionel No. 264 Forklift Platform as well. In Photo 7 both accessories are being served by the same siding. To add nicely to the scene, Walthers Cornerstone Series model kits offered a nice kit called the Walton & Sons Lumber Yard. I grouped the office structure from that kit together with the Lionel sawmill and the forklift platform, as shown in the photo. The office and the forklift platform looked like a natural mounted side by side.

The No. 264 Forklift Platform needed paint on the freight dock to make it look a lot more like a real wooden surface on a concrete base. I first painted the wooden part brown and then streaked some flat black and flat gray on it with random strokes. That made it look more like aged freight dock wood. I added silver paint on the tire treads to make them look as much more believable representations of metal treads. Adding some black powder makes those silver treads look like some rubber from tires from forklift trucks. Now all I need to do is add some Woodland Scenics ST1453 Asphalt Top Coat (see chapter 16) on the steel forklift driveway to make it look much more like blacktopped pavement rather than shiny steel.

Two of my favorites are in Photo 8. The No. 345 Culvert Unloader and the No. 342 Culvert Loader match up perfectly together using the No. 345-10 Connecting Ramp. In the photo they are seen in their original colors. I never could figure out why the two buildings were molded in red plastic. The two bases are molded in light brown plastic, and the two roofs are molded in gray plastic. I kind of liked the two crane structures in orange metal since that looks like a safety color for an industry with crane towers.

Here's what they look like now in Photo 9. I painted the two plastic bases an aged concrete color to make them just a little more believable. After carefully cutting out the raised letters molded into the sides of the buildings, I painted both red buildings with a flat light gray color and trimmed all the windows in a flat dark gray. If you plan to add some interior lights, also paint the interior of the buildings in light gray as well. That way light won't shine through the walls of the building. The roofs were painted in the same contrasting dark gray as the window trim.

The vertical wooden ramp sides were also painted with the light gray paint to more closely identify with the two building structures. All small parts such as the hand railings along the ramp walkways were also trimmed in the dark gray color. Later on I will add some appropriate signage in the remaining rectangles on the sides of the buildings.

In Photos 9 and 10 you can see that the edges of the barrel ramp are painted in the same safety orange colors as the two crane towers. I figured that workers might need that little extra orange warning to keep their fingers and feet off the ramp when the culverts are rolling down. It's a nice accent that draws attention to the accessory.

The big secret to keeping these accessories working beautifully is to actually trap the bases of each vibrating accessory onto the train tabletop. That directs the vibration from the mechanism to make the accessory operate better. Photo 10 hides the fact that the bases are trapped tightly by plastic angle glued to the table, which also serves as a dam to keep the gravel from getting to the accessory base.

Note also the break in the rails. That enables you to fasten the track down on the accessory, thereby allowing you to build both accessories and the track onto one removable base to provide easy access for servicing. If I need to work on them, I can remove the two as a single unit, unplug them from the layout, and take them into the workbench for adjustments.

Finally, in Photos 11 and 12 I've added some darker gray streaking to anything that looks like it would get a lot of traffic or industrial grime, such as the wooden base to the tower control office and the wooden backing wall where the culverts slide off the traveling hoist.

To finish off these accessories, they are just begging for some more Arttista workers placed here and there to add additional human drama to the scene. I can see where I can easily work in one or two workers in the control tower offices, as well as some more on the back railings and the concrete bases. When I also install some tiny lights inside the control towers, the workers inside the buildings will stand out nicely. But all these are just suggestions. What are your ideas? How about making some thin walled building sides to completely connect both accessories together into one large building? The culverts could go into one side of the building for, let's say, some special industrial coating to be applied. Then they would roll out of the other side for shipping on some future train. Use your own imagination to make those old toys into something new and better for your own layout.

CHAPTER 19 - A Facelift for the Horse Corral

Lionel's original Operating Horse Corral (#3356-150) and the later version (#70-9224) have always been a favorite of mine ever since I found out how to make them work better (Photo 1). The secret I found out long ago was to freeze the base of the corral in a socket of material on the layout to dampen its movement when the vibrating mechanism was working. Once that has been accomplished, horses or cows move silently and smoothly through the corral accessory. They also load into and out of the horse or cattle car much better.

But what about that plastic look? When we were kids, that looked great. But now I want things on my hi-rail layout to be as scale-like in appearance as I can possibly make them look. For years I had given up on my Operating Horse Corral because it looked about as real as a 3-dollar bill.

Then I saw my friend Bob Bartizek's Pennsylvania and Western layout, and he had the best looking stockyards I've ever seen (Photo 2 below). Bob's is obviously a beautiful scale layout with scale attention paid to the appearance of the corral. Now there is only so much you can do with an operating accessory to dress it up yet have it still work, but Bob's stockyard inspired me to see what I could do.

Take a look at the Operating Horse Car and Operating Horse Corral. Obviously, the part that sticks out as the worst appearing to me is that white plastic looking corral fencing that had to be raised up so high to provide space for the motion mechanism beneath it. Sure, I know horse ranches have white fences all over Kentucky, but this corral is meant to be railroad property. I just don't think those corrals had pristine white fences. If they ever did, they weren't pristine white very long.

I had just finished using some basswood to make a wooden bridge elsewhere on the layout. I figured I could hack this corral accessory up and improve its appearance quite a bit by making some real wooden fencing for the horse corral.

I began by carefully cutting away the white plastic fencing (Photo 3). When you do this, leave the small plastic nubs at the bottom of the fence posts, as shown in Photo 4. They will serve as a guide to show you where to attach the new fence posts.

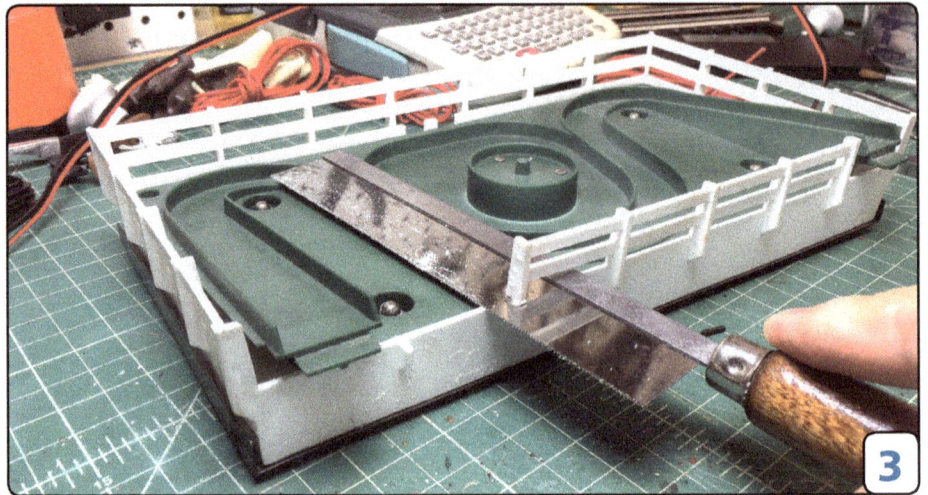

Here's a tip on how this wonderful operating horse corral works. Everything that is white plastic is firmly connected to the metal base and is not supposed to vibrate. Everything green in color is a vibrating platform and definitely is supposed to move. If it doesn't, the horses go nowhere. No part of the green plastic base may touch the white corral portion. We can add and take away things to the white corral part and we can add or take away things to the green part, but we cannot do anything to cause the two parts to touch each other.

The other thing we can do to improve the illusion is to hide that clunky base part of the corral. After some careful measuring, I determined that about an inch of the base needs to go away. We can do that by hiding it with built up earth to disguise it a little. Anytime I do this, I almost always use cork road bed as a buildup, but since we need a whole inch, I decided on getting some high density Styrofoam from a home improvement store. Sometimes that material is pink, sometimes blue, and sometimes green. It all depends on whose brand the store is selling. But don't use the white Styrofoam since that is usually low density foam that easily crumbles and is hard to work into shape.

Photo 5 shows some green Styrofoam chunks added to the sides and back of the corral. The black spots are drywall screws temporarily holding the Styrofoam down waiting for the Elmer's glue to dry. That clunky corral base is already starting to go away.

In Photo 6, I've removed the screws, filled the screw holes with putty, and shaped the Styrofoam down using some rasp files. You can shape the Styrofoam with wood rasp files or even the open end of your vacuum cleaner hose. That technique works well for me since it also sweeps up all the filings as I go. Add a little earth tone paint (Photo 6), and the result is really starting to look good. I took the time to carve in a little flat depression for a gravel service drive leading up to a place where I plan to show a gate in my finished corral.

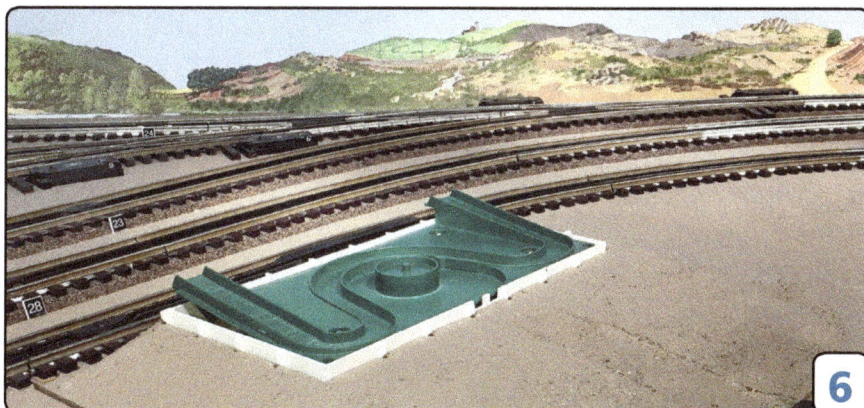

Little things make a big difference in scenery. I cut out a piece of leftover foam core board and made a paved apron leading off the edge of the road going into the corral. I'll add gravel later, but look at how good that makes the approach to the future gravel service road look.

The sizes of basswood you will need are 1/4″ square stock for the fence posts, 1/32″ x 1/4″ flat stock for the bottom fence rail only, and some 1/16″ x 1/4″ stock for the middle and upper fence rails.

Using Minwax Classic Gray #297 (Photo 7), I pre-stained all the wood I will need for the corral. It's important to do the staining before you glue any wood together since the stain will not penetrate any glue you have on the outside of the wood.

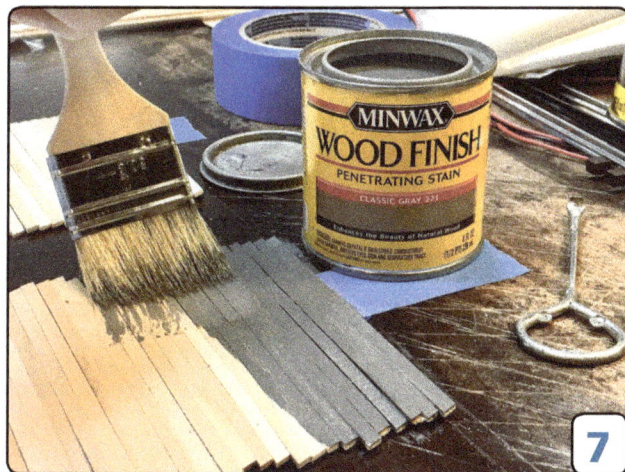

In Photo 8, I am applying the thin (1/32″ x 1/4″) wood fencing on the bottom of the corral directly over the white plastic of the base. Cut the pieces to fit exactly between the plastic nubs left over from cutting off the plastic fencing. An easy way to handle these small pieces of wood is to pierce the thin wood piece with the corner of a modeling knife allowing you to hold it while you apply two or three dots of CA glue to the wood. Then position the wooden plank with the knife, hold it in place, and remove the knife, as shown in the photo.

Photo 9 shows the lower fence board in place. Note that the fence board on the long side of the corral needs to extend past the end of the short side. Don't trim that off until later after you have attached the corner post to the fencing.

I liked the looks of the loading chutes on my friend's corral and started out simulating them on the operating corral for this project, but then I made a disturbing discovery. The enclosed chutes hid too much of the fun of watching the horses going into and coming out of the horse car. When modeling the real world, there comes a time when you have to make some "style" choices. Which is more important to you, the scale appearance or the operating fun? In this case, for me the operating fun won out, so I didn't model the enclosed chutes for the operating corral.

I decided to paint the green plastic base of the corral with a soft brown flat acrylic paint, as shown in Photo 10. Note also the placement of the two corner fence posts that attach to the fencing. Because I wanted my fencing to be smooth on the inside of the corral, the corner posts do not actually attach to the corral base. They are held in place by the fencing slats themselves, outside the fencing on the corners. It is easiest to do the bottom fence rail, then the top fence rail, followed finally with the middle fence rail. A Q-Tip is a good tool to use to apply some stain to the exposed ends of the basswood fence posts. I also touched up any of the exposed plastic pieces that still show on the corral base with some gray and/or brown acrylic flat paint.

Note also the good-looking horses! Don't forget to give those goofy rubber horses a facelift as well. Who wants all the horses to look like globs of brown or black rubber? Do a Google online search for some pictures of horses to get some ideas for colors. That's what I did, and now my horses are proud to be seen hanging out in a good-looking horse corral.

Wow! Look what happens when we plunk that big clunker corral base into our Styrofoam earth buildup, as seen in Photo 11. Now all that's needed is to do something with that funny green clunky plastic thing in the middle of the corral. Its reason for being is that the magnet underneath it on the base pulls on a metal plate riveted to the underside of the green plastic. The vibration translates into a slight twisting vibration that moves the horses along. Why couldn't that be a watering tub?

In Photo 12, I've added a piece of wavy translucent blue plastic to simulate some water (Plastruct #91802 Agitated Blue Water, catalog #WPSB-308). I found it at a local hobby shop that stocks plastic sheet materials.

First, I cut away that funny little plastic nub sticking up in the center of what is to become my round water tub. Then I looked around my shop and found a metal washer that fit perfectly into the depression in the tub. Using the washer as a pattern, I traced around it onto the blue plastic with a black Sharpie pen. Then I cut around the line with a good pair of scissors to make the water insert fit perfectly in my trough. It isn't a big deal, but little details like that really help the illusion. I finished off by painting some silver paint on the outside of the green water tub to simulate some galvanized sheet metal. I then added some soft scenery weeds and grasses around the corral along with a gravel service drive (Photo 13).

Compare the finished product in Photo 13 with Photo 1. See what a difference there is? It is possible to incorporate some of the working accessories from Lionel's earlier era right into your modern hi-rail layout. Sure, it still doesn't look like the wonderful scale corral on Bob Bartizek's masterpiece, but it certainly looks a whole lot better than how it started out.

BEFORE

AFTER

Chapter 19 *Building A Layout* by Jim Barrett

CHAPTER 20 - Reliable Remote Uncoupling

In the 1940s and 1950s, Lionel came up with a perfectly clever way to have fun performing freight operations just like the real railroads did. The operator could press a button on a remote control box and energize a magnet built into a special section of track called the UCS (uncoupling section). The magnet would pull down a steel plate on the bottom of the coupler, causing the coupler's knuckle to open. That would let you uncouple a train to add or remove cars anywhere within the train. With a UCS track section, the train operator could uncouple where he needed or wanted to in order to "set out" a freight car or to add one into the train.

This system worked relatively well until later manufacturing economy measures replaced the metal plate with nothing more than a metal thumbtack on the end of a plastic arm that held the coupler pin. That resulted in an appalling drop in reliability and couple performance. Then along came several new manufacturers of couplers and uncoupling track sections, supposedly compatible with the original operating coupler system Lionel came up with. But there was, of course, no standard established among the different manufacturers, and there still isn't. The result is couplers that look like they should work, but they simply don't. How awful!

The recent alternative was to make the coupler on the back of the engine work by pressing a button on the remote. Trouble is all the rest of the couplers on the train were sort of left in the dust of modern technology. I wanted a way to be able to open couplers anywhere in the train and to do it reliably by remote control, just like we do with the coupler on the back of the engine. I found the way to do that using the MTH DCS and some magnets salvaged from old Lionel O27 remote track sections, but more about that shortly.

The biggest problem is getting couplers to work like they should to begin with. It doesn't make any difference how much work the modeler puts into making couplers work by remote control. If they physically don't perform reliably, then all the bells and whistles don't make a bit of difference. I researched many different makes of couplers available today. Some are good, and most are just plain junk.

I found that the two most reliable operating couplers currently available are the MTH RailKing freight trucks with the hinged plate on the bottom that opens the coupler and the sometimes available original Lionel postwar coupler design from the 1950s, which used a metal plate as well. Lionel still uses that original design truck and coupler on all operating cars that need an accessory slide shoe.

The trucks and couplers of both the postwar Lionel style and the modern MTH style open easily using a magnet in the track. Also, both of these manufacturers very compatibly coupled up with each other. But equally important, when they coupled, they stayed coupled!

Since the RailKing truck operates with needle point bearings on the axles, it makes them far preferable to the old postwar Lionel style trucks of the 1940s and 1950s. They are also far more available. The coupler arm of the RailKing truck also swivels at its base where it attaches to the frame of the freight truck, making the arms more functionally flexible when they need to be. In addition, there is a manual "nub" on the coupler shaft that allows the operator to open the coupler easily with a finger if all else fails.

With that in mind, I have set about converting every car with a known coupling problem to one or the other of these two types of trucks and couplers to make them work flawlessly. It really isn't the scary job I thought it was going to be. RailKing trucks and couplers are readily available from MTH (#30-89001). Of course, not all manufacturers' freight cars are alike, so some modifications to the undercarriage of certain cars might need to be made. But where there's a will, there's a way. It required a few trips to the hardware store to get the right size (and the right thread) of miniature screws, washers, and bolts to do the job, but it was well worth the effort.

Keep a goal in mind to mount the new truck as high as you can into the underside of the car in order to keep the center of gravity as low as possible. Sometimes, when converting trucks and couplers on manufacturers other than Lionel and MTH, it may mean that you need to cut out the plastic bolster on the underside of the car body itself if that's how it was made.

Here's another very important consideration: When you're finished, weigh the car using something like a kitchen food scale. Why is this important? Because evenly weighted cars couple much more smoothly. When each car has actual mass, coupling works much better. In fact, there is a published guideline for the recommended weight of freight cars. For O gauge, the National Model Railroad Association (NMRA) has recommended a guideline of 5 ounces per freight car plus 1 additional ounce for every inch of car length. Therefore, a 10″ O gauge boxcar should weigh right around 15 ounces. If you follow this guideline, you will be amazed at how well cars will couple with all other cars.

You can get very creative about where and how you add weight to some cars. Some of my flatcars now carry farm tractors, some gondolas have scrap in them, and some boxcars carry other forms of freight glued down to their floors in the ends. A good source for lead to add weight is any Bass Pro Shop. They sell a variety of lead weights in the fishing department. One of my favorites is lead ingots (weighing 5 oz. each). These can be easily cut up to make smaller weights, but most importantly, they are flat and can be attached to cars with glue (I used Walthers Goo, and it worked very well). These ingots are great for flatcars and other exposed areas of freight cars. You can get a bag of 16 of these 5 oz. bars for about 27 bucks.

Also available is something called Reusable Split Shot that comes in a packet of 20 for about four bucks. They are loose and somewhat round lead balls. Those are good for hopper bays. Some Goo in each hopper bay, and the lead shot will stay put for good. Now every car I have "plays well" (couples and uncouples well) with every other car. That makes model railroading so much more fun!

Another critical part of the equation is what you use to uncouple the cars. Even though I have Ross and Gar-Graves track, I was bound and determined to make my layout truly "coupler functional." The essence of my solution is pictured in Photo 1.

As I have reported here in the past, making use of scrap Lionel O27 uncoupling track magnets is the key. These track sections can be found all rusted up under sellers' tables at train shows and can be bought for as little as 50 cents to a buck apiece. They look like what you see in Photo 2. Remember, you don't care what they look like... nine times out of ten the all-important magnet still works. What you want are magnets like the ones shown in Photo 3. Check the plastic covering on the top of the magnet to make sure it isn't deformed from overheating. Those magnets aren't reliable.

2

3

Every magnet has two wires (or more accurately, two ends of the same wire). One must connect to any AC common going back to the transformer, and the other must connect to AC+. To control the magnet, you need to be able to activate the AC+ connection for only a short spurt. In the old days we used a button for each uncoupling magnet. My method uses the MTH DCS. Since one TIU (Track Interface Unit) can operate up to five AIUs, that amounts to up to 50 accessory devices that can be operated from a single remote control handle.

My system will use two TIUs, each with three AIUs connected. That will result in up to 60 uncoupling magnets (or other accessories), all controlled by a single remote control handle. Oh yes, and it will be able to control up to 60 track switches as well. In addition, any and all of what you put onto one remote can be easily "cloned" onto as many other remotes as you like. That enables anyone in the operating session to control any uncoupling magnet, any switch, or any engine. The fun thing about this is you can pair up crews of engineers and switchmen to work together. One person operates the locomotive while the other operates the uncoupling action and freight operations.

Remember when I wrote that the wire wound around the magnet's core was coated with lacquer to insulate the copper from each other in the windings? It also means that the copper wire won't solder to anything. That's not good! You need to be able to solder to both wire ends. To do that, you need to scrape some of the lacquer off the wire ends.

Carefully straighten the two ends of the wire coming off the bottom of the magnet. Gently scrape the two wire ends on all sides as depicted in Photo 4. Do that ever so gently until you see the bright copper color of the wire with the lacquer scraped off. It is very easy to accidentally cut the copper wire when doing this, so be careful to only gently scrape the wire and don't push down on the knife blade and cut it off. With a soldering gun, heat each wire end and coat the copper with solder (this is called "tinning" the wire). That will also help strengthen the wire from the scraping action.

Here's something to think about: As soon as you evenly weight your freight cars, you can couple on curves just as easily as you can on straights. The system I'm going to show you lets you plant your uncoupling magnets into a curve just as easily as in a straight track. If you are coupling on a curve, all you need to do is to open both couplers before you attempt to couple up the train.

A Lionel O27 uncoupling magnet is a simple device. It is a short steel rod about 1/4″ in diameter and only 7/16″ long, wound with hundreds of turns of a fine lacquer-coated wire. The lacquer coating serves as insulation on the fine copper wire so it won't short out within the coils. When you press a button and allow about 14 volts of electrical current to pass through the wire from one end to the other, it makes a very powerful magnet out of the little steel rod it is wrapped around. That will attract the metal plate on the bottom of the coupler, and "tada" the coupler opens.

4

Hold the magnet up to the center rail where you want it to be mounted, and you will notice that the plastic top of the magnet spans just about perfectly from the edge of one tie, past two more ties, and to the edge of the third tie. Use that as a guide to show how much center rail you need to cut out. In any case, be sure that you do not remove more center rail than needed for the magnet plastic to fill back in when you're done. Using a Dremel rotary tool and a fiber cutting disk, cut the center rail at those two locations and cut the ties near the inside edge of the outer two rails, allowing you to remove the center rail piece with its two tie chunks attached. If you already have added ballast, that's no problem. Cut through the cork as well and remove the cork roadbed, too. The result should look like Photo 5.

Cut up some short lengths (8″ or so) of 20 or 22 gauge wire and drill a hole (slightly larger than the diameter of the wire you're using) through the table at each end of the opening you've made in the track (Photos 5 and 6). Strip one end of each wire and tin with solder. Poke the unstripped end of each wire through the holes as shown in Photo 6.

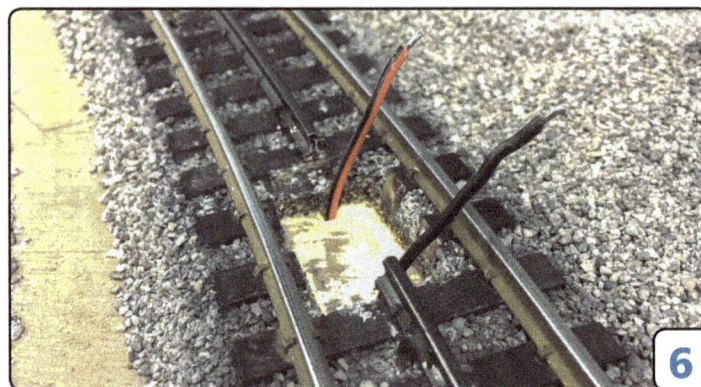

If in the process of making the cut in the track you also cut into the cork roadbed, cut a piece of cork and replace it in the opening between the wires as shown in Photo 7.

Soldering the super-thin wires of the magnet to the ends of the two bigger wires is somewhat delicate. Until the magnet is mounted and glued in, it is easy to break off the small wires of the magnet. For this reason, I've settled on this method to minimize that happening. Hold the magnet by the body and position the thin wire of one end of the magnet against the end of one of the large wires sticking up from the table. It makes no difference which magnet wire goes to which table wire. Apply heat from a soldering gun until the solder melts and merges together. Hold it still until the solder has set and repeat the procedure for the other wire from the magnet. The finished result should look like Photo 8.

Position the magnet, carefully guiding the wires down through the holes, and glue it in place as shown in Photo 9. Use Walthers Goo since you may need some adjustment time before the glue sets up. Center the magnet in the opening, making sure that there is no gap between the center rail and the plastic on top of the magnet. Fill in the open area with some ballast and brush it in place (Photos 10 and 11). It doesn't hurt to leave the ballast loose around the magnet. You may have to replace the magnet someday, and it is a lot easier to do if you don't re-glue the ballast back in place.

Remember that you actually broke (electrically) the center rail to put this magnet in, so you need to reconnect the center rail electrically. I use a Dremel tool bit with a rotary grinding ball on the end to clean the plating off the center rail at two locations close to the uncoupling magnet. Using a soldering gun, heat the center rail at the cleaned spots and allow solder to flow to and join with the rail. This is called "tinning" the rail. At that point, drill two more holes down through the table right beside the cleaned off spots you just made on the center rail. Make the holes slightly larger than a piece of 16 or 18 gauge wire.

Cut a piece of 16 or 18 gauge wire about a foot long and then strip and tin both ends of the wire with solder. Poke one end of the wire down through one of the holes. Slide the tinned end of the wire down to the bottom of the center rail and solder it to the rail. Push the other end of the wire up through the other hole and solder that end to the center rail on the other side of the uncoupling magnet. When you are done, touch up the top of the magnet and all solder spots on the center rail with black paint. If you look closely at Photo 12, you can see where the red insulation of the end of the wire is peeking up through the ballast.

Connect one of the wires from the magnet to the nearest AC common under the table. Connect the other end to a wire that will go to your AIU and attach it to position #1 of one of the accessory ports on the side of the AIU (Photo 13). The brown wires in the photo are all going from the AIU to various uncoupling magnets on the layout. The "IN" port at all 10 of these accessory posts is where you will attach the constant voltage that you are feeding to each of your uncoupling magnets. A word to the wise: If you have done all your other work as described, you will not need more than 14 volts for the uncoupling magnets to work perfectly. In fact, more voltage than that, or even long presses on the momentary button with that voltage, will result in the magnet overheating and melting the plastic on the top of the magnet. When that happens, you will need to dig the deformed magnet out and replace it with another one. Another note: Don't attempt to use wire larger than 20 gauge for the AIU ports. Also, tin the ends of the wire before you insert them in the hole at the port of the AIU. When you tighten the screw to attach the wire to the AIU, if the wire isn't tinned little strands of wire can venture over and touch other contacts, thereby driving you crazy. Follow the directions from MTH about adding in accessories to the remote. The system actually lets you label each accessory in addition to the system applying a number. Take a good look at Photo 14. For uncoupling spots 7 and 8 on the layout, I've added some signs glued into the ballast to let me know what number they are and where they are. In the remote I've typed in abbreviated descriptions for where they are as well. Look carefully at the remote in the bottom of the photo and you will notice that there are five keys at the top of the remote. The one on the far right has "ACT" over it, which means that button will "actuate" or act like a momentary push button for accessory #7 in the window. Pressing that button will energize the uncoupling magnet labeled #7 in the photo.

To recap, here's your project for the next two months:

1. Get all your couplers working correctly at 14 volts or less.
2. Salvage a bunch of old O27 uncoupling magnets.
3. Mount them in the track where you want them to be located.
4. Hook them up to your AIU(s).
5. Weight your freight cars correctly.
6. Done!

You are now set to have more fun than you've ever had with switching operations!

CHAPTER 21 - Creating Scenery Access Ports

Back in chapter eight, we made a removable roll away section of the layout. If you look at Photo 1, you can see that section locked into the main layout. I have a lot of work to do yet on the trestles and other scenery, but this is an opportune time to talk about and show what I call scenery access ports. These are loosely defined as key locations in the scenery that can, when needed, be easily removed to allow access to things inside or behind the scenery like a train that may have derailed inside the mountain, for example.

Look carefully in the lower left portion of the photo and you will see the scenery module separation line in the hillside. In the near future that irregular line will be easily disguised by weeds and other foliage. That line is the separation point of the movable module that will contain the valley you see in the photo, as well as three railroad trestles that will be there when the scenery is finished.

The rollout module idea was born of the necessity to get behind the trestle assembly both for construction of the back of the layout and also to be able to service hidden trains when they need attention.

The movable trestle assembly is the largest scenery access port I've ever attempted. At first it seemed like an impossibility, but when I found a source for heavy commercial grade wheels, it really became doable. If maintenance is ever needed, the trestle module will be unsnapped (note the suitcase-style snap in the foreground of the photo), and all three trestles plus the canyon itself will separate and roll out of the way to gain access deep inside the mountain. Compare Photo 1 with Photo 2 to see the beginning of the trestle rollout module.

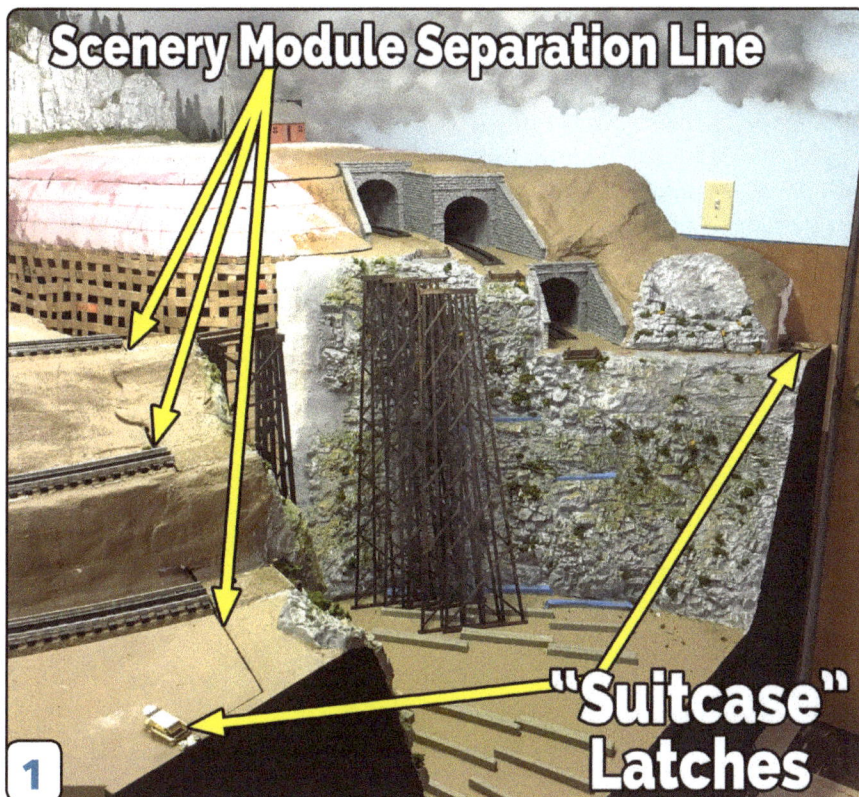

Scenery Module Separation Line

"Suitcase" Latches

1

2

Photo 3 might not look like much, but it shows the early stages of making the ravine that will lead back into the mountain. The back of the ravine will be dominated by a waterfall coming from a mountain stream that will emerge from under the highway bridge. The waterfall will end with a river running down the floor of the ravine (painted brown for the time being).

The riverbed floor has a trick built into it. The disappearing drop-down riverbed is hinged on both sides with an irregular saw cut split down the middle, which will be disguised by the river water itself at a later date. Kicking the single hinged leg inward, as shown at the bottom of Photo 3, allows both halves of the riverbed to drop out (Photo 4). That will allow me to walk all the way back to the face of the mountain just behind what will become the waterfall area.

Right behind the highway bridge over that future waterfall, shown at the back of Photo 4, I will need to get access through to the inside of the mountain. Just inside or behind the mountain, right at that point, is a hidden track switch. Yes, to be sure, try to avoid this if at all possible because Murphy's Law says that if it is possible for a train to derail at the most inaccessible point, it will. But when you can't avoid it, always plan on being able to get to the trouble spot quickly and easily by incorporating some easily removed scenery sections so you can get to the derailment or other problems without too much trouble. In my case, Styrofoam lends itself to making easily concealed access ports in the scenery.

My mountain is composed of two large cast mountain scenery pieces raised up on some pink Styrofoam to give them enough height to cover (mostly) a vertical sewer stack. I stacked up three pieces of 2″ Styrofoam to make the base for this mountain. Just behind the base is that critical track with a switch that allows the upper-level train to spiral down through the mountain. That will present another great mountain scene where the train pops out of the mountain tunnel opening onto one of the three trestles stretching over the huge river gorge and then back into the mountain, continuing its spiral down to the lower-level track.

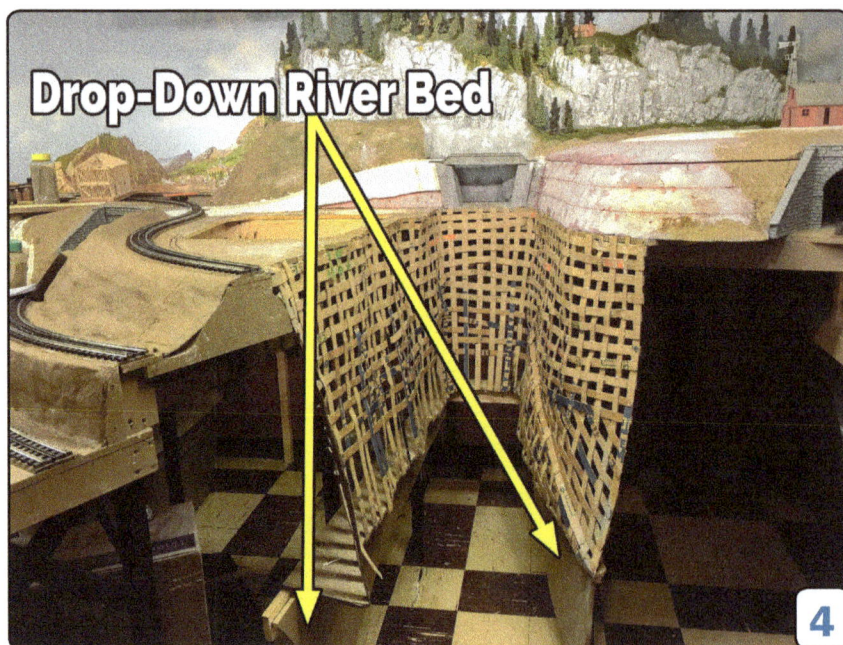

As shown in Photo 5, I have lifted out my highway bridge to expose the chunk of movable Styrofoam that in Photo 6 has been pushed back inside the mountain. In its finished form, I will not be able to remove that Styrofoam access port by pulling it forward and removing it from the front. That's because the scenic materials for my future rip roaring mountain stream will be right in front of the access port area. The build up of that scenic water material will prevent me from pulling the Styrofoam chunk out of the wall to open up the scenery port. That means for the access port to work, it will have to be able to push back inside the mountain and out of the way. By doing that, I will be able to gain access to the track switch inside (Photo 7). That will enable me to fix the mockup derailment of the UP hopper shown in the photo.

Once any operating problem is solved, replacing the movable piece is easy and quick. In the Styrofoam I put a couple of holes large enough for a thumb and index finger (Photos 5 and 6 again) so I can easily pull it back in place when I am finished (Photo 8). Don't worry about those two holes; they will be easily disguised with scenery tricks like foliage or bushes. If space permits, you can even place a tree on the wall to use as a handle for the Styrofoam port. A word to the wise: Leave a nice small battery-powered LED utility light inside the mountain so that you'll be able to see the problem by peering through the access port. Even something as simple as a single AAA battery-powered LED keychain light will work nicely. Thanks to LED technology, something that small will provide an amazing amount of light. These little things are available at hardware store checkout counters at a very low cost.

If there isn't any scenery water to worry about on your layout, perhaps just a simple piece of scrap Styrofoam with trees "planted" in it might work. The removable piece could be simply lifted out of the way to expose a nice open access hole.

Styrofoam Access Port Closed

Styrofoam Access Port Open

Anything that gives you access to hidden parts of the layout can be a movable scenery access port. It doesn't necessarily have to be just finished rural scenery. If your layout has urban scenery, such as offices or commercial buildings, they, too, can form a scenery access port. In Photo 9 my Ameri-Towne #941 Barrettsburg Factory looks like an impressive part of this industrial park, but what it really does is hide a tunnel through the wall just on the other side of it. If there's a problem in the tunnel, the whole building can simply be lifted up and out (Photo 10). That will allow access to the tunnel as well as to the siding going inside the building. All the building needs are some locator pins inserted into the layout table at the interior corners of the building. In Photo 10 one of those locator pins is visible below the red gondola with the culvert load. That pin allows the building to be set back in the same place every time.

Because of the sheer size of O gauge, we need to be smart about how we use layout table space. Any trick we can come up with, such as removable scenery access ports, helps us use that space wisely. Keep the concept of removable access ports in mind as you build your own layout and as you design scenery. Any trick like this that enhances the overall effect of your layout adds to its "wow factor."

CHAPTER 22 - A Trestle Trick

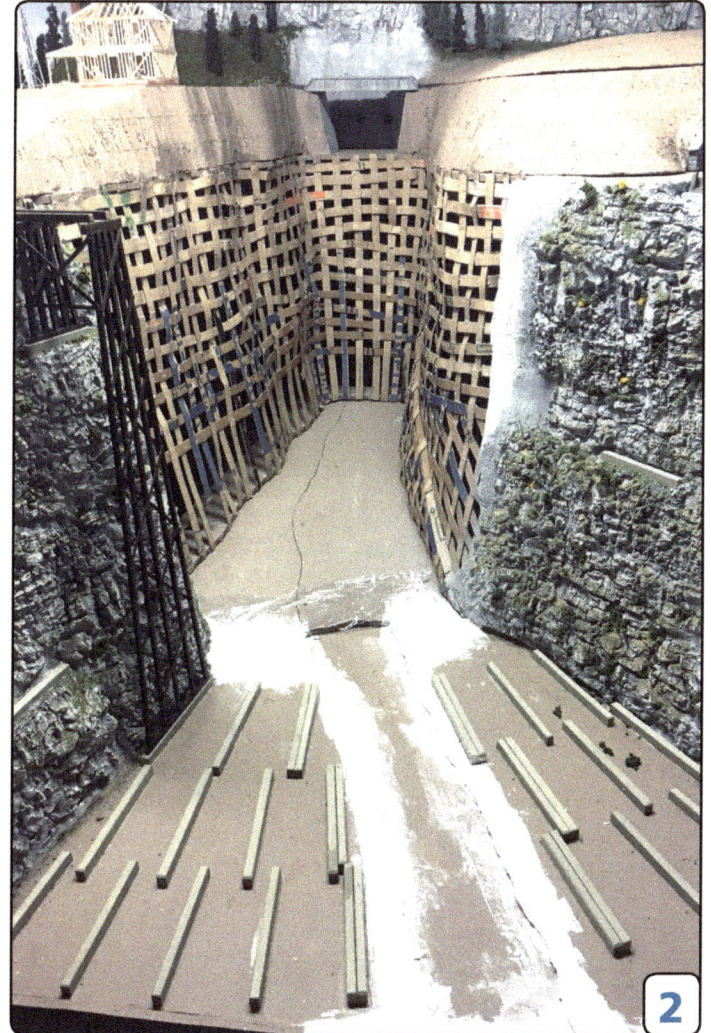

In chapter eight I discussed how to build movable roll-around sections of the layout. The purpose of that project was to build a platform that would contain a triple trestle on something that moves around so I could get behind it if I ever needed to. Photo 1 shows the floor of that movable piece tucked neatly under the slanted floor of what will become the river in a deep valley.

Photo 2 shows the addition of the rock sides of the trestle valley with preparation for the river that will run under the trestles. The gray pieces on the floor of the valley are carefully positioned, simulated concrete foundations that will support the three completed trestles. There are some double foundations on each side of the river for all three trestles. The extra trestle bents at these locations will be used to support the steel bridge over the river. The bed of the river is made by using some spackling compound to slope the ground up on each side of what will ultimately be the river area. In the future I plan to describe some model water tricks that will make that shallow stream bed look more like a deep rushing stream.

Now is the time to add scenery detail to the floor of the valley under the trestles. Access to the valley floor will be severely limited after the trestles are completed, so it is important to do that ground work now before building the trestles.

In Photo 3 I've added some ground cover from Scenic Express (#EX896E, called Dead Fall Debris), filling in around the concrete foundations to further define where the river is going to be. This is a nice rough mixture of foliage and tree bits. I applied a coating of Elmer's glue to the painted wooden surface of the valley between and around the concrete trestle bent foundations and followed that with a sprinkling of the ground cover material. I then followed with a spray of "wet water" (water with a few drops of dish detergent mixed in). That wet water application will saturate the dry scenery material on the valley floor with a liberal dribble of diluted Elmer's glue. The wet water allows the diluted glue to mix thoroughly with the dry scenery material. Don't worry, when it all dries, the glue disappears.

On my layout, there will be three long trestles crossing this deep gorge. The tallest of the three is in the background of the photo, complete with one finished trestle bent standing on the left. It will not be climbing or descending but simply crossing the valley. There will be another trestle in the foreground. It will be just a little shorter but will also be simply crossing the valley.

The trestle in the middle is the present focus. It will be both the most challenging to build and the most difficult one to get to when all three are finished. This one will be a graduated height trestle ascending from left to right as it crosses the valley. I already have the track in place on the left and right of my removable trestle module for all three track beds. I will tackle this graduated trestle first, which is the one in the middle. The big construction challenge will be to make a smooth, continuous rise in the trestle going from the lower elevation of the track on the left to the higher elevation on the right of the valley.

There are many different ways to go about solving this engineering problem with the most common one being to actually build the track on a sloping piece of curved plywood supported by temporary vertical supports. Then when the roadbed and track are complete, the temporary supports and plywood would be removed, leaving the track sort of hanging, to be subsequently replaced with trestle bents and the completed trestle. This method, as I see it, is a long, tedious procedure fraught with a lot of chances for uneven construction. So I have come up with what I think is another outlook on solving this construction problem.

Photo 4 below illustrates my solution. It involves carefully making a joint between two long pieces of 3/8″ square balsa sticks by sandwiching the ends between two thin 1/32″ x 3/8″ x 4″ balsa strips using some ultra-thin CA glue. Look carefully and you can see these strips on the upper and lower sides of the long beam, slightly to the left, far above the river.

Splice Joint

3/8" Square Balsa Wood Sticks

In Photo 5 you can see the joint in the big beam hanging precariously out over the opening in the gorge.

I should point out that there is a major difference between balsa wood and bass wood. Don't confuse the two! Although bass wood is the wood to use to make trestle bents, this little trick will only work with balsa wood. Balsa is the softer of the two and has just the right amount of flexibility to pull this little trick off. Bass wood will not do.

Using super-thin CA, cement one end of the long 3/8″ stick to the lower end of the track's roadbed, right in the middle of the track bed (Photo 6). Carefully bend the stick to form an even curve over the valley and cement the far end of the stick to the high end of the roadbed (Photo 7). Before you cement the second end in place, sight along the balsa stick, as well as over the top of the stick, to keep it generally centered with where the middle of the track will eventually go. It isn't critical that it be exactly centered, but it should be bent to pretty much represent where the middle of the track will be. If you look back at Photo 5, you can see what I mean.

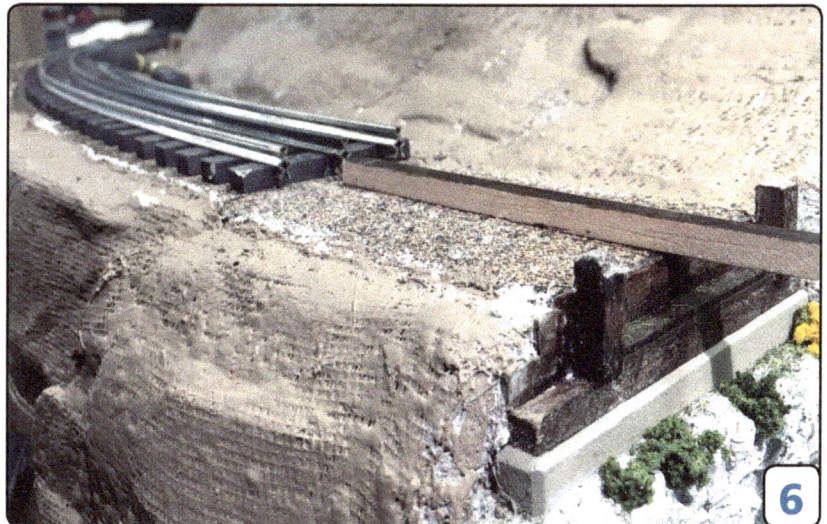

When you get just about the right amount of bend in the stick, glue the upper end of the balsa stick to the middle of the roadbed at the high end of the grade as seen in Photo 7. What you have just done is make the bottom of this curved stick represent the exact height where you want the ties of the track to be when the trestle is finished.

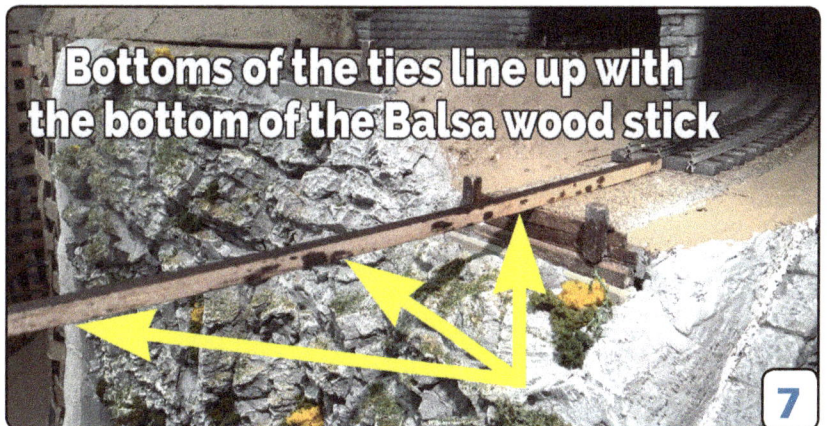

Now stand back and take a look at the 3/8″ balsa stick from the side (Photo 8). Depending on the length of your opening, you may detect that the stick is sagging lightly in the middle—it was in my case. Temporarily prop up the middle of the bend and accurately measure the distance from the trestle bent's foundation to the underside of the stick at that point. Construct your trestle bent for that point to a height that will exactly fill that opening.

3/8" Spacer between the top of the trestle bent and the 3/8" Balsa wood stick

Be sure to use a temporary 3/8″ spacer between the top of the trestle bent and the underside of the balsa wood stick. Note the spacer on top of the trestle bent in the photo. That spacer represents the bass wood stringers you will use to support the track ties (Photo 9). Construct the first trestle bent to fit the height you find between the concrete foundation and the underside of the balsa stick. Do the same for the second trestle bent. Be absolutely sure that the trestle bents are totally vertical. Use a carpenter's square to verify this before you cement the trestle bent into place on its foundation.

Using some 3/8″ square bass wood stock, cut the track stringer beams to fit between the earth foundation point and the first trestle bent. Make sure the ends of the bass wood runner stick fall right in the middle of the trestle bent's support beam. Photo 10 shows some trestle bents complete with the track runners cemented in place and with a piece of track positioned on top of the track runners.

The large gap over the river has been bridged by two very long and unrealistic runners. Those runners will be covered by some bridge girder material from Scenic Express later in the project to make that gap much more structurally believable. The end effect will be that the steel bridge is supporting the track.

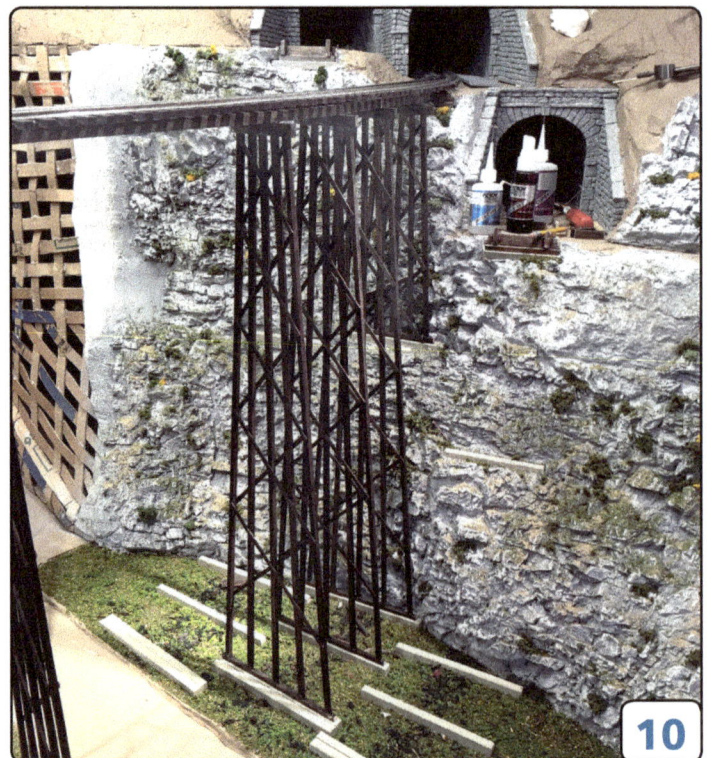

Photo 11 shows the trestle bents in place and strengthened by some cross bracing. Do some research on real railroad trestles. If you Google the phrase "wood railroad trestles," you will see hundreds of photographs showing how trestles were built, dependent mostly on the particular problem to be solved. At the very least, each railroad seemed to have its own standard. Pick one of those standards and follow it for your own circumstances on your model railroad. I made my cross bracing from bass wood stock that was 1/16″ thick by 1/4″ wide and then cut to length as needed. That would scale out to roughly 3″ x 12″ boards on the prototype. You may want to reduce yours to 1/32″ thick stock by 3/16″ wide (2″ x 10″). I stained all my bass wood stock with walnut oil stain. The finished appearance looks a lot like creosoted lumber.

Your particular cross bracing pattern will depend on which pattern you want to emulate. In our modeling world, it may be okay to follow a pattern of bracing but not necessarily as intricately as the real railroad did it. That's because just a little bracing will go a long way to show a dramatic effect on a model railroad, especially if there is going to be two or three tracks crossing over adjacent trestles. I chose to leave out much of the interior bracing of a trestle simply for expediency.

Photo 12 shows cut and fitted flexible steel girder material resting on Scenic Express #FL6039 Bridge Shoes with the flexible bridge girder material #RR0010 Girder Bridge Plate. I glued the cut and trimmed girder material to the side of the bass wood stringers. I then made an additional trestle bent cut to fit beneath the girder material as it is shown appearing to rest on the bridge shoes.

13

14

In Photo 13 above, you can see the top of the new bridge support trestle bent with a triple sill beam, topped with three scale 12″ square beams creating a pad for the cast bridge supports. The completed effect is shown in Photo 14 and is very impressive!

GarGraves makes a special trestle track with extra wide ties (Photo 15). I use this track for the trestle. On real trestles, wider ties were used to support a wood plank service walkway along the track on the trestle. Railroad maintenance workers used this walkway to inspect the track.

15

Photo 16 shows the track ties positioned evenly over the trestle stringers beneath the ties. Attaching the track can be done either with small black screws or even by gluing the ties to the trestle stringers at some strategic spots along the trestle. Even over the bridge steel, the track can be attached to the stringers that show up just inside the steel girders (Photo 17). The finished effort is shown in Photos 18 and 19.

Building the two other fixed height trestles will not require anything more difficult than making the trestle bents of each trestle all the same height. Then after adding the stringers to the tops of the trestle, the track can be laid on the stringers. In the future I will add the planking and railings for the walkways, and this part of the layout will be complete.

This project is a little daunting, but don't get discouraged by its complexity. This is the first finished trestle I've ever built. Sure, I made mistakes along the way, but they were easier than you might think to correct. I even made some improvements!

16

17

18

19

CHAPTER 23 - Electrical Break-Aways

It's a Cinch!

Previously I've shown you how I built a break-away roll-out module that will eventually have all three track trestles on it for my main lines where they cross my deep ravine (Photos 1, 2, and 3). The purpose of this section is, of course, to be able to get to areas of the layout behind the trestles that will need regular service for cleaning as well as for getting to derailed trains.

Although I thought it was a wonderful idea for whole complicated sections of the layout to be easily rolled away, it wasn't going to work out very well unless I could also make all the electrical connections break away as easily as the layout module itself.

It truly is a cinch to do this, but only if you use Cinch electrical connectors. If you do a Google search for "Cinch Jones connectors," you will come up with the Cinch manufacturer's web page and any number of sources where you can buy these items via mail order. Although Cinch makes all manner of electrical connectors, keep in mind our unique need in model railroading, which is for relatively high-amperage connections (10–12 amps) as compared to any other use in the electrical and electronic community. For this reason I settled on what they call the Cinch 300 series Jones connectors. The logic for this is that this series of connections all handle a hefty 10 amps per pin in the connector. The only thing you have to decide now is how many pins you need for your connectors.

I have three different tracks on this roll-away module, so that is going to require six connections. But I don't know how many other things I might want to locate on this module later on in addition to the tracks themselves. How about a campfire scene with a glowing fire? How about a kid on a swing? How about a log cabin with a smoking chimney? Each of these accessories will need its own AC (or DC+) source and an AC common (or DC-) source as well.

I may want some or all of these accessories or even something else when the time comes, but I won't know until much later when I'm in the finishing stages of building my layout. I decided to play it safe and use the Cinch Jones S-312-CCT (in-line socket) and P-312-CCT (in-line plug). The "12" designation is for 12 pins, which will allow for my six pins needed for the tracks and still leave me six more for other things. That means I can have five separate accessories using different voltages and one common pin for all accessory AC (or DC) "-" connections.

You may not need that many wires for your module. If there's one thing that building a layout has taught me over the years, it is that you never know how many things you're going to put on a particular part of the layout until your layout is "done." And when does that ever happen?

It's great to have more pins that you think you'll ever need in a connector rather than find out you don't have enough after you've done all the work to make up a wire harness with a plug and socket. Keep this in mind: If you don't want all the pins in any given Cinch Jones 300 series connec-tor, you can easily remove individual pins in both the plug and the socket, making them easier to plug and unplug.

Photo 4 shows both the Cinch Jones S-312-CCT (socket) and the P-312-CCT (plug). These are a nice, brutal plug and socket that can take a ton of abuse and keep on performing perfectly. In both the plug and socket, you will see a retaining pin partially pulled up.

A pair of long-nose pliers will allow you to remove the pin completely, which will allow the separa-tion of the housing from the plug or socket base (Photo 5).

Photo 6 shows in detail what is on the back side of the base of either the plug or the socket of the Cinch connector. If you look closely at the base, you will see that each pin has a number. The left row, vertically, is designated as 1, 2, and 3 from top to bottom. The next row is 4, 5, and 6, and so on across the base. This numbering system is carried across the base from the plug to the socket. That makes it easy for us. I will designate 1 through 6 for the AC + and - of my three tracks and the remain-ing six pins for my accessories. Since I don't yet know what I want to eventually use these pins for, I'll make it easy for myself and simply run six different colors of wire for each of the six pin numbers I want to des-ignate for accessories. That will give me up to five different AC or DC voltages for five different accessories and one for the AC or DC (-) for all of them.

While I'm on Photo 6, I want to make one more point. If you do much intricate soldering such as you will do on these Jones plugs and sockets, your best friend will be the tool shown in the photo. It is a Panavise Model 381 with model 380 vac-uum base and 303 standard head. It will let you hold anything, at any angle, for as long as you need. That may not seem like much, but that tool makes a job like this a breeze. You would be wise to invest in one of these as there seems to be no end to the applications for it in the O gauge train hobby. These tools are available in full-line hobby shops or on the Internet.

Now for the most important part of the project, make a note card of each wire and its pin number (Photo 7). When you begin the next phase of the project, this card will elim-inate any problem getting the wires and pin numbers con-fused. Starting with a middle row wire, solder the tinned wire to the tinned pin (tinning is applying heat and solder to the wire and heat and solder to the pin before soldering them together). Finish all the middle row wires before pro-ceeding to the upper or lower row wires. That makes them all easy to reach when soldering.

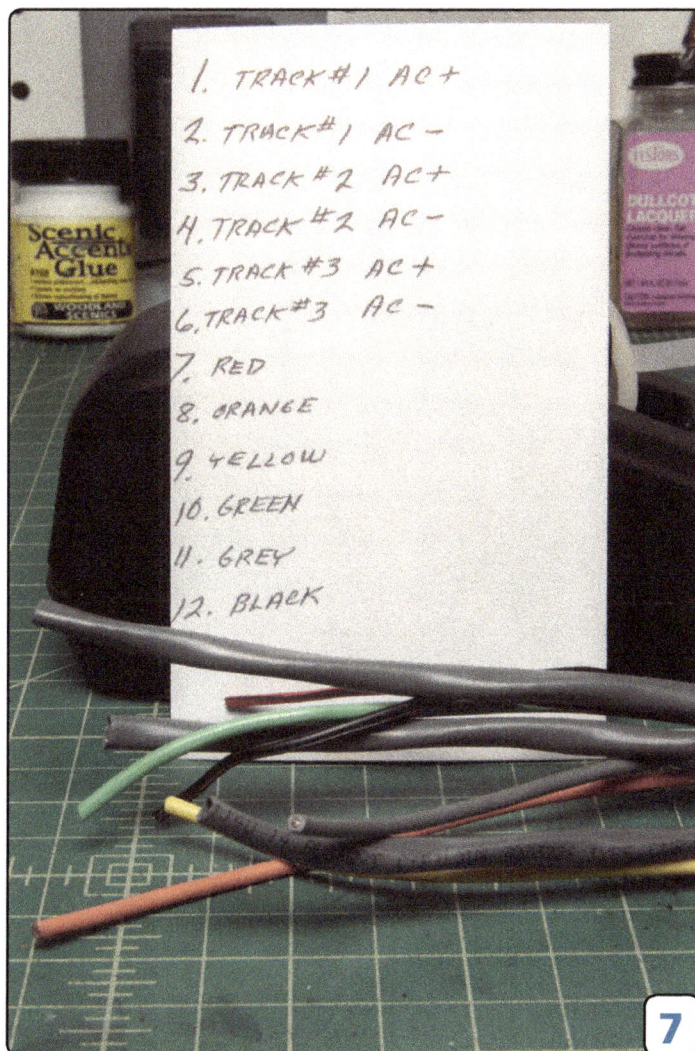

Photo 8 shows each wire soldered to its designated pin. If your soldering skills need work, learn the correct way to solder before attempting this part of the project. It is easy to "cold solder" a connection just to have the wire break off the pin later and drive you nuts. There is only one way to correctly solder. Heat the pin and the wire equally. Any other way will result in a cold solder joint, which is weak and will fail easily. If you do things correctly, a team of wild horses couldn't separate the wire from the pin.

Once you have all the wires soldered to all the pins in both connectors, smooth out the wires leading away from the plug or socket base. Remove any kinks in the wire all the way out to the ends. Gather all the wire ends together, snip them all off evenly, and thread them through the hole in the housing for the plug or the socket (Photo 9). Slide the housing cover up the wires and gather the wires together closely at the plug and socket bases. When you push the cover housing down over the wires, they will need to be closely grouped so they all fit easily inside the plug or socket housings. Insert the pin into the side of the housing and through the plug or socket base. Then tap the pin home with a tack hammer.

I used several wire ties placed about 4″ apart along the wires to form them into a cable (Photo 10). The plug and the socket ends of the wire harness are shown plugged together in Photo 11. Using a volt/ohm meter, connect the leads of the meter to the two exposed ends of each wire color to verify that all connections in the plug and socket are performing correctly.

Photo 12 shows the wires from the plug harness feeding into the module. Each of the paired track wires will go to the tracks when they are all mounted onto the module. At present, only the middle track is ready to be connected. The other two will be ready once I finish the other two trestles. Until then, their wires can be fed up to the track roadbed waiting for the track to be installed. All the future accessory wires are fed into the inside of the module where I can get to them later and hook them up as needed.

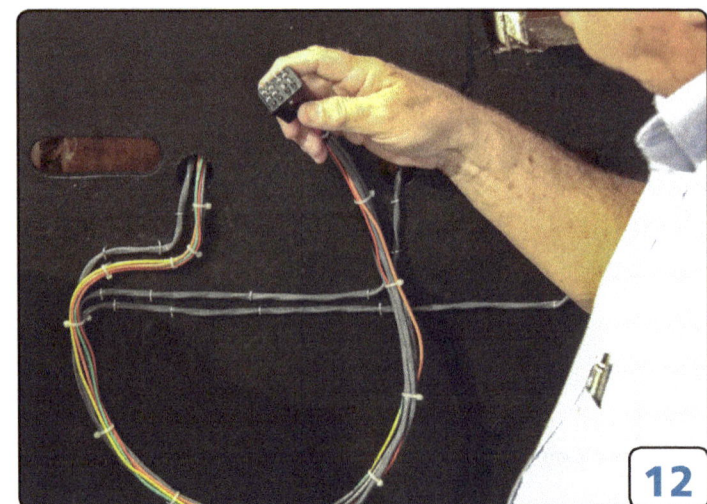

In Photo 13, the matching track wires for the socket harness are connected to the power sources on the layout for the tracks while the accessory wires will await connection to the right voltages for future accessories.

Photo 14 shows the two harnesses being connected together before closing up the module.

Now your roll-out module can be easily disconnected from the layout physically and electrically every time you need to gain access to the inside of the layout, all with the least amount of inconvenience. Two suitcase snaps and one plug will separate all of it at the same time.

CHAPTER 24 - Bench Testing
Trackside Accessories

A thought occurred to me when I was making the wire harnesses for the roll-out trestle module in the previous chapter, "Electrical Break Aways." Why not use the same electrical connections for any module I use on the layout, such as all the operating accessories in Photo 1? That would let me make up a universal test harness socket for my workbench identical to the socket harness for the trestle module where it connects to the layout. There's a very good reason to do that.

In the previous chapter I introduced you to the Cinch-Jones connector that allows the hookup of multiple wires at the same time (Photo 2). I use the Cinch-Jones 300 series connector because it easily handles our relatively high O gauge amperage requirements of 10–12 amps per wire. I settled on the 12-pin Cinch-Jones S-312-CCT (in-line socket connector) and the P-312-CCT (in-line plug connector).

For the most part you won't need all 12 pins, but there might be some instances where you will need that many.

Trackside operating equipment made by Lionel almost always relied on a vibrating mechanism to perform its magic. Either the vibrating mechanism was used to advance a string around a pulley to translate into rotary motion or the vibrator moved a platform to move things in a linear motion along the platform. The trouble is, if the accessory is not anchored firmly to the layout, the vibrating mechanism shakes the whole accessory instead of just the horses, the barrels, or the rotary device used to drive the loading and unloading mechanisms. That causes the accessory to work poorly.

Servicing the accessory is most often accomplished by removing the item from the layout and taking it to a workbench.

Now we've lost the established layout placement and its effect on keeping the accessory well anchored. Any testing and adjustments made at the workbench will not be quite the same when you reattach the accessory to the layout.

The solution is to take a piece of the layout with you to the workbench, duplicating the effect on the accessory whether it's on the layout or on your test bench. I've tuned an accessory to work perfectly only to get it back to the layout and found that it won't work well at all.

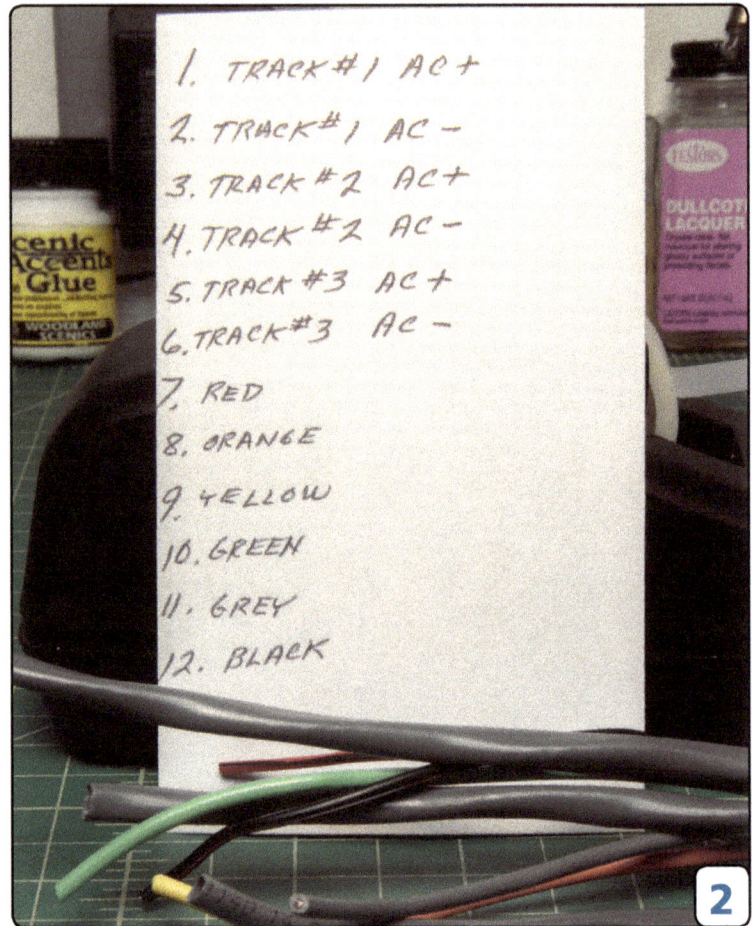

Following that same electrical wiring diagram I used for the trestle module in Photo 3, I can make any part of my layout that has trackside operating accessories totally removable, track and all.

Photo 4 shows the two Lionel operating culvert accessories: the No. 345 Lionel Culvert Unloader and the No. 342 Lionel Culvert Loader. These were two of Lionel's most wonderful accessories, but they didn't work worth a hoot until fastened down to the train table along with the track that they served. I cut the table plywood under both the track and the two accessories making the whole scene removable.

Photo 5 shows the open spot on the table where these accessories used to be. I added scrap wood to the edge of the underside of the plywood hole in the table to provide a firm resting bed for the accessory module to sit in. I can unplug the whole scene as one complete module, remove it from the layout complete with the track, the operating car, and any lighting, and take it to my workbench.

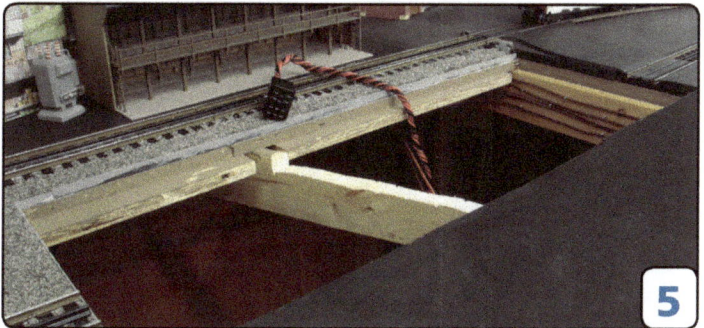

Following the same wiring diagram I used on my removable trestle module, all I need to do is make up another wiring harness with an in-line socket outlet, as shown in Photo 6.

I used a nice long wire harness, in my case about 6′ or so. I wired it to a universal connection board I made so that I could apply any test transformer's wires to any wire in the harness using an alligator clip (Photo 7). The socket of that harness is then plugged into the mating plug harness that goes to each removable operating accessory module.

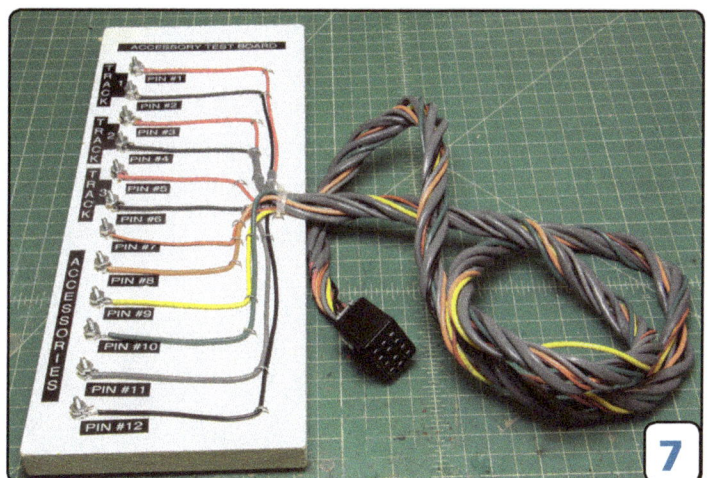

Any section of track that you attach on the removable module only needs to be wired the same way as the rest of the siding for trains to work on the accessory module the same as they do on the rest of the layout. No track pins are needed. Just make the plywood accessory module fit snugly into the table so the ends of the track align perfectly. Wire the track, the accessories, any other lighting, and so forth through the Cinch-Jones plug using the wiring diagram and use the different wire colors for anything on the module the same as you do for anything on the table wiring. Make a matching Cinch-Jones socket under the train table wired the same as the plug for the accessory module.

When anything on the culvert accessories doesn't work right, I simply unplug it, remove the whole assembly from the train table, and take it to my workbench (Photo 8).

There I plug it into my socket harness at my workbench, make the necessary voltage connections on the workbench's harness patch board, and adjust the accessory until it works perfectly. When it passes this testing process, I unplug it, add it back into the layout, and reinsert the plug.

Even if you've already finished your layout, you can go back and make your trackside accessories and their respective lengths of track removable. Just come up with your own universal wiring diagram and make them all easily serviceable at your workbench. This little piece of layout planning and construction makes your layout a whole lot more fun and much more easily serviced, when needed. You won't believe how much more fun all of the old Lionel trackside accessories will become when they are actually dependable.

CHAPTER 25 - Building the Trestle, Part 1

Trestles are one of the most dramatic fixtures in railroading, including model railroading (Photo 1). If you don't believe that, use Google to search for the term "wood railroad trestles" on your smart phone or your computer and look at the hundreds of photographic examples of real railroad trestles. In the 1800s, when we got serious about spanning the nation with railroads, wood railroad trestles were the technological breakthrough of the time that allowed us to do it.

Beginning in the eastern half of the early United States, as well as the western half as we migrated to the Pacific coast, trestles became a common solution to overcoming valleys, canyons, and marshlands. In fact, as much as 1 to 1-1/2 percent of all railroad trackage was installed on trestles.

As our cities grew, urban sprawl dictated that railroads needed to go either below or above ground to get out of the way of ground transportation. Going below ground with railroads was reserved for intercity trains, servicing passengers traveling within points in the city. Through trains had to elevate above the streets and often did so with wood trestles, many of which were eventually filled in with earth brought to the site by the trains themselves.

Trestle construction started in the east as a necessity to get past the rugged terrain of the eastern mountains and valleys. Railroads were always built the cheapest way possible at first with improvements coming later when revenue from operating trains allowed for this. Most early wood trestles were immediately filled in with earthen landfills poured directly from trains at the top of the trestles. Where earth fill wasn't practical, many wood trestles were replaced with iron and then steel trestles as the railroad's economy and technology would permit.

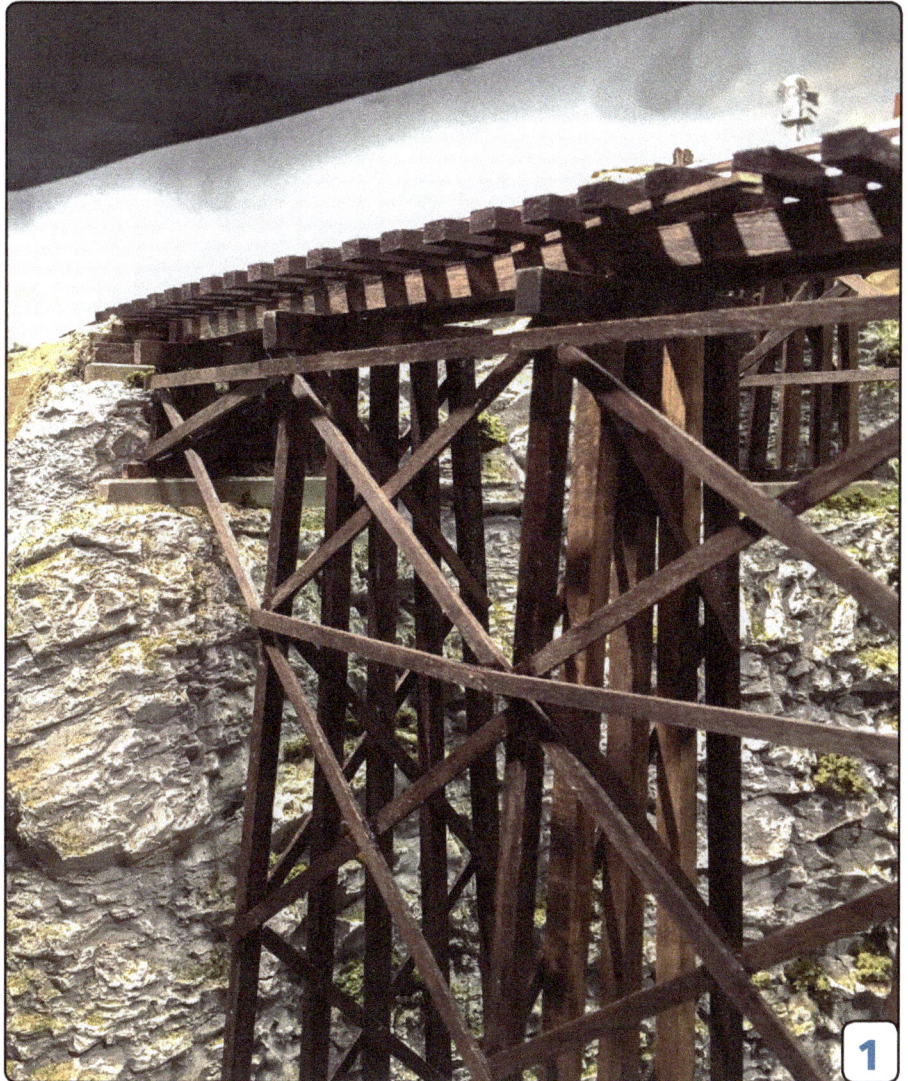

As railroads went west, they encountered massive standing forests of tall trees. The price of premium grade lumber for trestles therefore was just right: free. The advancing railroad provided its own transportation of these tall trees to its own temporary sawmills. The railroads quickly found that squared-off timbers were far superior to round logs for construction of intricate trestles.

At first glance, trestles look very complicated and difficult to understand, much less build (Photo 2). If you get past the initial shock and awe of seeing an intricate trestle, you soon learn that they are actually very simple assemblies of basic components. The vertical sup ports, called trestle bents, support all the weight. They are joined together by stringers, which are nothing more than short, massive bridge beam assemblies spanning the distance between each ver-tical support (trestle bent). Then, finally, the whole assembly is strengthened by a clever system of wood bracing.

So let's take this one step at a time. As noted earlier, the main substructure of a trestle is the trestle bent. Don't ask me why or how they ever became known as bents since there were no bends anywhere in the timbers making them up. Trestle bents are vertical assemblies supporting all the weight of the train on the trestle. These assemblies are spaced evenly every 15′ to 24′ depending on the railroad's design standards and the geography they had to span.

A trestle bent assembly consists of support posts joined together under one timber beam at the top called the cap. That assembly is anchored to a timber at the bottom called a sill. The whole trestle bent assembly then usually rests on a concrete footer. Esthetically, I decided to use 16′ spacing (4″) for my O gauge trestle bents. If your trestle is going to be in a straight line, then 5″ (20′) spacing is perfectly acceptable.

There appears to be almost as many different designs for trestles as there are for... well...trestles. I've settled on a design the Southern Pacific Railroad used on most of the trestles they built on the original trans-continental railroad. I've made two O scale drawings (1/4″ to the foot) of the SP design as shown here. The SP design features five massive squared-timber support posts, each measuring a 12″ square. They were joined at the top by the trestle cap measuring 12″ wide by 18″ tall. The sill timber is 12″ x 12″ square, like the support posts. Bracing was most often made up of massive 3″ x 12″ lumber. The trestle bent assembly rested on a poured concrete footer measuring 18″ tall by 24″ wide.

I like the SP five-post trestle bent design mostly because that design is easy to model. It features one totally vertical center support post right in the middle of the trestle bent. That makes it easy to locate each individual trestle bent on the valley floor. All we need is a center line on the valley floor where the track is going to be located above the valley. Each trestle bent is then mounted to the floor of the valley with its center support post directly above the track centerline drawn on the valley floor.

The trestle in the drawing represents a trestle height of about 34′ (8-1/2″). Make several copies of that page of the magazine. If your bent needs to be shorter than the one drawn, simply draw a new set of lines representing the top and the bottom of the sill and its supporting concrete footer so the overall height of the finished trestle comes out where you want it to be.

If your trestle needs to be taller than the drawing, add some paper to the bottom of the drawing copy. Additional height can be added to the trestle bent drawing by project-ing the image of the support posts (at their existing angles) downward onto the added paper (Photo 3).

Notice in Photo 4 that once you get your own trestle bent height worked out with your addition to the pattern, it's a good idea to cover your adjusted drawing with a single sheet of waxed paper. Use blue masking tape if possible since that kind of tape will allow you to remove and replace the waxed paper as needed without tearing the drawing beneath it.

Use that pattern for a one-on-one assembly pattern for your trestle bents. The waxed paper cover sheet will still allow you to see the design while protecting your revised pattern from damage from the CA glue.

In all cases, model your trestle with basswood, not balsa wood. Basswood is a hardwood which simulates the strength of full-sized wood timbers much better than balsa. Hobby shops which lean toward model airplanes will almost always have basswood as well as balsa wood. Get acquainted with basswood, and you will understand why basswood is used for model train trestles.

If you cannot find an ample source of basswood shapes, use Google to search for the term "balsa and basswood," and you will see a world of information about the two, their availability, and their pricing. One good source is www.nationalbalsa.com. That's a misnomer because they market and sell basswood as well. Go to the web site and progress through to "Basswood Sticks" and then to the 36″ or 48″ bass-wood stock.

The basswood stick sizes you will need are 1/4″ square (all support posts and sills), 1/4″ x 3/8″ (trestle bent caps), 3/8″ square (stringers), 1/16″ x 1/4″ (all bracing), and 3/32″ x 3/16″ (guard timbers and hand rails, if used).

One of the nicest things about bass-wood is how well it takes true oil-based wood stain. To simulate the creosote appearance of treated trestle wood, I had great results by getting some cabinet grade oil-based wood stain in the walnut color (Photo 5). When brushed or wiped over the basswood sticks and wiped off, you have what looks like beautiful timber treated with creosote.

Staining is something to do to the wood before you cut the basswood stock into the individual parts you will need. Sure, you'll have some ends that need to be touched up before you assemble them into your trestle bent, but that's easy. If you wait until you have finished construction of your trestle bent, any glue you use will ruin the ability of the wood to absorb the stain.

If you don't have a Micro-Mark table saw, you will need to get at least an X-Acto Razor Saw or equivalent. Also get an aluminum miter box to guide the blade. Those tools will come in handy for this project. Be sure to get an ultra-fine toothed saw blade since you will be cutting hardwoods. If you do have the table saw, this project will be a breeze.

You'll want to mass-produce some parts of your trestle before you begin construction. After staining the basswood, cut the following shapes into quantities you think you'll need:

- 1/4" square sill pieces
  (cut to the length determined by your drawing)

- 1/4" square center support timbers
  (cut to exact height your drawing shows that you will need). Resist the urge to also cut the other support posts with angled ends; they need to be individually marked, cut, and fitted as you make each trestle bent

- 1/4" x 3/8" x 3-1/8" caps
  (one per trestle bent)

- 3/8" x 1/2" concrete footers
  (one per trestle bent)

The following parts can be mass-produced but need to be cut a bit too long and then individually fitted and trimmed during actual construction of the trestle bents and the finished trestle assembly:

- 1/4" square support posts
  (trim to length and end angle needed per your drawing)

- 1/16" x 1/4" sway bracing
  (cut to length per your drawing pattern)

- 1/16" x 1/4" horizontal bracing
  (cut to length per your assembly pattern)

- 1/16" x 1/4" cross bracing
  (cut to length per your trestle bent assembly pattern)

All assembly is done with a CA-type glue similar but not limited to BSI/Bob Smith Industries brand, also known as Insta-Cure (Photo 6). The Insta-Cure line of CA is commonly available in most hobby or model airplane shops. I use the Gap Filling Medium consistency CA (purple label) with the Insta-Set spray Accelerator. This combination will let you add a tiny drop of CA to the surface to be joined. Position the two pieces of wood and then add a very short spray of the Accelerator for a nearly instant bond. Any excess Insta-Set fluid can be harmlessly wiped off without defacing the treated wood.

Your waxed paper covered drawing is your cut-and-assemble pattern for the basswood for each trestle bent. By placing a stick of basswood directly over the drawing and marking the cut line, you can mass-produce many of your individual parts of the trestle as needed. The most practical parts to mass-produce are the center support posts, the caps, the sills, and the footers. Resist the urge to mass-produce the other support posts since they need to be measured and cut individually for a proper fit. It is also important that you mark the exact center of all the caps, sills, and footers. An easy way to do this is to put all the same parts together and scribe a scratch line across all sides of the pieces. Since you have already stained all the parts, the scratch you made will show up as a light wood line. When you have finished assembly, just dab a little stain over all the center marks, and they will disappear.

Begin by gluing the end of the center support post to the center of a sill beam. Being careful to maintain the square, keep the two pieces directly on top of the pattern and add a short spray of the CA Accelerator to the joint. Then add the cap to the top of the center support post in exactly the same manner and glue it in place.

When that assembly has cured, cut the two outer support posts to the length and angles needed and then add them to the assembly. Set the base of the outer support post on the sill by the amount shown on the drawing (about 3/8″). Match the top location with what is shown on the drawing pattern as well. Dry fit the pieces to check for fit and then apply a spot of CA to the ends of one of the outer support posts, fit it into place, and spray a shot of CA Accelerator on the two joints. Repeat this with the other outer support posts. Follow that with the two inner support posts (between the outer support posts and the center support post) matching your drawing pattern precisely.

Before going to the next step, trim or cut away any glue that may have accumulated in the corners for the support posts end joints. Using the drawing as your cut pattern, measure and cut as many pieces of sway bracing as you will need for your trestle. Don't forget to add sets of additional sway bracing to the lower end of your drawing if your trestle bent pattern has been extended downward far enough to need another set. Attach the finished trestle bent partial assembly to the waxed paper with some short pieces of blue masking tape on the sill and on the cap (Photo 7).

You are now ready to begin attaching the sway bracing. Position your precut sway brace timber directly over the support posts as indicated on the drawing to check that it fits properly (Photo 8). Remove it and add a tiny drop of CA glue to each support post where the drawing shows the sway brace will be crossing over. Spray a tiny amount of CA Accelerator at the ends of the sway brace to secure it at the correct location. Then add some pressure to the sway brace to flatten it down on the support post timbers (Photo 9). Apply a small spray of CA Accelerator at each joint. When finished, carefully remove the trestle bent, turn it over, and reattach it to the waxed paper. Repeat the process for the other side.

When you are finished, use a Q-Tip to dab some stain on any ends of the wood that still remain white from the cuts. Once you have precut pieces of basswood parts for your trestle bent, and with a little practice, you can complete a trestle bent at the rate of about a minute apiece. As you will note, the finished trestle bent assembly will be an amazingly rugged, strong support for your track when it is assembled with the others for your finished trestle.

Make as many bents as your trestle will require. Some of them might need to be shorter. Determine the height of shorter ones by measuring up from the top of the footer mounted on the sloping wall of the valley. For now, work on completing your trestle bents. We'll finish the trestle in the next chapter.

The Trestle Templates

On the following pages are two trestle bent templates, printed at full O scale size.

You can download these templates in PDF format from our web site at

ogaugerr.com/trestle/

TRESTLE BENT PATTERN - SIDE VIEW

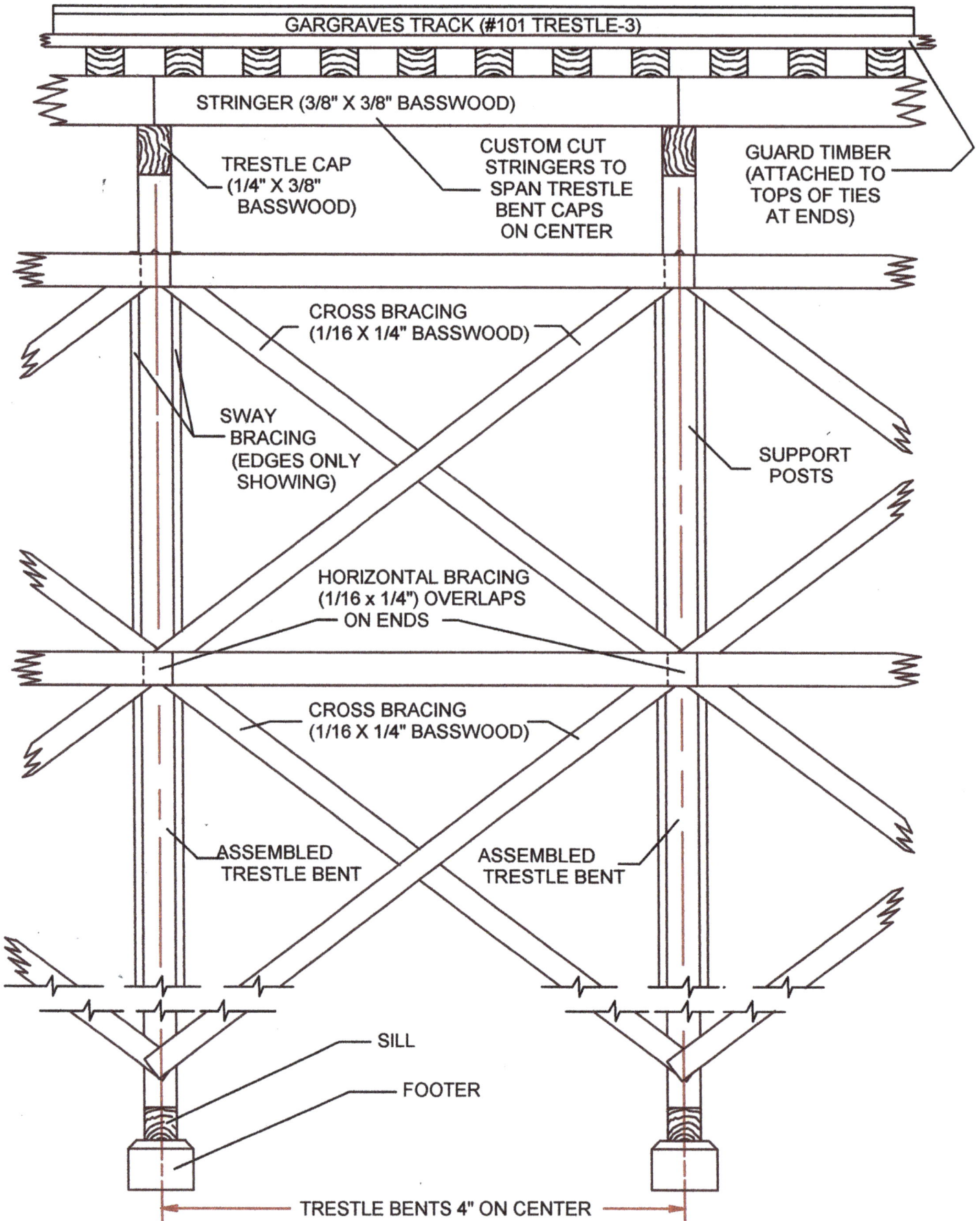

GARGRAVES TRACK (#101 TRESTLE-3)

STRINGER (3/8" X 3/8" BASSWOOD)

TRESTLE CAP
(1/4" X 3/8"
BASSWOOD)

CUSTOM CUT
STRINGERS TO
SPAN TRESTLE
BENT CAPS
ON CENTER

GUARD TIMBER
(ATTACHED TO
TOPS OF TIES
AT ENDS)

CROSS BRACING
(1/16 X 1/4" BASSWOOD)

SWAY
BRACING
(EDGES ONLY
SHOWING)

SUPPORT
POSTS

HORIZONTAL BRACING
(1/16 x 1/4") OVERLAPS
ON ENDS

CROSS BRACING
(1/16 X 1/4" BASSWOOD)

ASSEMBLED
TRESTLE BENT

ASSEMBLED
TRESTLE BENT

SILL

FOOTER

TRESTLE BENTS 4" ON CENTER

CHAPTER 26 - Finishing the Trestle

In the previous chapter we built all the vertical supports known as trestle bents you will need for your project. In this chapter we'll locate the trestle bents on the valley floor and add cross bracing and horizontal bracing to complete the trestle framework. Finally, we'll add the track to complete a dramatic trestle.

Look again at the two actual-size drawings on the previous pages. The one titled Trestle Bent Pattern Side View shows the sides of two trestle bents, the stringers on top of each trestle bent bridging the space from one to the next, and a piece of GarGraves #101 Trestle 3 track. Just a note: GarGraves Trestle 3 track looks like its regular track except it comes with the beautiful 3″ wide ties, as shown in

Photo 1. Don't mind Lulu, my cat. She's anxiously awaiting the lower trestle to be completed to her tunnel. Those wide ties come very close to the scale 12 or 13-foot-long ties used by the real railroads for trestles.

Locate all the trestle bent assemblies along a centerline where the trestle will be placed. I like the 16′ spacing (every 4″) simply because it looks good. If it is a straight trestle, add some squared-off lines crossing the centerline at each 4″ interval to show exactly where the finished trestle bent footer is to be located. If the trestle is curved, approximate the 4″ spacing along the curved centerline by using a guide made from a scrap of wood and mark the centerline for each footer accordingly.

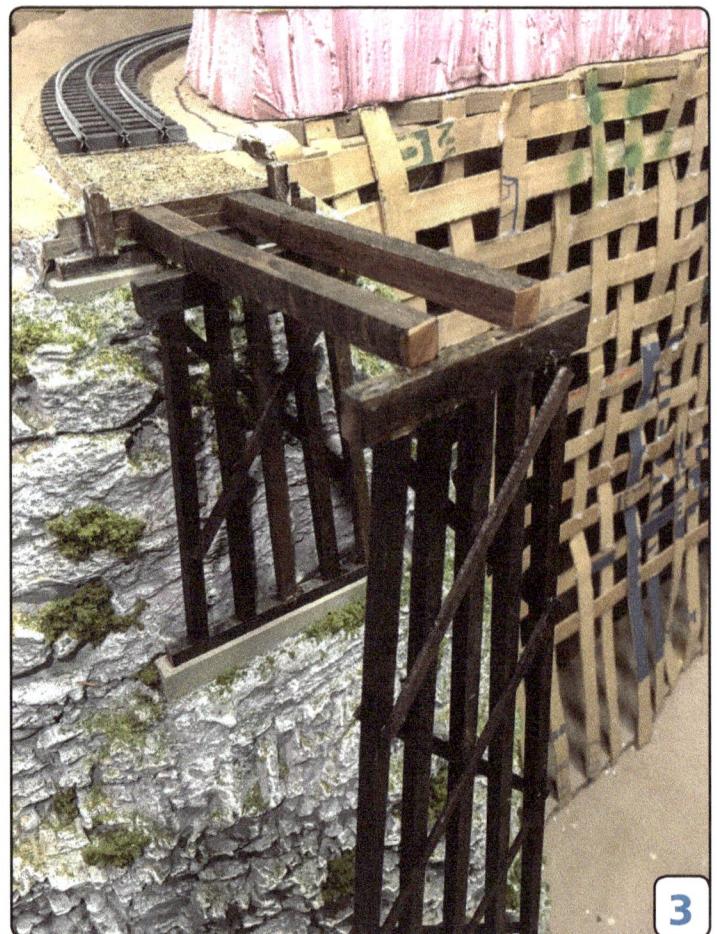

Note that the resulting locations of the trestle bent footers will make the spacing of the inside of the trestle bents closer together than the outside of the trestle bents. That's okay. That's the way it worked in the real world, too. If you have a curved trestle centerline and it's time to draw the line for each trestle bent footer, eyeball each trestle bent footer line so the ends of each bent will appear evenly spaced on the inside and the outside of the curved trestle. Photo 2 shows that curve spread of all three sets of footers for my three trestles.

Do a little finish work on the footers before gluing them with CA in place on the valley floor. I filed the top edges and ends of each basswood footer to resemble concrete and then painted it with gray paint to resemble finished concrete. Each footer was then glued to the table surface being careful to center it up on the trestle centerline and to space the ends apart as needed for the curved centerline. Remember, with the slower acting time of the gap filling Insta-Cure glue, you will have plenty of time to accurately locate the footer, hold it in place, and spray the CA accelerator on the base of the footer. I found that it helped to make small pencil marks centered at the ends of the footer pieces to line up with the lines drawn on the valley floor.

Always remember that the end goal is to make each trestle bent perfectly vertical. The taller the trestle, the easier it is to spot any variation from true vertical. There are a number of different ways to do this, but here's mine: I put just a small spot of CA on the bottom of each end of the sill and position the trestle bent on top of the footer by eye as vertically as I can. Remember, the gap-filling CA will not immediately set up without the accelerator, which will work in our favor. Using a carpenter's square, find and hold true vertical on your trestle bent and then spray the CA accelerator at the ends of the sill and wait for a couple of seconds until the CA sets up (Photo 3). Check again to make sure the trestle bent is truly vertical and add a bead of CA along the outer edges of the sill where it touches the footer. Add a little spray from the CA accelerator, and the trestle bent is now attached to the train table and correctly plumbed to vertical.

I know it's pretty scary-looking and rickety, huh? Don't worry. Adding the stringers bridging the tops of each trestle cap will vastly stabilize the trestle bents. Stringers were the most brutally strong part of the trestle. They were the massive wooden beams placed directly under the wheel rails carrying the load of the whole train and distributing it to the trestle bents. The Southern Pacific design bolted together three wooden beams each 6″ x 18″. The finished assembly measured 18″ square (3/8″ square in O gauge).

As much as possible, stringers need to end up directly under the wheel rails of the track that will be placed above them. During this phase of the construction, you have one more chance to check and easily correct any variation from true vertical that you may have ended up with when attaching the trestle bents to the concrete footers.

Since the width of the wheel rails in O gauge is about 1-3/8″, this makes each wheel rail 11/16″ from the center (rail) of the track. Mark the tops of all the trestle caps 11/16″ off each side of the center mark made earlier, and that will be the location of the middle of every stringer. I make pencil marks 11/16″ from the center on both sides of every cap. These marks will end up under both the stringers and the rail ties when the trestle is complete. Don't worry, the marks will never be seen from above after the track is attached.

Install your first stringer between your land footing and the first trestle bent. The top of the stringer needs to fit even with the top of whatever you are using for roadbed. In my case, I used cork roadbed so the ties of my track rest on the cork roadbed until they get to the trestle. At that point, the top of the stringer lines up with the surface of the cork roadbed, so the track ties march smoothly off the earth road-bed and onto the trestle stringers (Photo 4).

The first pair of stringers needs to span from the earth landing of the trestle to the exact middle of the width of the cap on the first trestle bent. Once again, check the top of your first trestle bent for true vertical. If it is still off a hair, determine the small amount the top of your stringer cap needs to move and then measure and cut your first stringer to that dimension. Apply a small amount of CA glue to the bottom of both ends of the stringer. Hold it in place on the earth landing timber and on half the thickness (or width) of the trestle cap. Spray the CA accelerator on each end of the stringer. Be careful not to leave any excess CA glue at the end of the stringer where it rests and attaches to the cap. That must be kept clean for the next stringer. Check again after the second or so the CA needs to set and you will find that the trestle bent is now at true vertical. Repeat the process for the second stringer on the other side of center.

Be sure the stringers only use up half the thickness of the trestle cap beam. That will allow for the next stringer to bridge the gap from the first trestle bent to the next one. Each of these stringer beams must be measured and installed separately. Make all saw cuts as square as possible. There just isn't much room for error on the tops of all the trestle caps. Continue this process all the way to the other side of the trestle where it makes its landfall. A gentle to moderate tug on the trestle assembly will show you how amazingly strong it is even without the cross bracing applied.

In an effort to keep things separate in your mind, sway bracing is what is installed on the faces of each trestle bent to make it rigid from side to side (no sway). Sway bracing is what we dealt with in chapter 25 that is shown in the drawing on the Trestle Bent Pattern Face View page.

Cross bracing is what is installed from one trestle bent to the next to make the trestle rigid along its length. Study the two trestle drawings for a few minutes with both types of braces and their locations.

As you look at the Trestle Bent Pattern Side View drawing, beginning at the top end of the sway bracing on one trestle bent, we will start the cross bracing spanning from the top ends of the sway brace pattern of one trestle bent to the bottom of the same sway brace pattern on the next trestle bent. Make the lower end of the cross brace you are about to install meet about in the middle of the trestle bent support post. That will allow you to put the next cross brace continuing down to the next trestle bent end to end with the upper cross brace you just attached.

Complete all the cross braces going in one direction. Don't start the cross braces going in the other direction until you have completed all the cross braces in the first direction. That is necessary to keep the pattern the same throughout the trestle.

Begin the cross braces in the opposing direction by starting at the top of a trestle bent and butting up the new cross brace to the sides of the cross brace you just finished. Cut and fit each new cross brace to meet the side edges of the existing cross bracing from bent to bent.

We're now ready to begin the horizontal bracing. This operation will clean up all the exposed ends of the cross bracing by laying them directly on top of the joints. Begin the horizontal bracing by spanning the distance from the meeting place for all the cross braces on one trestle bent to the meeting place for all the cross braces on the next trestle bent. Each subsequent horizontal brace begins by overlapping the end of the last horizontal brace until that pattern, too, is complete.

Finish the assembly by carefully going over the whole trestle and dabbing some stain on any openly white wood showing from cuts and scrapes. Also you might need to touch up the concrete appearance on the footers a little. I scarred them up by dropping the square a dozen times at least while building the trestles on my layout. You will not believe how rock hard and sturdy your trestle now is!

If your trestle is curved, pre-bend your GarGraves Trestle track close to the finished curve you will need before you begin attaching the track to the tops of the stringers. That will eliminate stress on your trestle. I pre-bent and then trimmed the rail ends as needed, using a Dremel tool equipped with a fiber cutting disc, to line up with the next section. I've tried several different methods, but I believe the best method for attaching the wooden track ties to the wooden stringers is an occasional small dab of CA glue and a short burst of CA accelerator. All you need is one small dab on each stringer every five inches or so along the trestle. Doing it this way will still allow you a very minor amount of track flexing as you go to closely follow the stringers.

Some final notes: You may find that the support post angles of 4 degrees and 8 degrees I show on my side support posts still won't let you make super tall trestles, if that is what you need to make. On my tall trestle (31" or so) the trestle bent got far too wide at the bottom. If that is the case on your layout, adjust the angle down by a degree or two. I think I ended up with 3 degrees and 6 degrees for all three tall trestles on my layout (Photos 5 and 6). That's the nice thing about trestles...they are so dramatic it's likely that nobody will even notice if you had to cheat a little to get them to fit on your layout.

Yeah, I know, it looks a little scary if you've never done this before. It's more tedious than scary. As long as you follow the pattern I've drawn, you will have fantastic results and a very dramatic effect on your layout.

Photo 6 at the right, shows the what the three big, curved trestles looked like when Jim passed away.

He was about to start work on the river when his final day came.

CHAPTER 27 - Adding a Bridge to the Trestle

Wood railroad trestles were the best way for a railroad to overcome a valley or any other open gorge obstructing its intended path. Geography almost always dictates that the bottom of a valley will find a natural water run-off, such as a stream or river. If it was less than 15 or 20 feet wide, the stream would fit nicely between two of the trestle bents making up the full trestle. But for anything wider than that it was necessary to leave out one or more trestle bents and incorporate an overhead bridge in the trestle to span the distance over the river.

Photo 1 shows my three trestles built to the point where they need to cross over the riverbed in the bottom of the valley. Following the Southern Pacific's design guidelines, I will add girder bridges to span the river.

Let's use the same 3/8″ square basswood stock we used before for stringers, as I showed you in chapter 25. Cut to fit two stringers to span the distance between the existing trestles on each side of the riverbed (Photo 2). Obviously, this distance is too great to expect these overly long stringers to support the railroad. We are going to use the wooden stringers to attach the bridge plate material to make a much more believable correct-to-prototype bridge.

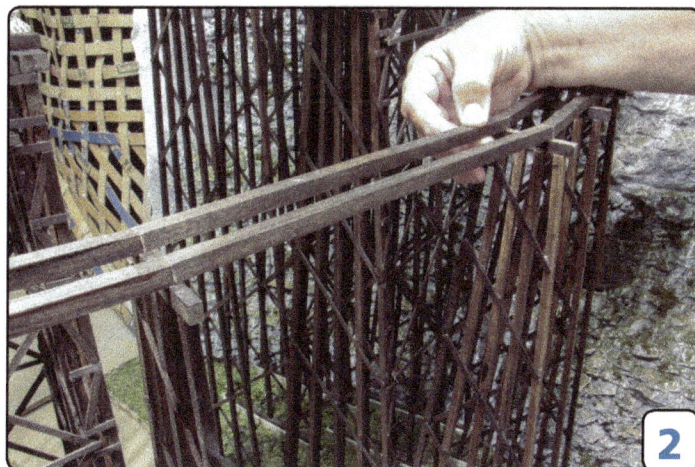

In this golden age of layout building we are lucky to have such a wide array of structural and scenery products available to accomplish nearly any project we undertake. Scenic Express at www.scenicexpress.com has two products that will greatly simplify any bridge project.

The first of the two items we want to use is called O-Scale Girder Bridge Plate product #RR0010 (Photo 3). This girder bridge material is flexible, 1-13/16″ high and over 2′ long. It is easily cut to length using an X-Acto saw and miter box to enable you to make girder bridge sides to span any distance.

The second product you'll use is O-Scale Bridge Shoes product #FL6039 (Photo 4). They are exact models of the real thing and measure 1/2″ tall. They are designed to fit perfectly under the girder bridge steel and spread the weight of the bridge and its load over a larger footprint.

Photo 5 shows the two girder bridge plates cut to fit exactly between the trestle bent caps on each side of the river. A little CA glue followed with a spray of CA accelerator on the outsides of each stringer will hold the girder plates in place.

Hmm, now we have our girder bridge plates hanging precariously over the river with no visible means of support, not to mention the railroad above the bridge section, which will be added later. To hold this girder bridge up, we will need to make two more trestle bents just like the ones we already made in chapter 26, with one very important difference. Both of these trestle bents must be made exactly 2-1/8″ shorter than the trestle bents used to make up the trestle proper. This dimension allows for the height of the girder plate, the bridge shoes, and the wooden pads for the bridge shoes.

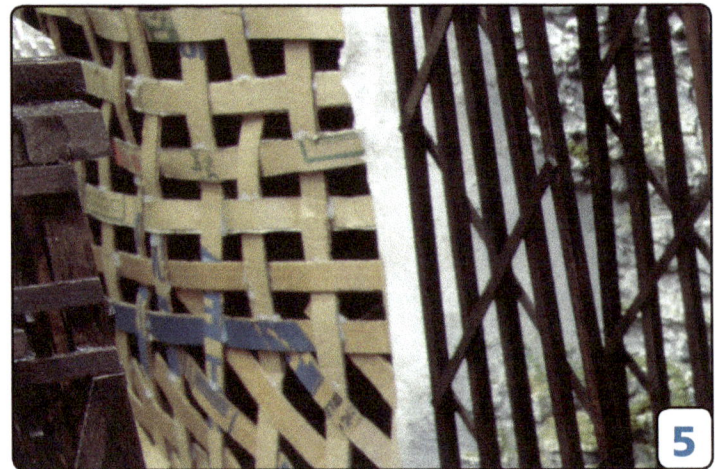

In chapter 22 I showed how to make simulated concrete footers for trestle bents. Because the trestle bent supporting our girder bridge will be right beside the trestle itself, an additional concrete footer needs to be added right beside the existing footer for the trestle on each side of the river (Photo 6).

Photo 7 shows the first of two additions needed to be made to the bridge support trestle bents. On one side of each of these trestle bents, add an additional wooden sill beam right beside the one making up the bottom of the trestle bent.

When this new trestle bent is added to the new footer, the additional sill beam will maintain a 1/4″ gap between the bases of the two trestle bents (Photo 8). That spacing gap is needed due to the side bracing on the inside of the two trestle bents.

Also, at the top of the bridge support trestle bent, add an additional cap beam to both sides of the existing cap of the new trestle bent (Photo 9. This will effectively make the cap beam assembly on the bridge support trestle a full 3/4″ wide.

Using the same 1/4″ square basswood stock used to make up the main beams of the trestle, cut three pieces exactly 3/4″ long and glue them side by side to make up a wooden pad assembly measuring 3/4″ square. You will need four of these assemblies for your bridge.

Photo 10 shows one of these 3/4″ square wooden beam pads positioned at the top of the bridge support trestle beam directly underneath the steel girder plate on one end of the bridge. Aha, now you can see what is going to hold this bridge up!

When you glue the trestle bent onto the foundation, also glue the side of the new 3/4″ wide cap beam to the existing trestle and the 3/4″ square wooden pads onto the tops of the wide support cap.

Finally, add in the O-Scale Bridge Shoes to complete the structure (Photo 11). Once you are sure of their fit and location, attach each of them with a drop of CA glue. Now you have an extremely sturdy support for your girder bridge and the track to be added later.

When the trestle cross bracing and horizontal bracing have been added, as covered in chapter 25, you still end up with the bridge support trestle bents needing some bracing to more firmly attach them to the main trestle.

Photo 12 is an interesting railroad solution to two parallel trestle bents. In southern Indiana along the B&O railroad I found this automobile bridge going over the track. The B&O built two parallel trestle bents on each side of the tracks to support a wooden floor for the automobile bridge. B&O connected the two trestle bents with that interesting Z-shaped cross bracing.

I followed that pattern to join the trestle bents on my bridge supports to the adjacent trestle (Photo 13).

Our finished girder bridge project is shown in Photo 14. I love the use of the basswood bracing to give a permanent look of rigidity to the trestle and the bridge. It is a very believable solution for combining a steel girder bridge and a wood railroad trestle.

The Trestle Templates

You can download full-sized, properly scaled trestle templates from our web site at

ogaugerr.com/trestle/

CHAPTER 28 - Recycling Mountains

Layout scenery doesn't have to be expensive. Previously used layout scenery, in fact, is very cheap. Many of us know someone who is taking down a layout or otherwise scrapping part of a lay-out to redo it in some way. But most of us don't realize that layout scenery can be refurbished and reused pretty easily. The trouble is we don't often consider how easy it is to redo something to make it part of a whole new scene.

On my layout I'm incorporating a very large mountain to hide two turnarounds at the end of two loops of the main lines located at one end of the room. I've also figured out a way for the mountain to partially hide a helix of sorts that will allow me to move trains from one level to another.

Some time back, a friend of mine dismantled his layout and gave me a foam casting of a rocky mountain face. It was painted and partially detailed with trees, shrubs, and other scenery materials. As big as this mountain casting was, it still wasn't big enough to do what I wanted it to do, but it was a start. I stored it away for future use and mostly forgot about it.

On a recent trip to Scenic Express, I found what I thought was another large mountain casting that was somewhat different from the one I already had. No problem, I thought! I bought it and figured I would find a way to work it into my mountain along with the old casting. It wasn't until

I was already back home that I found that the new unpainted mountain casting I had just bought was, in fact, the very same casting as the one I already had. They just appeared to be from different molds due to the fact that one was already painted and bore little resemblance to the new one.

The trick was going to be to match the color and style of the two pieces and mate them up to create my larger mountain. I also needed to disguise the two pieces just enough to make them a little dissimilar yet incorporate them both into one big mountain.

Photo 1 shows how I began that project. One of the main objectives of the mountain was to hide some vertical pipes in that part of the basement. I blocked the new mountain casting up about 6″ to hide as much of the pipes as I could. It is indeed hiding most of the black pipe from the view of the camera. Also shown is a mock up area for a future highway curving up into the future mountain. If you look closely, there's a break in the background of the highway where a bridge will go over a stream. The water in that stream will end up going over a deep waterfall and down into a large gorge planned just to the right of the curved highway piece. There will also be another bridge in the lower-left foreground of the photo represented by a thin board. The mountain needs to be at least twice as long as it currently is with just one casting.

Photo 2 shows both castings on my worktable. The new one is the one on the left, and the old one is the one on the right. I made another trip to my favorite paint store counter. I had them mix up a flat latex wall paint sample for my basic rock gray, which I selected from a paint chip at the store. Using the sample paint thinned 50-50 with water, I painted both the new and old mountain pieces with my airbrush to match each other. Don't worry if your old scenery casting has flocking, a fine scenery material, covering some of it. Paint over it anyway.

A quick spray coating of Testors Dullcote will be applied over this and any other scenery paint used on the layout. The flat appearance of Testors Dullcote is what really makes painted scenery look so believable. It is an important step that should never be left out.

Here's another secret to making rock look believable. After the Dullcote is applied, use a cheap, small 1″ to 1-1/2″ paintbrush and drybrush some pure flat white latex paint on the tips of the rocks (Photo 3).

Photo 4 shows the before-and-after effect with the mountain casting on the left touched up with some flat white on the rock tips.

Photo 5 shows the dramatic effect of the white paint followed by adding a very light airbrushing of black or gray paint into the recesses of the rock to further show the contrast of the rugged rock features.

In Photo 6 I've raised up the closest rock casting by another 2″ thickness with Styrofoam to cover even more of the vertical pipe. The rock casting in the back is intentionally left one level lower and just slightly back to make it appear farther away than the close rock casting. The pink Styrofoam is secured with Elmer's glue and a few drywall screws, with both rock castings securely attached in the same manner. Don't worry about the slight mis-match between the two rock castings because I'll show you how we disguise that later.

I've located the tunnel portal and black shadow box and have begun my process of adding cardboard strips adding on to the depth, height, and length of the mountain castings. This cardboard strip method actually makes it quite easy to close off the tops, add to the base, and join the two castings together smoothly.

Photo 7 shows the addition of more cardboard strips to the top of the rear mountain casting as well as tying the castings into the base of the mountain foreground. I'll probably make my finish layer to the top of the mountain foreground easily removable to allow for scenery work on the mountain rock work.

In Photo 8 I've added a rock casting to the front of the mountain to close it off better. I still need to patch up the very visible crack and camouflage things with some trees and other scenic elements later.

Photo 9 shows my very favorite scenery material. PlasterWrap is a neat way to make thin-shell scenery. It is quite literally gauze cloth on a roll, impregnated with plaster. If you've ever had the misfortune of having a broken bone in a cast, you may have come across this material in hospitals in the past. Scenic Express sells this product for about $12 per roll. It is easily cut into any size sheet from the 8″x 15′ roll dipped in a tray of water and smoothed onto the cardboard strips or screen wire or any other means of forming a suitable base to lay the cloth on.

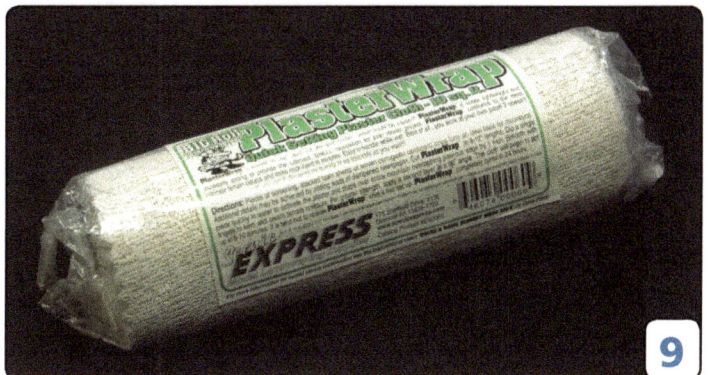

Photo 10 shows how this material is placed on both the casting base and the cardboard strips to begin closing up the terrain. You can also easily scrunch up some wet plaster cloth to close up any gaps between any two mountain castings. The result is a hardened thin layer of scen-ery when the plaster dries and has taken a set. Be sure to use some blue masking tape on all finished painted walls or backdrops to keep plaster or airbrushed paint off the backdrop.

When you are done, you may want to thicken the finished surface or to con-tour some texture into it. That is easily done by adding more plaster to the surface. Photo 11 shows a Plaster of Paris carton available from home improvement stores. You might as well get a couple of cartons when you go to get your custom-mixed paint samples. Plaster of Paris is sold in the same department as the paint. The plaster is mixed one part plaster to two parts cold water. When you mix it, you now have only about 10 minutes to work it before it takes a set. I use a rubber kitchen spatula and some spoons to mix it. I apply it with spoons and contour it with a rubber basting brush. The rubber brush tips let you get the hardened plaster out of it without ruining the brush.

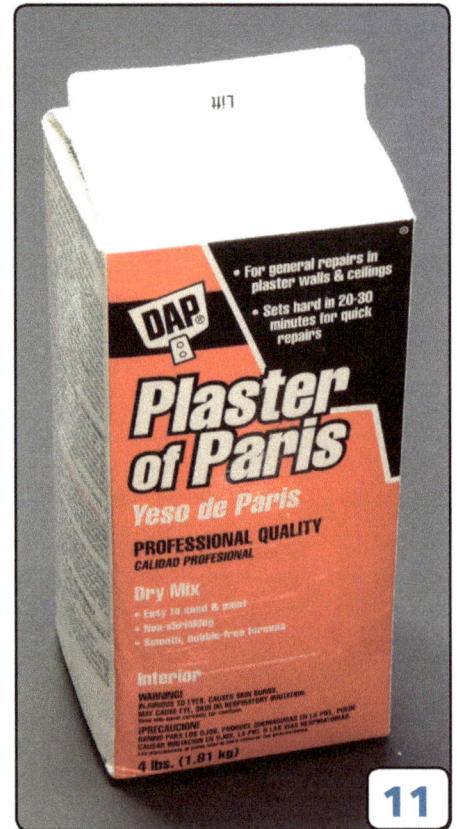

Photo 12 shows the finished coats of plaster and some of the airbrushed paint blending in the gray of the top of the mountain with the rock castings. Also note the airbrushed brown earth to those areas where you think you might want some green covering later. When in doubt, make all the surfaces gray and add the brown as you find you need it. I've still got some pipes sprouting out of the top of the mountain, but maybe some carefully placed trees will hide that later.

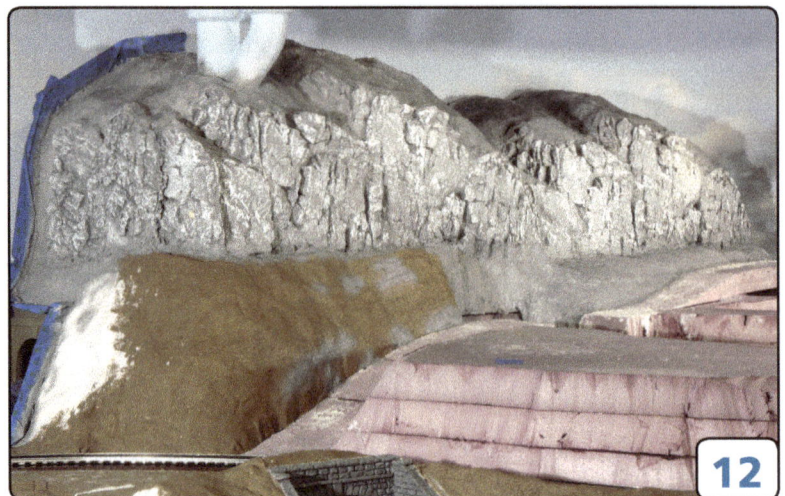

Photo 13 shows the dramatic result of the mountain at this stage. Obviously, it won't all be rock at the top of the mountain after we add some greenery for forest ground coverings, but it's always good to make it rock color at first. That way, if you have some of the forest covering wear off later, it will correctly show some rock color peeking up from beneath it.

Photo 14 shows the crack between the rock castings is now nearly invisible. I've painted some green shades into some areas of the brown earth and on top of the mountain rock as well. Note that the addition of the foreground Styrofoam has now clearly defined the future highway going up the mountain.

Photo 15 shows quite a few things. Ground cover has been added by coating the gray mountain surface with Elmer's white glue. I used a small 1″ trim brush to apply the glue. I then sprinkled some Scenic Express Farm Pasture Blend (#EX886C) on the top of the Elmer's glue. When that is done, spray the entire finished area with a mixture of tap water with a few drops of dish washing detergent mixed in. That is called wet water in the scenery world and will let the loose flocking mix in with the glue better.

When that is done, I use a carpenter's pointed scratch awl to punch a hole in the plaster shell and then add some hot glue to the hole and plant the trees. Be sure to use a few different types and heights of trees just as you would see in nature.

You'll see the results thus far in Photo 16. What used to be a bunch of bare Masonite, Styrofoam, and plywood is dramatically taking on the finished appearance of a mountain, complete with a forest and with sky and clouds in the background. I think I'm going to shop for a little HO log cabin and place it in the clearing on the top of the mountain at the upper right.

If I, as a somewhat mechanically inclined but woefully artistically challenged person, can make this look good, then so can you!

CHAPTER 29 - Planning for Realistic Operations

The difference between model railroading and simply running toy trains is the layout you build and how realistic you can make parts of your train world look. As an example, when we were kids we all loved the operating accessories Lionel made that added fun to the operation of our O gauge trains. That's what separated our O gauge trains from any other scale. We had operating trackside accessories that gave reason for the train to be there.

We had an Operating Lumber Loader and an Operating Log Dump Car that allowed the operator to control the train car to unload logs and then load them back up into that or another car. The same was true for the Operating Hopper Car and the Operating Coal Dump Ramp. Another combination was the Operating Barrel Car and the trackside Operating Barrel Loader. Or, how about the trackside Operating Culvert Unloader coupled with the Operating Culvert Loader? Those were unique Lionel accessories that made O gauge trains more fun than just running scale looking model trains.

An interesting thing happens as we grow up. When we are children, our imagination fills in the blanks for things like realistic looking railroad scenery. We don't need all the exacting detail to get the thrill factor out of running electric trains. All we need are the train, the living room carpet, and the transformer. Our imagination fills in all the rest.

Then as we and our hobby interests develop, we strive to add realism to the railroad to get that same thrill factor. Our trackside scenery becomes a hobby in itself with trees, grasses, rocks, roadside gravel, and track ballast among other things vying for inclusion. Clunky looking trackside accessories with their bulky bases, toy like plastic appearances, and sometimes goofy looking human figures just don't fit in with scale appearances.

Another thing we suddenly ask ourselves: Why are we unloading barrels, logs, and culverts onto a loading ramp just to load them all back up again? That sure doesn't seem like any kind of realistic operating train layout!

With a little imagination and some careful scenery placement, we can find things that simply go together to make the scene realistic. In Photo 1 there's a Lionel #3562-25 Operating Barrel Car (with the clunky worker figure removed and an Arttista worker set in its place) and the #362 Operating Barrel Loader along a highway on my layout. To eliminate the clunky looking base on the barrel loader, I painted it with a concrete colored paint and decorated the plastic wooden frame by painting it flat black and adding some gray aging stains. But most importantly, I added a piece of black foam core board to the surface of the parking lot and slanted it up from the road to the top of the barrel loader base by inserting a couple of scraps under the edge closest to the barrel loader (Photo 2). The barrel loader base is already starting to look better. Once I get to the point of adding some gravel, that "concrete" base will blend right in with the parking lot.

It dawned on me that something that goes together nicely with Lionel's Operating Barrel Ramp is the MTH #30-90133 Brewery with Operating Smoke (Photos 3 and 4). In this case, I took the plastic brewery building apart and added white mortar material to make it look more like the brick building it is supposed to be. Now the operating barrel car, the operating barrel ramp, and the brewery all have a reason to be on the model railroad. When the railroad spots the barrel car on the siding, the new empty barrels are unloaded. Then at some later time, the brewery workers bring them in, load them with finished product, and roll them back out to the loading dock. The railroad once again spots the barrel car on the siding, the workers load the beer barrels, and the yard switcher picks them up and adds the car onto a passing freight.

Some other work needs to be done to match up the accessories and make the scene even more believable and less toy like. Since I'm going to cover the parking lot with gravel later, I'll need to reduce the edge of the parking lot foam core board slightly so the gravel isn't higher than the pavement of the road it joins to. That is very easy to do with a rubber mallet and a piece of scrap wood (Photo 5). The foam core board easily crushes up right along the edge of the road to allow for the gravel to be applied later.

There is a slight mismatch of floor heights between the brewery and the barrel ramp, which is easily overcome by adding some more black foam core board to the floor of the brewery dock (Photo 6). That will let me extend the floor out and over to the barrel loader ramp to give brewery workers a place to roll the loaded barrels out to the loader.

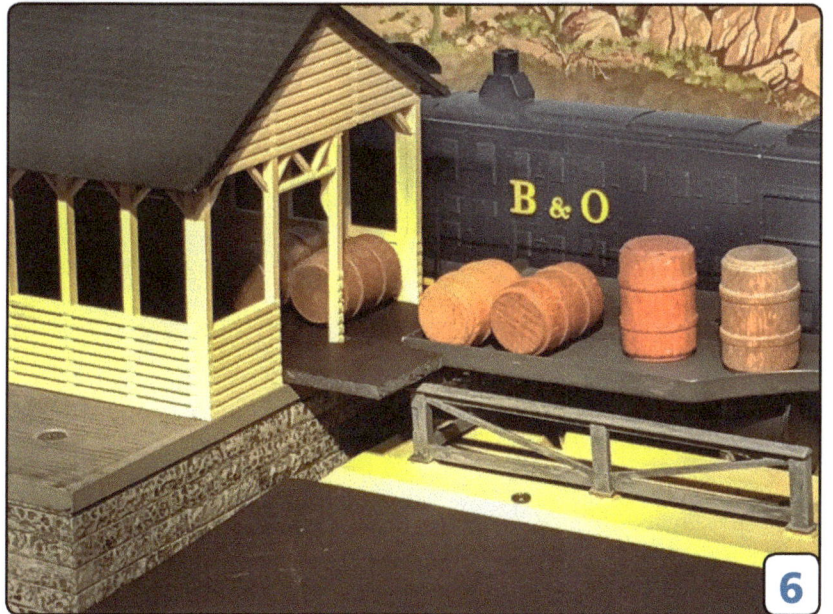

That was also a natural spot to add in a piece of scrap stair material down to the parking lot (Photo 7).

Photo 8 shows the far end of the parking lot and the need to do something about improving the looks of the pavement and the end of the barrel loader ramp, too.

In Photos 9 and 10, I've begun adding some spackling compound to the edges of the foam core board to gradually slope the parking lot down to the lower surfaces. Scenery gravel was added to the surface by pouring it out to a thin layer and spreading it evenly using a soft 1/2″ paintbrush. When this is done to the point where you are satisfied, gently spray the entire gravel surface with water diluted with a couple of drops of liquid dish detergent, a mix known as "wet water" in the model railroading world.

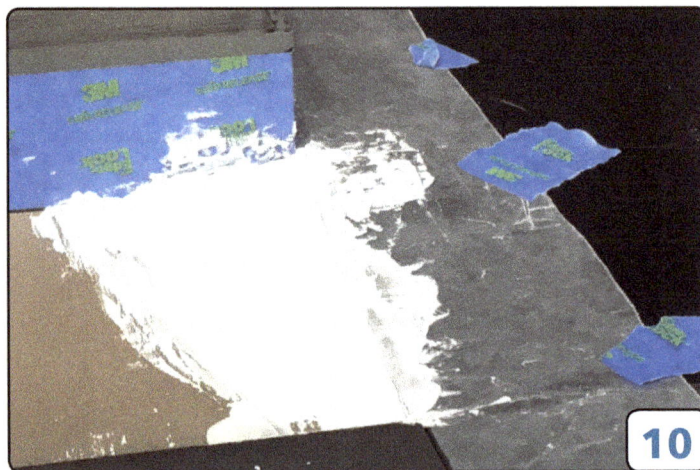

Then while still wet, dribble on a mixture of Elmer's White Glue diluted 1:1 with water. It isn't necessary to pool the thinned glue mixture up on the surface of the gravel; just pour it in until it all seems to lightly and evenly saturate the gravel. The spray water with the drops of detergent added will allow the diluted glue to soak into the gravel and spread evenly through it.

When it dries (usually a day later), the effect you get is shown in Photo 11. Also note in the photo that I've added a handrail to the stairs using some scrap basswood and CA glue and also some carefully placed workers from Arttista in O scale. Simple things like the walnut stained basswood sticks for the handrail add so much more realism to the scene.

Note in Photo 12 how much better the base of the barrel loader looks with the gravel parking lot running right up to the top surface of the concrete base. Note, too, that adding something like a scale sized worker to help roll the barrel off the ramp and onto the barrel car makes the scene so much more believable.

A local pickup is depicted in Photo 13 on the new gravel parking lot along with more figures to add to the realism. Smudging some black stain onto the plastic stone foundation and the dock of the brewery makes it look more like real stone and old wood rather than just different colors of plastic.

The combination of the MTH Brewery, the Lionel Barrel Loader and the Operating Barrel Car just naturally go together to make a great model railroading scene (Photo 14).

Nothing was sacrificed, and I now have the best of Lionel operating accessories from the postwar era and an MTH trackside accessory all working together to make a nice hi-rail model railroad scene. I have many more details to add to the road like edge gravel, stripes, signs, track ballast, as well as saw grass for the terrain around the building.

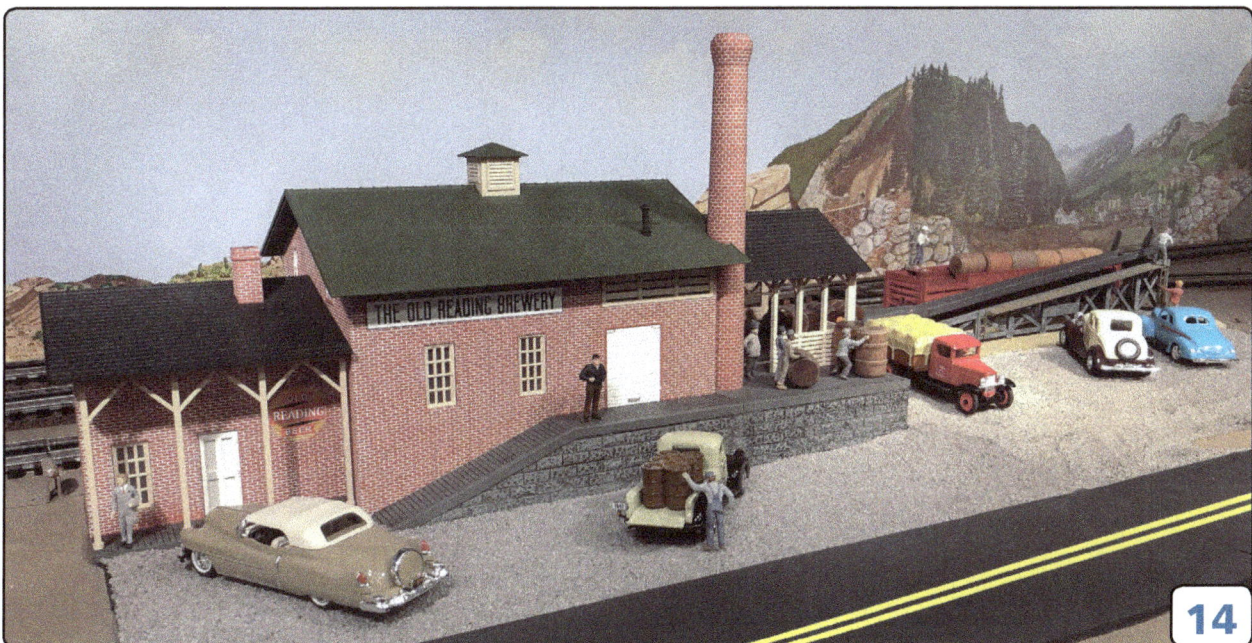

CHAPTER 30 - Connecting Two Levels

If your layout is designed to be one that is viewed only from the front and sides, like mine is, then to use the "vanishing perspective" effect, you will want to put close things down lower and far things up higher. I followed that idea right from the beginning. I built my layout table at basically two different levels with the one in the front lower than the one in the back (Photo 1). That also allows nice use of tunnels for the lower-level tracks to disappear under the upper level to do such things as hide the fact that they are turning around when you reach the end of the room. To hide the obvious turnaround, I put a wye in the lower-level track and made it look like one leg is going underground to some distant place while the other leg goes to the trestle, farther to the right in the photo. What they actually do is connect in one big turnaround loop.

Photo 2 shows that I have a highway on the upper level that is in sore need of a bridge over that lower track. The bridge is a project for a future date. I need to make a believable little ravine for the railroad to enter into that tunnel portal. At the right of the photo is some of the previous hillside scenery I brought to a certain point and that now awaits being joined to the scenery to be put in.

There are lots of ways to make scenery elevations, but my favorite is still the one I have used since I was a kid. It involves making use of some available scrap cardboard, some plaster cloth, a hot glue gun, and some cheap interior latex house paint. Cut the scrap cardboard into strips about 5/8" wide. I bend one end in to make a tab and then apply some hot glue to the tab, sticking it to the tabletop (Photo 3). Space the vertical strips 5/8" apart, about as far as they are wide. At the tops of the strips, fold the excess over the edge and snip it off with a pair of wire cutters, like the ones shown in the photo. Learning to use the wire cutters is much faster than trying to tear the strips apart.

You can get hot glue sticks at a whole lot of places, but the ones I like best are sold by Woodland Scenics #ST1446, shown in the package in the photo, because they need less heat to work well. That means you don't have to spend a whole lot of time waiting for the glue gun to heat up.

Glue the tops of the strips to the upper level, as shown in the photo. Let the cardboard strip "balloon out" just a little so the finished product won't look like a vertical wall.

When you get to something like a tunnel portal, glue the bottom of the strips to the back face of the portal and curl the strip up to the top layer of the layout, also shown in the photo. Also note in the photo that you need to interlace horizontal strips from the ground up, spacing them about as far apart as they are wide, just like the vertical strips. Think of it like a card-board pie crust.

After you've run about a square foot or so of strips, apply a spot of hot glue at every cardboard strip joint and slip a clothes-pin over the joint, as shown in the photo, until the glue hardens. Since I use the low temperature glue sticks made by Woodland Scenics, the hot glue joint will set up hard enough to remove the first of the clothespins by the time you get the last of the pins on.

Photo 4 shows continued progress with all the cardboard strips in place. It's very easy to get a stray strand of hot glue on the rails, so be careful. It's tough to see and difficult to get cleaned off the track. By all means, get all the gluing done before you apply any ballast to the tracks. If it is hard to get hot glue off the rails, it is nearly impossible to get it out of glued down ballast!

Note in Photos 5 and 6 that I used CA glue on a scrap of wood at both ends of the location for the future bridge and painted them a concrete color to represent the foundation for the ends of the bridge. It's best to do that before you put the cardboard strips in place since the earthen scenery will look like it runs right up against the concrete.

Photo 7 shows the finished cardboard strip work for the next phase in the project. Now is a good time to get some blue painter's tape and cover the rails, the tunnel portals, and the concrete abutments to keep any stray plaster off the places where it shouldn't be. Be especially careful to cover switches and switch motors since nothing will ruin

them faster than getting plaster and water in the moving parts. Note how well the cardboard strip system lets you blend new terrain in with the older terrain. Here's the fun part! Shown in Photo 8, plaster cloth is something available from Scenic Express, part #EX0060, and other sources and it is shown on the right side in the photo. Similar material is also available from Woodland Scenics as well as other sources. Check your local train store as some of them stock this material.

The Scenic Express material, shown in the photo, comes in rolls. It is a gauze cloth impregnated with plaster. Unroll it and cut it up into squares or strips. I cut squares and half-squares, as shown in the lower left of the photo. It is very simple to use! Dip the plaster cloth square or strip into water and drape it over the cardboard strips. Start with the small strips around the details such as the tunnel portal or the concrete bridge foundations and then finish the large areas with squares of plaster cloth. It has some working time, so smooth it with your fingers and note the plaster becomes more paste-like overlapping one strip or square to another. Photo 9 shows the finished results with the tape removed from the tunnel portal and the concrete bridge abutments.

BEFORE

1

AFTER

10

Let the plaster cloth dry over-night and paint the hard-shell surface with the same earth tone brown latex paint we've used in previous chapters. After the paint has dried, remove the blue masking tape. Wow! Compare the result in Photo 10 with Photo 1.

Our new contoured terrain is ready for a bridge project and then the final scenery effects such as grasses, weeds, scruffy bushes, trees, and ballast for the track.

CHAPTER 31 - A Wooden Railroad Overpass

U ntil a few years ago, if you traveled along US 50 in southern Indiana, you might have seen a very unique and historic railroad overpass (Photo 1). It was totally made of wood. It's gone now, but it survived at least 60 years that I know of. I've seen this wooden overpass multiple times ever since I was a little kid riding in the back seat of my dad's car on trips to visit relatives. Even back then I thought it would look neat on a train layout.

I stopped one day many years later and took the time to climb down to the train tracks underneath this bridge. I had the good sense to take some measurements and a few snapshots so I would have something to look at some time later if I made a model of this bridge.

Photo 2 shows a couple of engineering ideas that allowed something like this to last for so many years. If you notice carefully, the 2″x 10″ floorboards (1/32″x 3/16″ basswood stock) are installed on a 20-degree angle onto the 12″x 12″ (1/4″ square basswood stock) floor support beams. These beams are spaced with scale 12″ (actual 1/4″) gaps between them.

The floorboards are evenly spaced with a scale 1-1/2″ to 2″ (actual 1/32″) gap between each board. When you are underneath the real bridge, you can look up and see sunlight coming through between the boards. The diagonal spacing keeps the boards from being forcefully rocked back and forth as the tires go over them. The angled installation more evenly distributes the motion of each individual tire on any given board rather than two or more tires striking the same board at the same time. The gaps between each board also make for good rainwater drainage, allowing the boards to dry out better and last longer.

Photo 3 shows several things. The floorboards are anchored on the ends with scale 8″ square runners on each side and trimmed with a slight angle on the end. The 4′ high guardrails are made out of more 12″ square timbers and anchored not only to the support beams under the floor but also to the 8″ runners above the floor. It actually makes for a very solid assembly.

The vertical posts for the railings are spaced about 4′ apart. When you include the post itself, they are about 5′ apart. The inside of the support posts are anchored with 2″x 8″ planks midway up the inside of the posts and also along the inner tops of the 4′ high posts. The open grain on the tops of the posts is capped off with hefty 2″x 16″ planks covering the posts and the top edge of the upper 2x8s.

Photo 4 shows one of the concrete bridge footers on the far side of the ravine. This bridge project is fairly simple. The material to use is basswood. I decided to stain the basswood with the same walnut stain (to simulate creosote) that I used for my trestle project. But for the surface roadway boards and railings, I will use a light gray stain to simulate the years of sun bleaching that the upper woods would have endured. The stain I found was Minwax Classic Gray #297. All the lower timbers were stained with the same walnut stain used with my trestles.

Chapter 31 *Building A Layout* by Jim Barrett

I began by cutting several 1/4″ square basswood beams to the length I needed to span the distance between my two concrete footers already built into my scenery shell. Each basswood beam is resting on top of the concrete footers beginning with one on each edge of the footer (Photo 5).

I then spaced additional 1/4″ square basswood beams between the two outer beams, allowing exactly 1/4″ spacing between them until I covered the tops of the bridge footers from side to side (Photo 6).

I used some scrap pieces of 1/4″ basswood as gauges to evenly space out the ends of the boards. I found it to be a good idea to place a piece of Scotch Double Sided Tape on the tops of the two footers to keep the beams from shifting around during construction. Do not cement the beams onto the concrete footers.

Somewhere in the middle of the span, it's a good idea to glue using CA to some short 1/4″ square basswood spacers to keep the beams evenly spaced throughout the length of the bridge. If you look closely at the photo, you will also see a single piece of the light gray surface planking glued across the ends of the beams right where they touch the end of the pavement for the roadway.

When you have finished gluing the two gray end planks onto the ends of the 12″ square beams, gently lift the whole assembly off of the double-sided tape and relocate it to your workbench. All remaining operations are far easier to do sitting down at your workbench. Be sure to surgically remove any and all leftover double-sided tape from the concrete footers for the bridge. You'll see why later.

Photo 7 shows the beginning of the floor planks going onto the floor beams. Begin with the first full width plank and start at the lower corner as shown. Spot a tiny drop of CA glue (thick consistency, purple label) on the surface of each and every beam and then carefully place the first plank. Using a plank turned on edge to get the correct spacing, glue the next plank on and quickly remove the "spacer" plank. Note that it is not necessary to have every plank cut to the correct length. It is rather easy using a #18 chisel blade in a #2 X-Acto handle to trim off the excess board length even after it has been glued on. If however you own or have access to a Micro-Mark or sim-

ilar miniature table saw, then life is much easier. You can use that excellent tool to mass produce all the correctly cut planks you will need.

One of the more amazing things I discovered was that after the first few planks, I was able to set the planks at correct spacing without the use of a spacer board or the protractor. You just develop a very good feel for it. Photo 8 shows how good the overall effect looks.

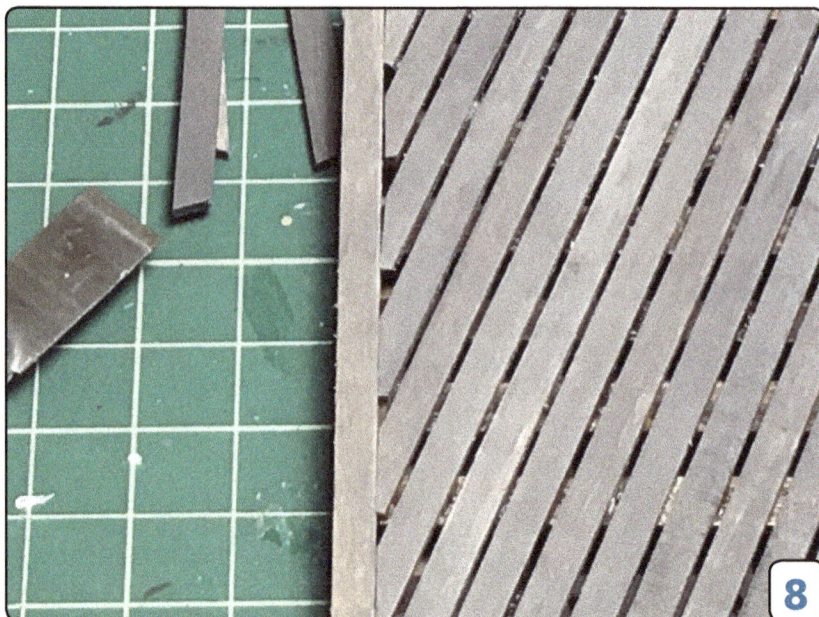

Photo 9 shows the remaining uneven ends of the final plank pieces. All that now remains is to turn the whole bridge floor assembly over and trim off the ends. Be sure to go back over the cut ends of any basswood and apply some touchup stain to the ends of the boards.

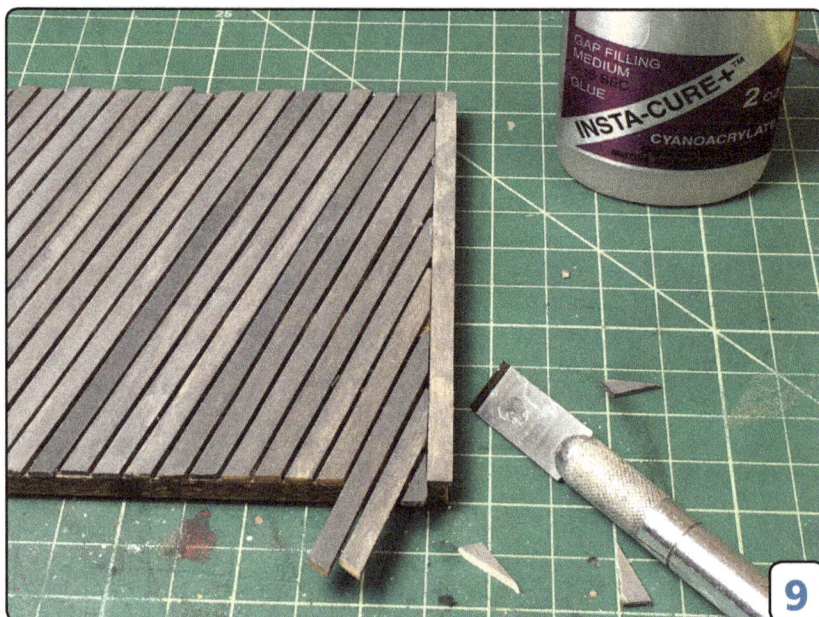

Photo 10 shows the attachment of the two 8″ square edge runners (scales out to 3/16″ square basswood) over the tops of the floor planks. Now it's time to set your whole floor assembly into the layout to check for fit. After that step, I began gluing the many 4′ high bridge railing posts onto the edge of the bridge floor assembly. Keep in mind that the posts need to be cut to 1-3/8″ actual length. That's more than the scale 4′ you need for the height, but you have to allow for the thickness of the floor planks and the support beams.

In Photo 11, I intentionally cut the runners to hang over the ends of the bridge by 1/2″. That lets me trim a final incline on the ends to somewhat match the real ones shown in Photo 3.

Also in Photo 11, the posts have been glued to the edge of the floor assembly, and the upper 2x8 plank (actual dimension 1/32″x 3/16″ basswood) has been glued to the posts as well as another 2x8 plank about halfway up the post. Note that I made the wooden planks for the railings go over the end of the floor assembly by some nominal amount equal to the typical spacing of the guardrail posts. Then I glued a final "floating" post to the ends of the boards as shown under the clamp in the photo. Final scenery will make it look like it is firmly anchored at the end of the bridge.

The end result is shown in Photo 12. Photo 13 shows something else that is kind of neat. Look how the overhead sunlight actually shows through the floorboard gaps exactly like the prototype in Photo 2. I like it when something works out like this.

Remember when I mentioned earlier to carefully remove all traces of the double-sided tape? This will now allow you to easily lift the whole bridge floor assembly off the concrete bridge footers and set it aside for doing things like climbing into the ravine to do scenery or get wayward railcar wheels.

The last step is the support beam work under the bridge. You will notice that nowhere have I specified how long any board or beam is to be cut. That is because those dimensions will be individually relative to the length and height of your own bridge overpass needs. Photo 14 shows what I came up with for the curved track and the bridge height I needed for my installation. I came up with the lengths I needed for my support structure by studying the photos I took of the real thing and somewhat scaling it to fit my particular need.

For your bridge supports, all the vertical and angled supports are made from 1/4″ square basswood stock with all bracing made from the same 1/16″x 3/16″ basswood stock I use for any and all trestle work. From an engineering standpoint I tried to mimic the same design as what shows up in photos at the beginning of this article. Photo 15 shows the final support work of the beams at the top of the double bridge support. This design comes from mimicking what shows up in the first three photos.

I was amazed at how easy this project was after getting the first few techniques down. If you build yours the way I've shown, the result will actually be three small projects: the bridge floor and the two vertical support assemblies. With the addition of a few round toothpick parts and some tiny holes, I ended up with all three pieces easily set in place and removable at will and allowing me to finish the ravine scenery and all the track ballast at any time.

CHAPTER 32 - Making Good Looking Guardrails

One of the things that has always bothered me about studying and photographing layouts is when a road or highway is positioned near the edge of the layout or the edge of a scenic cliff. All well and good but there almost never were any guardrails along the highway to keep the hapless O gauge driver from driving right off the edge of the earth. I vowed then and there to correct that situation on my next layout.

Ha! Easier said than done! What I had assumed would be a plentiful detail part in the scenery world of O gauge turned out to be one of the most elusive items of them all. There just isn't any good source of O gauge guardrails that can be used to enhance our scenery and roads to make them more believable. Sure, you can find HO guardrails for slot car racing sets or even larger ones for bigger scale slot car racing. But even then they aren't believable when it comes to a true O scale scenery detail for a good hi-rail layout. And that is such a shame, too. There has been such a literal explosion of great-looking, highly detailed cars and trucks for O gauge in the last few years, and road scenes have become as much a part of a train layout as the trains are.

While driving along streets and highways, I love to look for various scenery ideas, so I made up my mind to stop and take time to photograph some guardrails and take a few measurements as well. Doing so, it immediately became apparent that the era you are modeling becomes very important. In the real world, guardrails have changed a great deal in design and appearance in the past 50 years.

Since my layout is set in the 1940s through the mid-1950s, if you want to study what guardrails look like, you will have to find some nice old ones. Fortunately, America's back roads still have a bunch of them in use.

Take a look at Photo 1 above. This is what a basic guardrail from that era looked like. It was a deeply corrugated steel strip, although not mounted on steel posts like the one shown. Instead, it was directly mounted on 6″ x 6″ wooden posts or on wooden standoffs mounted on wooden posts. The steel guardrail was a hefty 12″ or so tall and had two bends or corrugations all along its length for strength. After measuring several, I found that the 1′ wide guardrail was nominally mounted so that the top of the steel was set 24″ above the road surface.

Scaling those figures down to our O gauge world (1/4″ = 1′) makes the steel part of the guardrail 1/4″ tall (wide) mounted on 1/8″ square wooden posts at a height of 1/2″ above the road's surface. It just so happens that Plastruct makes some styrene plastic sheet called O Scale 1:48 Corrugated Siding Part #91519, Catalog No. PS-24, as shown in Photo 2. Photo 3 shows the two sheets in the package. That sure looks like a sheet of guardrail stock to me!

If you space out two of the corrugations on the sheet and cut them off along the line in the valley of the corrugation between those two and the next two, you end up with an almost perfect 1/4″ wide corrugated strip looking just like the guardrail (Photo 4). Just hold down a straightedge and gently trim down the length of the plastic. A couple of passes and you will have single strips of double corrugations. This is almost too easy!

In Photo 5 I mounted the strips on some scrap foam core board with a couple of strips of double-sided tape. Using some Testors silver spray paint, I lightly coated the strips on one side and left them to dry thoroughly for the evening. The next day, I turned them over and did the same thing with the other side.

Bingo! I now have a very good imitation of O gauge silver-painted steel guardrail (Photo 6).

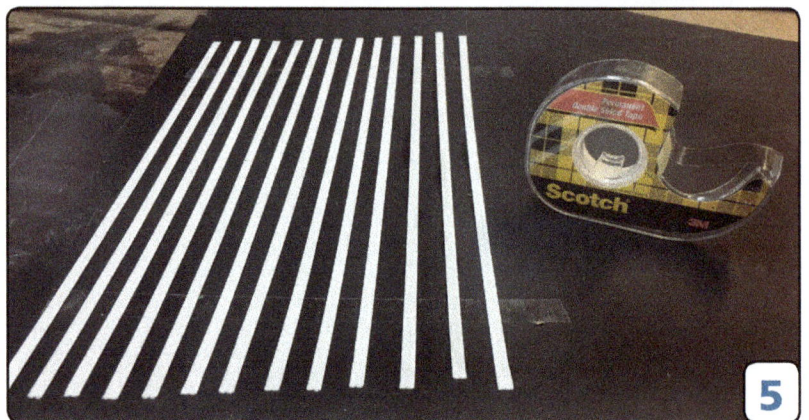

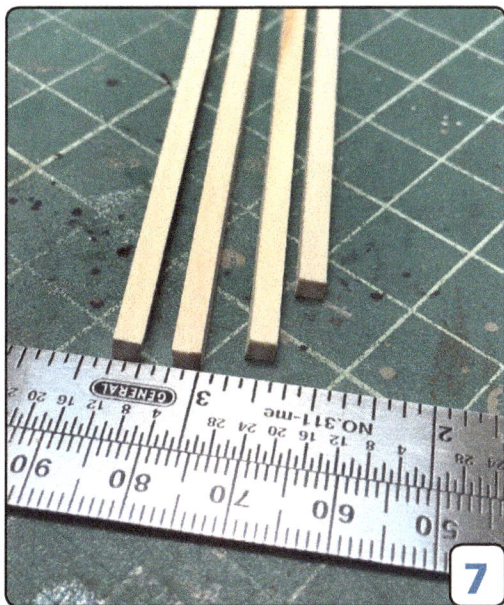

As I noted earlier, the real guardrails back in the 40s and 50s were mounted on 6″ x 6″ wooden posts spaced every 10′ to 12′ apart. That measures either every 2-1/2″ or every 3″ on our layouts. The 6″ x 6″ wooden posts in O scale need to be no bigger than 1/8″ square basswood (Photo 7). I first made a mockup of two lengths of guardrail: one at 10′ spacing and the other at 12′ spacing. I decided on the 10′ spacing because it looked just a little more rugged, but you may like the wider spacing.

I stained the lengths of the 1/8″ square basswood with walnut oil stain. That walnut stain makes the basswood look like a good facsimile of creosoted 6″ x 6″ wooden posts.

I debated on several different ways to mount the posts and finally decided that the easiest way is probably the best way. I know you've heard the old saying that square pegs don't fit in round holes, but they will fit if you make the round hole a hair bigger than the square peg. I drilled 5/32″ diameter holes through the scenery gravel and through the 1/2″ plywood table surface and pressed in the 1/8″ square basswood stock. I located the holes so the posts were 1/4″ to 1/2″ away from the road surface (a scale 1′ or 2′). I drilled the hole as straight as possible because you won't have much room to do any corrections when you are done (Photo 8).

Cut the 1/8″ square stained wood into 1-1/2″ lengths. Because the round hole is 1/32″ wider than the square post, the squared edges of the post can be gently forced into the hole nicely. Place the post onto the top of a hole and gently tap the post in until its top is exactly 1/2″ above the pavement (Photo 9). You will find that the 1/8″ square post compresses nicely into the slightly larger 5/32″ round hole. It also makes getting the height of the post to the exact 1/2″ above the road surface very easy to do.

In Photo 10 I've touched up the top of the posts with some more dark wood stain. Heck, that already looks good, and we haven't even attached the guardrail yet.

The beginning and ends of guard-rails today are a whole science unto themselves to make them safer when collisions occur at the exposed ends of the guardrails. But back in the 1950s, the safety factor consisted of nothing more than curling the ends of the steel guardrails to keep them from penetrating the car. Fortunately, that is easy to duplicate with styrene guardrails. Grasping the end of the guardrail with long-nose pliers, simply curl the end of the styrene guardrail around far enough so it will eventually hold the curl (Photo 11). You can see the finished effect in Photo 12.

Wooden clothespins are the best tools to use for this next step. Temporarily attach a length of guard-rail with clothespins, as shown in Photo 13. Position the guardrail so that the curled end is no more than 1/2″ past the first post. If your guardrail needs to be longer than a single length of material, overlap one end of the guardrail 1/4″ over the beginning of the next length of guardrail and continue on down your line of posts. Be sure to trim the end of the last guardrail to its final length after you have put another curl on the final end.

Position all of these pieces until you are satisfied with their final appearance and then put a tiny drop of thin CA adhesive on each post where the guard-rail is touching it (Photo 14). Also, put a tiny drop of CA on the overlapping ends of the guardrail sections.

Photos 15 and 16 show some final examples of a finished roadside guard-rail. As you can see, it is the little details that add so much to the finished effect of a model railroad. Try this project on your layout. It is surprisingly easy and very rewarding.

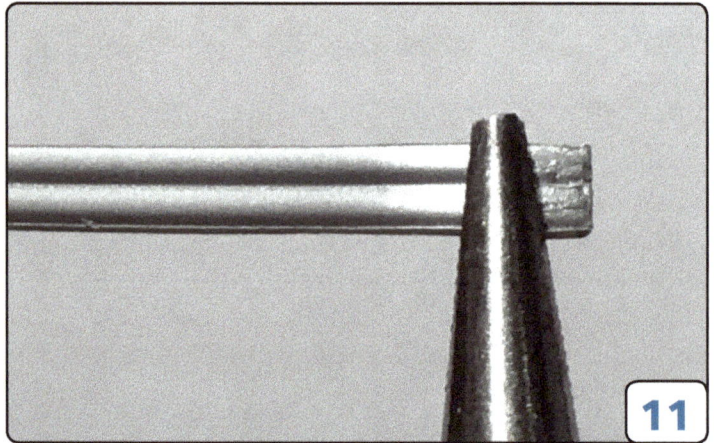

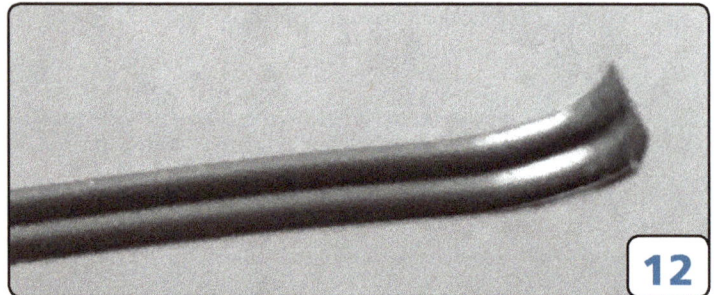

CHAPTER 33 - Making Old and Neglected Rail Sidings

Here's a scenery opportunity you may have never thought of. As you wander about the real world, note how many old rail sidings are in serious need of maintenance with heat-buckled track, weeds growing up all over the place, and very little if any ballasting of the ties. Also note that the heavily used mainline tracks are nicely maintained with fresh ballast and straight and level rails. Because the main lines are maintained better, note that the mainline tracks also tend to sit up just a little higher than a nearby neglected siding.

With a little pre-planning and some creative use of scenery materials, we can model that realistic feature on our layouts, too. Look closely at Photo 1 of the track on what will become an old and neglected siding behind the country store and the gas station on my layout. As a rule, I use cork roadbed under all my mainline tracks, but for this old siding I left out the cork roadbed and attached the siding track directly to the tabletop. That automatically makes the two mainline tracks to the left look like they have been more recently ballasted due to their height difference compared to the siding. Also note the slope down from the mainline track through the pair of crossover switches to the siding. It

demonstrates that the track gang has ballasted the main line, which now causes the crossover to have a serious downhill slope with a result of the main line being ballasted higher than the siding.

I wanted this siding to look sort of neglected, but still usable. It still services a brewery, a horse corral, and a barrel loader. The part of the siding behind the general store also serves as a nice place to park the switch engine while the crew goes inside for a soda break.

Before mounting the siding track to the table, I first bent the track section up a little in several places and then straightened it out. Since you can't get flexible track to perfectly straighten out once it has been bent, that left many little simulated heat kinks in the track. Check the finished installation to make sure that at least a short wheelbase switch engine can still navigate the wobbly track.

Also check to make sure that the switch engine can negotiate the slope between the two switches in the crossover to the siding. If it can't, it is a relatively simple fix to raise both switches to the same level and gently slope the siding track down in both directions away from the switch.

Another indication that the siding hasn't been ballasted in a while shows up where the gravel service road crosses both the railroad main lines and the siding. The road slopes down slightly from the main line to the siding. My gravel road is made from cut up pieces of black foam core board glued to the ends of the ties and then filled in on the edges with putty (Photo 2). After the putty dried, I painted the putty and the foam core board with Woodland Scenics #ST1454 Top Coat Concrete road paint. When that was dry, I covered it with road gravel—N scale ballast looks about like road gravel in O gauge. Using the concrete colored paint is helpful because the color looks a lot like the color of limestone road gravel that tops it. In tiny areas where the gravel doesn't totally cover, the paint also helps not to notice that.

You might be tempted to fill the roadway areas between the outer rails with gravel, but if you have any Lionel operating cars equipped with slide shoes for activation, like I do, that will cause a problem. The glued down N scale ballast for the road crossing will severely interfere with any operating car slide shoes passing over the gravel road crossing. Those slide shoes must be able to glide smoothly over that surface, which the gravel won't let them do. Instead I simulated the filler between the rails as asphalt using some more of the foam core board material, which I painted with Woodland Scenics #ST1453 Top Coat Asphalt paint. You may also have noticed that the gravel road seems to be abnormally high. It looks like that in the photo because the road is lifted up to the height of the rail it crosses. Don't worry too much about that. When the rest of the roadside scenery is added, it will look much more realistic.

When using GarGraves flexible track for these grade crossings, it is important to keep the foam core board thickness for the roadbed at 1/8″ or less. That leaves just enough room for a thin layer of road gravel to go right up to the edges of the rails without the gravel being higher than the rail. I debated whether or not to even ballast the siding track since it was going to be mostly overgrown with weeds anyhow. I'm glad I did though because the small patches of ballast that do show between the weeds look just like old sidings do in the real world. Most of the ballast is obscured with weeds, but some of it still shows through.

I use Scenic Express products for my weed projects. The smaller package in Photo 3 is WBP603 Summer Grass Tufts, which can be used anywhere by applying with a pair of tweezers and gluing in place with a dot of Elmer's glue. The larger of the two products is WBM051 Prairie Floor. It is a very thin brown vinyl sheet with random weeds and brown dirt patches on it. This material is easily cut with scissors to any shape needed. It was perfect for filling in the bare spot around the gravel parking lot of my gas station.

After I had cut the pieces I needed to fit the space I wanted to fill, I turned them over one by one, sprayed them with a light coat of contact cement 3M Super 77, and applied them directly to the painted brown table surface. While the contact cement was still drying, I was able to push the vinyl around until I made it fit very close to my existing open area. Don't worry when you notice that the cut vinyl edge is visible when you lay it down. A light covering of gravel brushed right up to and on the weed patch makes everything look perfect.

When all the pieces I cut were glued down and trimmed in gravel or ground cover, I finished them by spraying the edges with "wet water," which is water diluted with a few drops of dish detergent, and applying some drops of diluted glue to secure the loose materials. Diluted glue is made by mixing Elmer's white glue with 50 percent water and 50 percent glue. After it was thoroughly mixed together, I poured it into a little dropper bottle and applied it around all the taller grass tufts and over the shorter scenery materials between the tracks (Photo 4). Don't worry about the icky white appearance. Everything will dry clear and flat. Photo 5 shows the final result.

Also note some taller weeds and a few bushes around the horse corral in Photo 6. They came from the product WBSCW shown in Photo 7, which are bushes of different heights and colors.

Photo 8 shows the other side of the gas station. Back in chapter five I made table hinges that were modified to allow the opening of scenery panels. I made the statement back then about how they will be easily hidden by scenery. There are no less than two of them. Can you find them? Look carefully in the weeds and bushes on the side of the road in the foreground and behind the guardrail separating the gravel road from the gas station.

Photo 9 shows rows of weeds beside the track with the Great Northern hopper. There are more of those types of weeds in Photo 10 beside the caboose. Those products are CA0220, 0222, and 0223 random ditch weeds. Photos 11, 12, and 13 also show products NH07129 and NH016, which are more grass tufts of various colors and heights. They are premade rows of weeds in various colors like what you would find popping up between the ties of old, seldom used sidings. Their size seems about right for the weeds often found between the tracks and along drainage ditches. I got one of each.

Photo 14 shows the finished siding behind the store and the gas station. The gravel road looks much better with some weeds around the edges.

Here are some basic rules to follow about adding weeds to tracks:

- Don't make your scenery weeds high enough to snag things on the underside of the locomotives or rolling stock.

- Wheels and flanges need more room than you think they do. Don't put weeds or pavement material anywhere near the inner edge of the rails. You will find out immediately if you have weeds clunking up against the wheel flanges. Rolling stock can derail, and engines can simply stop running because the weeds act as insulators between the wheels and the rails.

- Don't coat the tops of rails with anything that prevents good electrical flow. You definitely need to clean the rails when you are done even if you can't see anything on the track.

- Make sure any weeds you add between the center rail and the outside rails are not too high. The slide shoes of operating cars travel along slightly below the tops of the outer and center rails and should not snag on stiff scenery weeds.

- Don't forget the areas immediately adjacent to the tracks, too. Bushes and taller weeds can be added one at a time by adding a spot of hot glue and placing the bushes on the glue spot before it sets up.

Scenery is definitely not my specialty, as you can see from this first attempt. I'll bet your efforts will be better than mine!

Chapter 33 *Building A Layout* by Jim Barrett

CHAPTER 34 - Hiding a Track Scenery Joint

Back in chapter five we discussed how to make a removable triple trestle module on my layout that would allow access to trains in the back of the layout, or under mountains. In chapters five, six, and eight I showed you how to make hinged sections of the layout to either swing up or down to allow passage through the front part of the layout into inner regions.

Also in previous chapters I showed you how to lay roadbed and track right over the joint line of the roll-away module, or at the lift or drop sections of the layout. Hiding that train table joint line with "green scenery" is relatively easy, but what do we do with the joint line where it goes right through the track ballast? That will require a tricky little track scenery joint.

A track scenery joint occurs anywhere you have a hinged panel or removable section of your layout that has railroad track with loosely applied ballast running over the joint. It is relatively easy to attach the track over the joint and to then cut the track where it crosses the joint (see chapter six), but the real trick is making a nearly invisible joint line right through the ballast—a joint that won't be easily noticed at a glance.

Loosely applied ballast is the hardest thing to make a nearly invisible joint line through. I've devised a way that seems to work very well and isn't really that complicated or difficult to do.

The trick is to make the scenery joint line between the track ties, then add ballast and ballast glue while still having the joint line hold up so it will be free moving through that process. My solution was to come up with a way to hold the ballast on both sides of the table joint tightly up against each other while the ballast glue dries. Of course, this all has to happen without the ballast glue actually gluing the two table sections shut.

Photo 1 above shows my triple trestle crossing over a deep gorge. As nice as that trestle scene is, the three trestles make it nearly impossible to get behind them to do any scenery work, or to get to any train derailments that may need attention behind them. To solve that problem, I built the entire trestle assembly on a movable module that fits perfectly into the layout train table.

Look carefully at photo 1. You'll see one of the joint lines between the trestle module and the train table in the foreground of the photo going from the front of the train table (the black surface) in a straight line over to the first curve, then progressing upwards through some loosely overlapping scenery base material to the inclined grade track. From there, it goes under and through the grade track, and up the wavy scenery base line material to the top track.

Photo 2 shows the straight line break in the train table through the lower track from an angle that really illustrates the problem of how to hide the track joint after the ballast is applied. Photo 3 shows a closeup of the table joint right at the track line.

Photo 4 shows what happens when the snap is unlatched and the trestle module is rolled away, revealing how the opening of the table goes through all three tracks. Since I like to place loose ballast over the ties followed by gluing the ballast in place, all six of the track joints on this roll out trestle module will have an ugly ballast joint line showing up. I needed a solution for how to make glued ballast track joints look invisible, yet still be able to roll the module out and back together again repeatedly. Since I tend to do some of my best thinking while lying awake in bed mulling over a problem, a solution finally came to me: Saran Wrap!

Chapter 34   *Building A Layout* by Jim Barrett

Saran Wrap (or any clear kitchen food wrap that adheres to itself) is the solution. As shown in Photo 5, I applied a piece of clear kitchen wrap against the end faces of both layout table sections right at the opened table joint (covering the black areas seen in Photo 4). I made sure that the piece I applied extended up and over the ends of the track on both sides of the joint. Once that was done, I gently closed the module back into the table, letting both sides of the super thin plastic wrap touch up against each other.

Photo 6 shows the closed joint with the plastic wrap extending above the track.

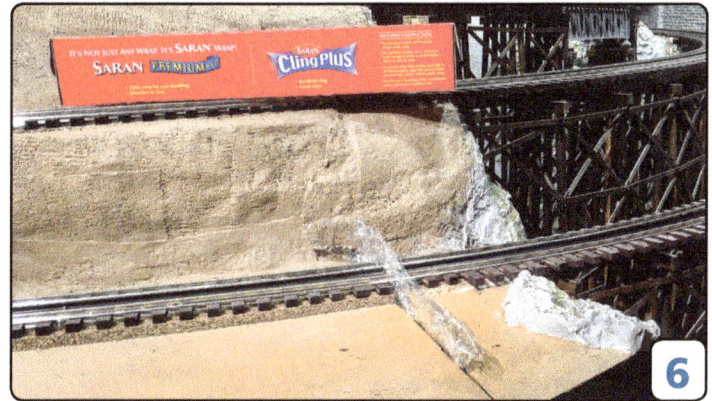

Photo 7 shows how you can clearly look right through both layers of plastic wrap and still see the track on the other side. This will become a very valuable visual aid to making this idea work.

In Photo 8 I have applied my loose limestone ballast to the near side of the joint, taking care to place the ballast right up to the clear plastic as if it wasn't even there.

Once that was complete, I did the same thing to the other side of the joint (Photo 9). The super thin clear plastic "wall" made up of the two layers of kitchen wrap allowed me to brush the ballast on each side of the table joint up against each other, using the weight of the ballast on the other side of the clear plastic wrap to hold both sides in perfect alignment. Being able to see through the plastic easily allowed me to make sure that the height of the ballast on both sides of the plastic wrap was exactly the same. When the plastic is removed later, that is what makes the joint line invisible!

Once I was satisfied that the ballast was correctly placed, I sprayed both sides with "wet water" (water mixed in a sprayer bottle with a couple of drops of liquid dish detergent). The "wet water" is a necessary ingredient for the next step because it easily allows the glue to soak down through the ballast when it is applied.

Photo 10 shows the application of the ballast glue (two parts water to one part glue, thoroughly mixed) applied with a dropper bottle over the top of everything, wood ties and all. You might note in the photo that the far side has already been done with the watered down Elmer's glue still visibly wet on the ties. The glue will dry flat and clear over the ties, as well as over the limestone ballast.

Another valuable function of the kitchen wrap is that it seals the flat ends of the layout and the trestle module from any stray glue that might soak down through the ballast, thereby inadvertently gluing the train table and the trestle module together. After waiting at least a day for the glue to thoroughly dry, slowly separate the two layout pieces. They will easily separate right on the joint of the two sheets of kitchen wrap, as seen in Photo 10.

After removing and discarding the sheets of Saran Wrap, Photo 11 shows that the joint line through the ballast has all but disappeared. You might also note that the ties themselves are less black and more weathered in appearance since the ballast glue has dried over the wood. After the ballast glue has thoroughly dried, and with the layout table parts separated, apply a very thin coat of Elmer's glue over the exterior edges of the ballast on both sides of the joint. That will further strengthen the ballast and keep the crispy edge from crumbling over time.

12a

12b

13a

13b

Photo 12a shows the same hidden scenery joint line on a "hinge-up" scenery panel. Note that as the open end of the hinge-up panel's edge passes through the ballast, it is hardly visible. Photo 12b depicts how the scenery remains undisturbed as the panel is lifted open.

Photos 13a and 13b show a hidden ballast joint line on a "hinge-down" panel. Note how well the individual stones in the ballast hold in against the wood ties even right through the separation line that was made by the kitchen wrap.

Don't forget to harden those ballast edges by applying some additional Elmer's glue onto the two edges after the original glue has dried and the panel is opened. Some additional trimming may also be needed using an X-Acto knife here and there. Be sure to form the ballast joint (using the plastic wrap separating the two surfaces) so the actual opening or closing of the hinged door doesn't damage the finished ballast joint line.

If you use loosely applied ballast on your layout, give this a try. Don't worry if you don't initially succeed. Sometimes it takes a little practice to get it right.

CHAPTER 35 - Making Short Work of a Long Rock Wall

When you build layouts in O gauge, you almost always end up working with (or against) a space problem. Sure, there might be some hobbyists who have a seemingly unlimited amount of space to build in, but most of us, like me, are challenged with doing as much as we can in a relatively small space. I've certainly learned a few things about layout space challenges in the course of photographing layouts all over the country.

One way to work more into a layout is to "go vertical" in any way you possibly can. Photo 1 illustrates what I mean. The total horizontal distance from the front of the layout to the back wall in this photo is only about 38″. If my layout was built all on one level, it would be tough to have four main lines, a town's main street, and the town itself all crowded into that narrow space. In fact, it would

look downright junky. This wasn't really a problem when we were kids. We were quite happy with a sea of tracks crowded onto a piece of plywood. But as we turn simple toy trains into a lasting hobby, the challenge we face is to let scenery play a larger role in the overall layout.

But look what happens when you drop the front 16″ of the layout down about 9″. That drop forces the eye to regard the scene on the lower level as a whole new scene, making the same number of tracks look not nearly so crowded as they would if they were all on the same level. The tracks appear to be further apart, and this also allows for more scenery ideas, seeming to add depth to the layout. This also gives the observer's eye more places to jump around to and take in more scenes.

Since one of my goals has been to feature as many of those nifty postwar-era operating accessories as I could on the layout, that elevation change also let me work in a long passing siding for the Lionel Ice House, the Lionel Lumber Loader, and the Icing Station from Atlas O. That last item is key in my case since I own a good many Atlas O reefers, and that facility gives them a reason for being active on my steam freight trains.

The problem is what to do with that long and ugly gap in the table heights? If I was creating an urban setting, the problem could be solved pretty easily with vertical retaining walls, which can be absolutely vertical and appear to be made out of concrete, brick, or some combination thereof. But I grew up in a small town and want to depict a main street scene looking much like my hometown, so I had to turn to nature for the scenery to fill in that vertical gap.

I gave some thought to rock castings like those I used on the valley with the railroad trestles (see chapters ten, twenty-two, twenty-five, and twenty-six), but that was a lot of work, and it took a lot of time, which I just don't seem to have anymore. Instead, I talked to my good friends at Scenic Express, and owner Jim Elster put me on to a great Heki-brand item called Flexrock, which is a flexible plastic rock sheet product (Photo 2). Check with your local hobby suppliers, but if they don't stock this product, you can find it by downloading the Scenic Express catalog at sceneryexpress.com. There you will find four or five different patterns of pre-formed, painted rock wall that can be mixed and matched for the effect you desire. Yes, this product may be a tad expensive, but considering the savings in time and effort, it is darn cheap. I ordered two different rock wall sections: #HK3503 "Dolomite Strata Cliff," and #HK3504 "Grey Limestone Cliff." These rock wall sheets are available in a couple of different sizes, and I ordered the ones that measure 14-1/2″ tall x 33″ wide. This stuff is great to work with! It is to some extent "crushable," allowing you to work it around tight corners if need be.

Since I needed to go from my lower level to the upper level, I had to add a "baseplate" of sorts to the lower level. It serves as a guide to the bottom of the wall and provides a place to securely attach the wall's bottom.

I made the base support with strips of 1/8″ thick x 1/4″ wide balsa wood (Photo 3). This size balsa, which is a soft wood, allows you to bend the strips enough to create gentle curves along the bottom level.

Using ultra-thin CA glue (blue label), I glued the 1/8″ edge of the balsa strip to the table top on the lower level, just behind a pencil line I made previously, as seen in Photo 4. This allows for adequate clearance of locomotives and/or rolling stock (see chapter eleven).

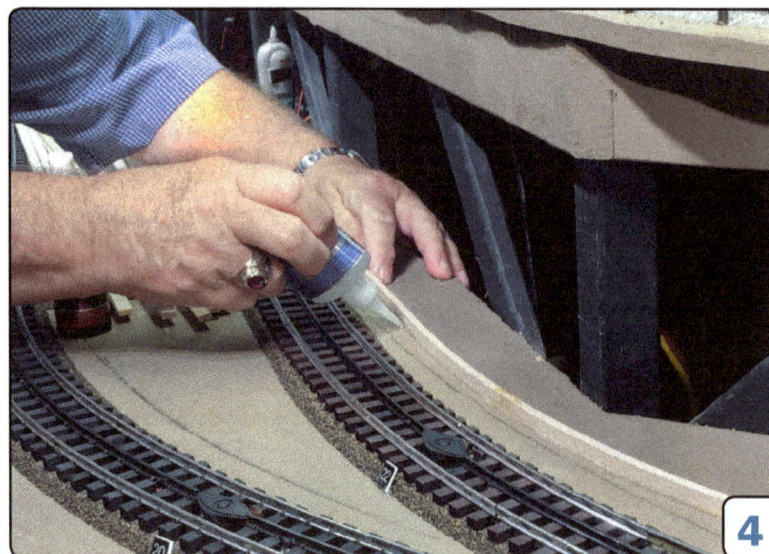

Using the CA accelerator spray, periodically spray the balsa strip and glue to cause it to set up nearly instantly. Bend the balsa strip along behind the pencil line as needed to form the base of the rock wall. Photo 5 shows the balsa strip glued in place, standing 1/4″ high all along what will ultimately be the base of the new wall.

Photo 6 shows how easily the sheet of plastic rock foil will conform to curves. I made a pencil mark about a quarter inch higher than the upper level of the layout on both ends of the rock wall material. You can always trim a little off later if need be, but it's more difficult to add a little back on if you cut it off too low.

On my workbench (Photo 7 below), I made a line connecting the two pencil marks on the sides of the plastic sheet and easily cut the plastic foil to the correct height with a pair of scissors (Photo 8).

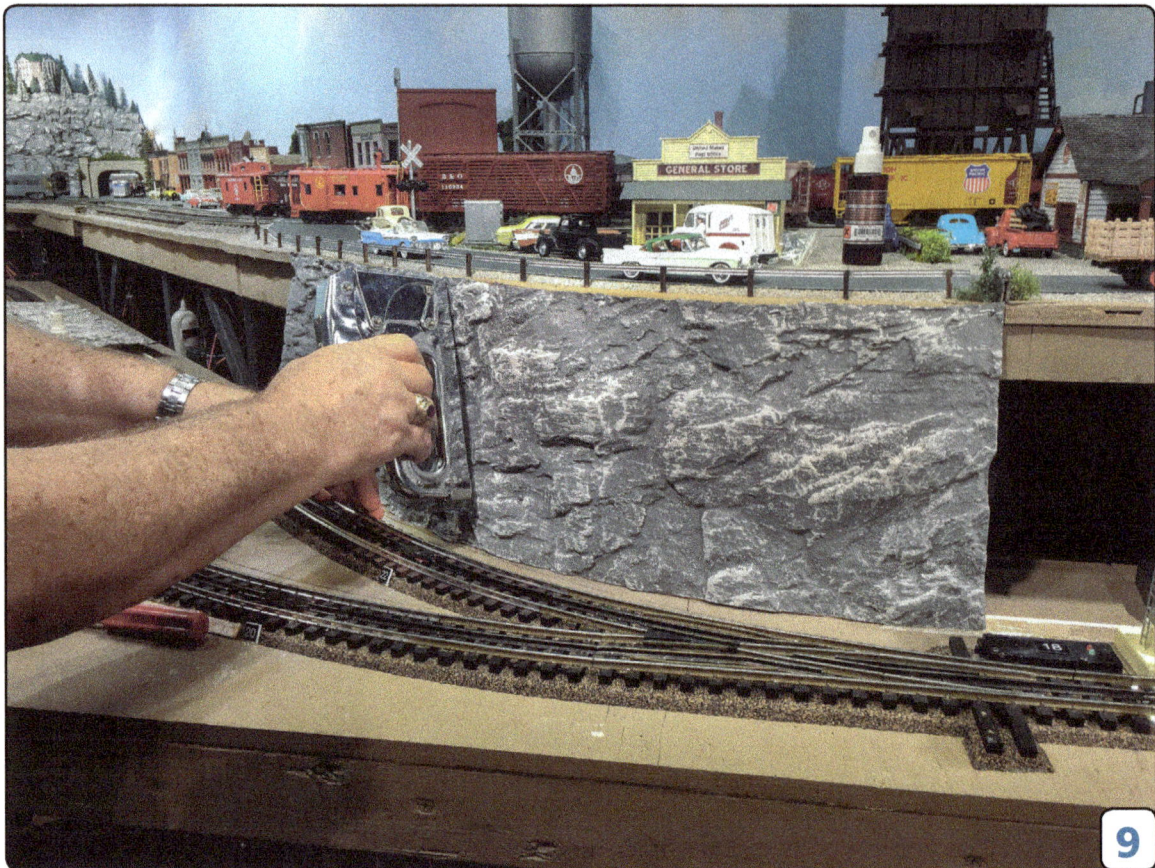

Now comes the fun part! Position the section of rock wall along the bottom table, up against the balsa wood strip, as shown in Photo 9. Using an staple gun (mine is an Arrow T-25) with 9/16″ tall staples, simply shoot through the top of the plastic rock wall material into the edge of the upper layout table along the full length of the plastic sheet about every three or four inches.

Stop short of the far end by about four inches and trim the ends of the rocks on the sheet in a manner similar to what is shown in Photo 10. It doesn't have to be perfect. Just round off the sharp edges of the plastic to resemble the ends of rocks.

You might find that the plastic rock wall wants to bulge out slightly in places along the bottom. To secure the bottom of the rock wall, use a large squeeze bottle of medium or gap-filling CA glue (purple label) and squeeze a bead of glue a few inches long along the bottom of the wall. Hold the plastic foil in place against the balsa strip with a scrap piece of balsa stick, and spray the CA accelerator in spots to hold it firmly in place. The CA will set up almost immediately, fastening the plastic sheet to the balsa strip behind it. Do this all along the bottom of the rock wall, but remember to stop about four inches before the end of the piece.

Repeat this procedure with another piece of rock wall material, slipping it in behind the loose end of the first piece. The worst edge you will end up with might look like what is seen above in Photo 11. A little vine material or a wild bush or two poking out behind a rock will nicely disguise that seam. Another thing you can do is to add a little gap-filling CA behind a piece of rock wall that is sticking out and push it back in place against the back piece of wall, spraying it with the CA accelerator. Photo 12 above shows how effectively that makes the joint seem to go away even more.

When your wall is complete, go along the top edge of rock and use an X-Acto knife with a long blade to trim off any portion that sticks above the upper level of the layout. Use a back-and-forth sawing motion as you work along the edge of the top surface. The plastic trims off very easily. Any gaps between the plastic and the table edge can easily be filled with bushes, grass clumps, etc.

Wow! Check out our completed rock wall in Photo 13! See how much better that looks than Photo 1. Add a couple of trains and some layout structures, as seen in Photo 14, and the improvement is dramatic. Now all I need to do is add ballast on the tracks, add some weeds here and there, and "rust" the sides of the rails.

I ran my wall down along the layout to a stopping point where I have one of those drop-down layout sections, as described in chapters five and six, which allow me to walk through the layout. For that area I'll have to do something just a little more creative to create an easily removable section of rock wall. I'll cover that solution in chapter thirty-six.

CHAPTER 36 - Making a Removable Rock Wall

In the previous chapter, I showed you how to make wonderful use of a product offered by Scenic Express called Flexible Plastic Rock Sheets (#HK3503 "Dolomite Strata Cliff" and #HK3504 "Grey Limestone Cliff"). It is a plastic foil-like product that does an outstanding job of simulating sheer rock walls (Photo 1). It solved my problem of taking up as little depth on my layout as possible to realistically connect two different levels of trains. By bending this product around curves in the ply-wood layers of the layout and fastening it to the edges with either staples or CA glue, it made the problem go away in short order.

But as you know if you've been following the construction of my layout, there are several places where I have hinged the layers of the layout either up or down to permit me to walk directly into or even through the layout in places. Check out Photo 1 again. It shows where I had left off making the rock wall because just around the corner of the curved wall to the right of this photo is one of the walk-in access points in my layout.

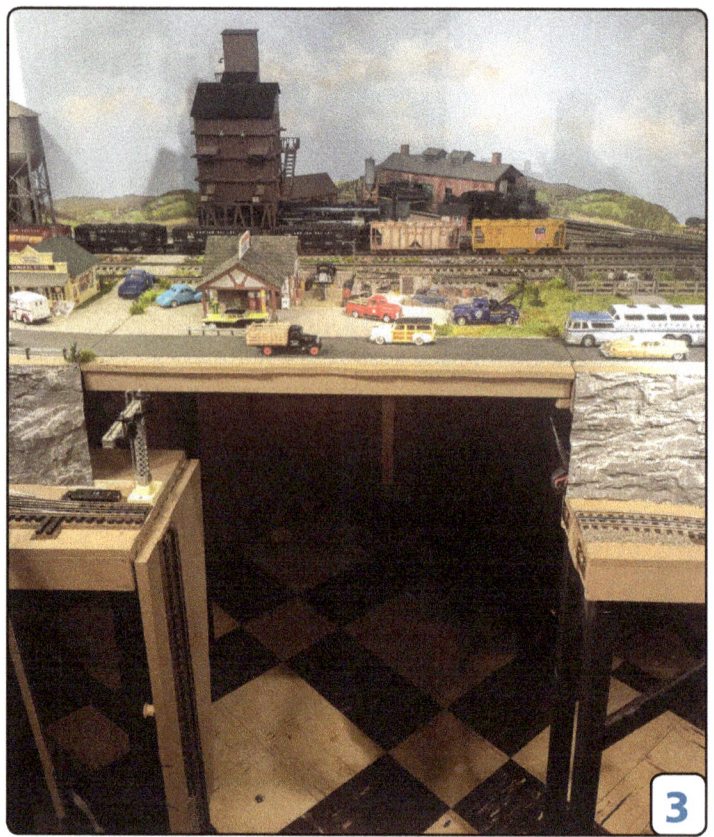

Photo 2 shows where my rock wall stops on both sides of the access walkway.

Photo 3 shows the lower track hinged down and out of the way, and Photo 5 shows the upper level hinged up and out of the way in case something in my engine yard needs a helping hand.

The trick is to make up a removable rock wall section to cover that gap shown in Photo 2. A trip to a big box home improvement store will show you a nice lightweight material that should be perfect for solving this problem (Photo 4). It is a 1-1/2″thick Styrofoam insulation product that can easily be sculpted with a hot wire or long blade utility knife, and can be shaped, if needed, by a wood rasp. Some stores sell this material in convenient 2′x 4′ sheets. It originally comes in 4′x 8′ sheets, which isn't so convenient. Try first to negotiate with the store to sell you a reduced size amount, but if that fails, see if you can interest some friends into jointly purchasing the big sheet to be cut up and used by all. The Home Depot near me had no problem with cutting it into 2′x 4′ pieces, but not all stores will do that for you.

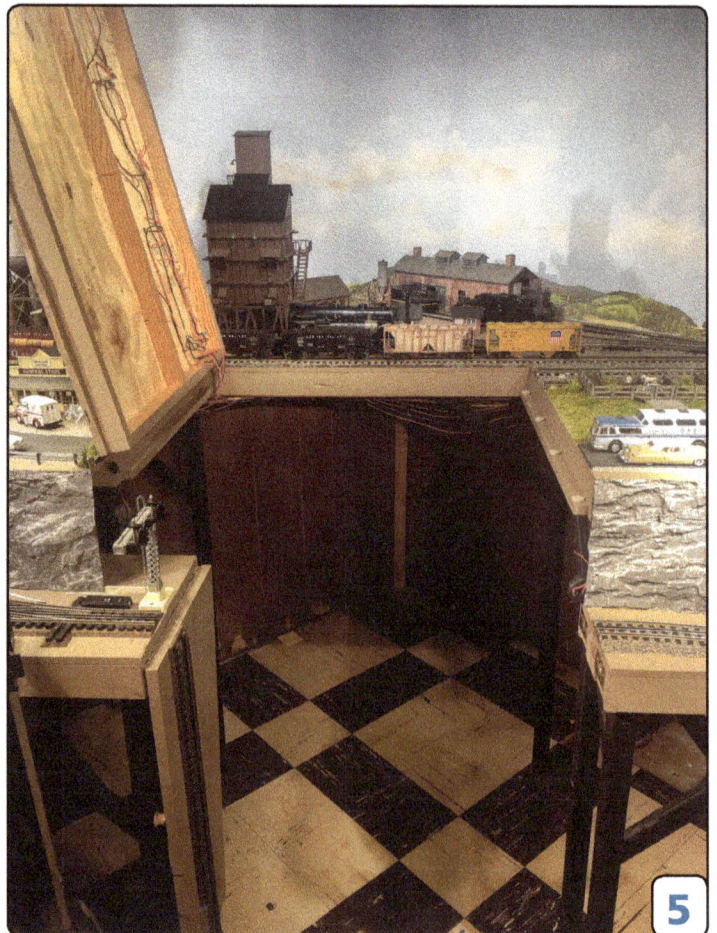

I have a table saw at home, so it was relatively easy for me to cut the foam to the width I needed to make up my fill-in piece. What you are going to end up doing is to make a very loosely fitting piece of the Styrofoam that will almost fill the gap between the levels. Make your piece at least one inch shorter on both sides than the gap you want to fill, and about an eighth of an inch shorter than the height needed. It should end up looking like what you see in Photo 6.

This Styrofoam backing board will be completely covered with the rock wall material and will not be seen at all when you are finished. For that reason, you need to install some wood stop blocks to make sure that it goes back in the same place every time your remove and replace it. At the top of my gap I have the frame around the bottom of the upper level of plywood that will act as a nice back-up block. But at the bottom I added a piece of 1/4" square balsa wood stick that will become the base of the Styrofoam block (Photo 7).

You will see in Photo 8 that the thickness of the Styrofoam insulation sticks out beyond the upper edge of the upper level on the layout. That's good. Using a red Sharpie pen, I drew a red line along the top edge so that I can see where I need to shape the Styrofoam to fit back into the top edge of the layout.

Right about now you should invest in a hot wire tool for cutting Styrofoam, if you haven't already. If not, try to borrow one from another hobbyist. Photo 9 shows how easy it is to shave off some thickness of the Styrofoam using a hot wire wand and get it to conform to the irregular shape of the front edge of the layout. Finally, add some blocking to the right and left of the Styrofoam piece so that it can easily lift up and out of the space for it, yet also be easily reinserted into the opening. Be sure to maintain the roughly one inch gap on both sides of the Styrofoam. We're going to get to that in a moment.

Photo 10 shows the start of fitting the rock wall material. Position a full piece of this material so that it overlaps on the left edge of the existing rock wall opening by another inch, or a full two inches past the Styrofoam edge. Place a piece of temporary masking tape at the bottom of the rock wall material, attaching it to the bottom level of your layout. That will hold it in place while you locate and mark the right edge of the rock wall material for cutting. Mark at least a full inch past what you need to cover the opening when you are done. Also, mark and cut at least a half inch above the top of the layout (Photo 10) to remove some of the excess rock material.

When you are done, you should have a piece of rock material two inches wider on both sides than the piece of Styrofoam you are going to attach it to. It should also be at least an inch wider on both sides than the rock wall you are going to cover.

For the next part of this project, use contact cement to affix the rock wall material to the Styrofoam backing board material. Due to the nature of the materials you are using, there are not many cements that will let you do this without damaging either the Styrofoam backing board or the plastic rock wall material. The only one I know of that is safe for this job is called 3M Super 77 contact cement. This is an aerosol can product that I use all the time with all kinds of scenery projects. It is available at Lowe's, Menards, or Home Depot, as well as many other stores of that type.

The key to laminating these two pieces together is to leave plenty of room on both sides to be able to slide it back and forth a little until you get a close match-up on rock strata appearance. To allow this to happen, fully three inches on both sides of the rock material must be masked before spraying on the contact cement (Photo 11). In addition, the upper inch of the rock wall material must also be masked.

A full inch on both ends of the Styrofoam must also be masked (as also shown in Photo 11). After placing plenty of scrap newspaper beyond the edges of the two pieces, spray coat both surfaces of the material to be joined. Refer again to Photo 11. Spray them with painting-like coats and let them dry to the touch.

When they have dried, carefully place the Styrofoam piece into the location in the opening of your layout. Then carefully center the rock wall material over the opening in the rock wall and slide it back evenly onto the Styrofoam backing piece. You will have only one chance to position these two together! Once they touch, that is the permanent home of the two, and they cannot be repositioned after the fact.

You can remove the finished assembly and continue to press it together, as needed. It should look like what you see in Photo 12. Replace the full assembly into its opening, and carefully trim off the excess rock wall material along the top as you can see in Photo 13. Using an X-Acto knife, dress up the rocks on the ends of the removable wall, as needed, to conceal the end joint lines. In my case, with just a little finesse trimming, the finished product looks like what you see in Photo 14. The end joint line does still show up at the right of the engine, but it is largely unnoticed in an overall view. As I finish the layout, adding a little loose green scenery fill material should make it go completely unnoticed.

Chapter 36 *Building A Layout* by Jim Barrett

CHAPTER 37 - Sneaky Switch Beacons

I have a need on my layout for two of my track switches to be able to visually show me which way they are thrown. That's no big deal, right? In almost all cases, you just look at the switch beacon or the switch lever and see by the color that is illuminated which way the switch is thrown.

My problem is that the two switches I'm talking about are both buried deep inside Mount Rewes, or what I call "trick mountain" on my layout (Photo 1).

Its "tricks" include things like the intricate trestles at the front of the layout that can actually separate from the layout and roll out of the way easily (Photo 2).

Another trick involves removable mountain tops that lift off easily, allowing access to things inside the mountain (Photo 3). That lets me get to all the tracks inside the tunnels to cure misbehaving trains.

You can see that not all my scenery is finished yet. Sometimes, projects like this have to be done before the scenery is complete. Scenery not only looks great, it often hides many construction sins! In fact, this mountain hides a lot of things. The mountain is basically at one end of my layout. Within it (and around the outside of it), scenery hides the fact that there are two big reversing loops lurking around the mountain as well as through it. One loop is for the upper circuit, and the other is for the lower circuit. Each of these tracks approaches the mountain from the left, then runs around the front of the mountain from the left side, visible on the outside. Then the two tracks encounter a giant canyon, which they cross on two tall trestles. At the end of the trestles, they both duck into tunnels on the right side of the mountain, where they continue underground through the back of the mountain. Both emerge from tunnels at the rear of the mountain on the left side, making their way back toward the opposite end of the layout.

If the mountain wasn't there, the scene would just be two boring half circles of track at one end of the layout, sending trains back the other way. The beauty of the mountain scenery is that it disguises those two simple reversing loops using vertical scenery tricks such as canyons and mountains.

In fact, the mountain also lets me do one other major thing that dramatically adds to the layout's function. It provides me with a place to make an access grade between the two levels, allowing me to switch trains from one level to another. In the world of train layouts, the term for this is a helix. This hidden helix was made with the addition of two track turnouts (switches, in model railroading parlance), one on the lower level and the other on the upper level.

The fun thing is that both switches and most of the helix are concealed within the mountain. That keeps layout viewers guessing how in the world trains go in one tunnel and might exit any one of three other tunnels.

As an example: A train on the lower main line can enter the lower level tunnel on the right of the canyon (Photo 4), switch off inside the mountain to the grade (helix) track, and emerge from the grade tunnel on the left side of the mountain (Photo 5), continuing to climb the mountain.

Then the train goes over another trestle while still climbing the grade. (Photo 6).

The train then reenters the mountain on the right side of the trestle, still climbing (Photo 7). Finally, the train emerges from the upper level tunnel at the left of the mountain (Photo 8).

So, the mountain already hides the two tracks and their respective turnarounds, the beginning and end of the grade track connecting the upper and lower levels, two different track switches, and one other thing I haven't yet pointed out. A strong hint to what that other thing might be is if you reverse the spelling of the mountain's (Mount Rewes) name. Yes, that's right! The vertical "stack" pipe from the upstairs bathroom is painted flat black and it hides nicely within the tallest trees on the mountain (Photo 9). The train layout itself finishes the disguise all the way to the floor of the basement under the layout.

Now before you all start clucking your collective tongues about burying track switches inside mountains, let me say that I fully agree with you. But sometimes you just can't avoid it. Since there was no other place on my layout where I could build a grade connecting the two levels, a helix within the mountain was the only answer. In the hope of making that a little less of a problem, I designed and built my mountain with several different ways to get inside it so that I can gain access very easily if trains or switches misbehave. Chapters eight, ten, twenty-two, twenty-five, twenty-six, twenty-seven, and twenty-eight, all cover, in one way or another, the removable, roll away trestle module and other such scenery planning tricks on how to easily live with track and switches inside mountains.

But there is one thing I didn't foresee. Since I use hi-rail switches equipped with DZ-1000 switch machines, the two switches inside the mountain are an obvious problem because they aren't readily visible at a quick glance. I also don't have a control panel since I use DCS. I use DCS not only for train control, but also for all switch machines and all accessories (the MTH AIUs are wonderful!). The only problem with DCS is that, while running the trains, there isn't a good, practical, and easily visible way to determine which way a switch is thrown.

Back in the good old days when I used lighted switch controllers, that was no problem: all you had to do then was glance at the bulb on the switch controller and quickly see which way the switch was thrown.

There is a relatively easy way for a hi-rail switch to tell you which way it is thrown without ever being able to actually see the switch. Any track turnout being operated by a DZ-1000 (or a DZ-2500) switch machine can also be equipped with an add on DZ-1008 Relay (Photo 10). This nifty little device gives you an extra set of electrical contacts, allowing the position of the track turnout to turn on or off an accessory voltage to do anything you want to do, such as light up light bulbs or any other indicator device. It can be conventional bulbs, LEDs, block signals, or dwarf signals, to name just a few examples.

On my layout I have a nice 1:48 scale farmer who volunteered to help out. My farmer thoughtfully installed two different outdoor security lights around his barn. The farmer chose security lights made by Life-Like, but they can be any manufacturer's light of any kind for our purposes. Regardless of whose light you (or your farmer) might use, each one has two wires. One wire needs to be connected to the constant AC+ voltage source (14-16 volts or so). The other wire connects to an accessory ground, or AC common.

The DZ-1008 relay comes with simple directions and diagrams on how to wire it up to a DZ-1000 or a DZ-2500 switch machine. After the DZ-1008 relay has been attached to the switch machine, there are four remaining wires: black, blue, gray, and white.

- Attach the **black** wire to your AC common connection.
- Attach the AC+ constant voltage source (14-16 volts) for the farmer's light to the **blue** wire on the DZ-1008 relay.

Set the track turnout to the switched direction (train to go to the climbing grade track). Using a volt/ohm meter, check either the gray wire or the white wire coming out of the relay. Only one of the two will have the accessory AC+ voltage passing through. That wire is the one to connect to the other wire on the farmer's outdoor light. The remaining wire from the relay will show no voltage in it. That wire will not be used.

The farmer's other security light is for the remaining track switch on the other end of the grade. Wire it up to a second DZ-1008 relay for the second switch so it will light up in the same manner as the first track switch.

When track turnouts are set in the normal direction (train proceeding along the main line through the mountain normally), we want the farmer's lights to remain off (Photo 11).

When the track switches are lined to allow the train to run via the hidden helix, we want the farmer's lights for those switches to come on (Photos 12). That will be our signal, obvious at a brief glance, that the switches inside the mountain are set for the train to divert to the hidden helix.

So now, from almost any point in the train room, you only need to glance at the farmer's barn area to know how the switches are set deep inside the mountain. Both lights "on" means that both switches are thrown for the train to climb the grade track. This system will also enable you to bring a train off whichever level it is on, move it over to the grade track, and pause it there to wait for a clear track. After resetting the track switches (both of the farmer's lights off), the train can wait there indefinitely for the other circuit to clear. As long as both of the farmer's barnyard lights are off, no train is in danger of hitting a train parked on the grade.

FARMER'S LIGHTS ON

The route is lined for the hidden helix which connects the two levels.

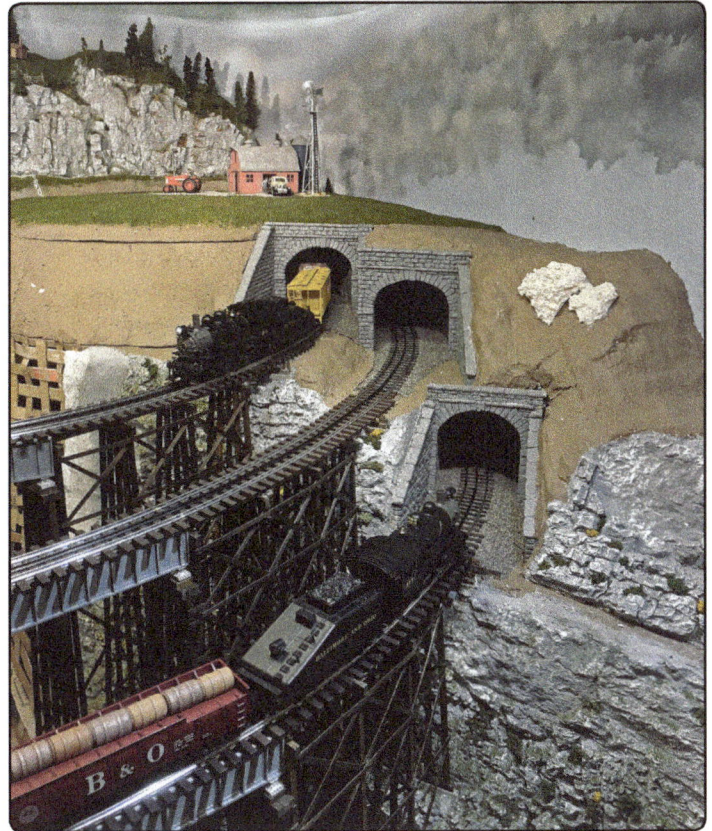

FARMER'S LIGHTS OFF

The route is lined for the main tracks.

Take advantage of your own scenery features. You may not have a farm, but you might have a couple of lights on billboards along a street or highway, or a lighted parking lot near a store. Maybe you just have two different porch lights, on a house, or something else. Any light that's easily seen from anywhere around the layout will do.

My point is that you can determine where you can use these indicator lights. Wire them in the same manner as I did with my farmer's two security lights and you will have your own visual indicators for hidden track switches.

I was just lucky enough to have a nice helpful farmer on my layout.

CHAPTER 38 - Installing Lighted Switch Stands

Lighted switch stands tell you which way the switch is thrown so you can determine which way the train is going to go (Photo 1). If you go all the way back to the post-war Lionel days, the huge oversized switch beacons told you which way the switch was thrown, and they were easily visible from halfway across the train room. If you have progressed to the point of realistic (hi-rail) track and switches, you might still have a color indicator from an LED on the switch motor showing either red or green to indicate how the switch was set. The railroad standard is that a lighted green indicator light meant the switch is set for the standard direction, and lighted red meant that the switch was set for the alternate or turnout direction.

I like to use Z-Stuff DZ-1000 switch machines like the one shown in Photo 2 because if the LED color indicators need to be reversed, they are easily plucked out of their respective sockets, reversed 180 degrees, and put back into the other socket. The provided tiny button pad used to activate the switch machine (not shown) has a set of matching color LED indicators on it to further help in identifying the switch position.

The only problem with the DZ machines is that you definitely need both the LEDs on the switch machine, as well as the LEDs on the switch button pad, to be wired together for the indicator colors to work. I have embraced the MTH DCS system with a TIU (Track Interface Unit) and a number of AIUs (Accessory Interface Units), which allow the operator to use the same hand-held DCS remote to work not only all the trains, but all the accessories ever built for O gauge trains, as well. Using the AIU to control switches means that you can eliminate any and all switch button pads and still throw all the switches by remote.

That one feature alone adds a whole new dimension to a train operating session with your friends. Now you can have an operating "crew" consisting of an engineer and a brakeman, each with a remote, and each with railroad responsibilities for the specific train they are operating.

The only thing missing is a way to determine which way a switch is thrown as you approach from a distance. Fortunately, there is something available from Steve Brenneisen at Ross Custom Switches that will solve that problem, and it works on every single track turnout that Ross makes.

Look closely at Photo 3, and you will see a Ross Custom Switch at the location where you would normally mount a switch machine to the throw bar of the switch. The switch machine can be mounted on either side of the switch. On the opposite side of the switch there are extended ties for the purpose of mounting an operating lighted switch beacon.

Out toward the end of those two longer ties, drill a 1/4" hole all the way through the table right between the two ties, as shown in Photo 4. Clean out the hole, removing any splinters or other debris. The 1/4" hole will make it nice and easy for you to thread the two tiny wires from the light in the switch stand down through the table.

Look closely at Photo 5. That is a #50 Brass, Operating Switch Stand Kit. Ross Custom Switches sells them on their website for $18.95. At first this may sound a little expensive, but when you look at how these switch stands are made and how they perform, they are actually quite a bargain. Note in Photo 5 that the kit consists of the brass switch beacon (brass, painted black), the internal brass crank mechanism permitting the beacon to turn ONLY an exact quarter turn, a wire throw bar attached to the crank, a light bulb with wires threaded through the crank and out of the bottom, and four little railroad spikes to attach the base of the unit to the railroad ties of the switch.

Note in the closeup Photo 6, that the switch beacon actually has a tiny Phillips head set screw right at the base of the beacon itself, between the white flag and the red flag indicators. That set screw allows you to turn the beacon to the proper direction once you have mounted the lighted switch stand to the ties on the switch. It will let you do one other thing as well: you can easily remove the rotating beacon itself and slip the bulb with its two wires up and out of the mounted switch stand if you ever need to replace it. Steve tells me that if you use only 10 or 12 volts for the light, it should last you quite a long time because it is rated as a 16 volt bulb. Setting your accessory voltage at 10 or 12 volts will greatly extend the life of the bulb. In addition, he promises direct LED replacements in the near future if you ever do need to replace a bulb. That will more than likely eliminate any future replacement maintenance. I found that if you use the following trick, it makes handling the bulb much easier and improves on the reliability of the switch stand, as well.

Begin by gently twisting the two wires coming out of the bot-tom of the switch stand together as shown in Photo 7. They don't have to be tightly twisted; just roll them between your thumb and index finger until they look like what is shown in Photo 7. When that is complete, gently loosen the tiny Phillips head set screw and gently slide the beacon up and off of the switch stand. When that is done, gently pull the bulb with its two wires up and out of the switch stand as well.

Photo 8 shows the three pieces separated, with the Phillips head screwdriver pointed to the location of the set screw.

When you do this, you will see that the bulb and its wires are in no way involved with the rotation of the switch beacon. The beacon attaches with the set screw to the rotating crank mechanism, which easily rotates while allowing the two wires to pass through the center of the crank mechanism without impeding its movement in any way.

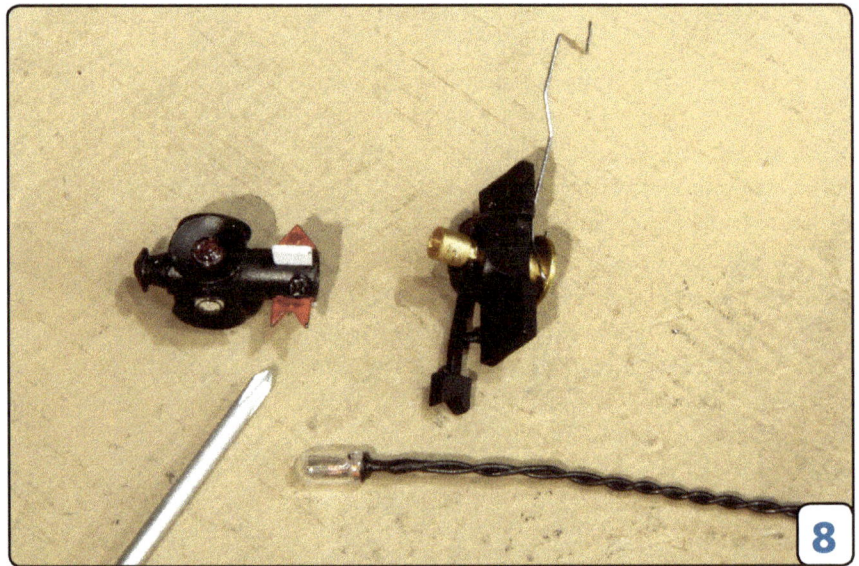

Photo 9 shows the two wires for the bulb after they have been passed through the tiny hole in the crank mechanism. Now is when you'll appreciate the twined pair of wires as compared to the two individual wires! Getting the two individual wires to pass through the tiny opening is like trying to herd two cats!

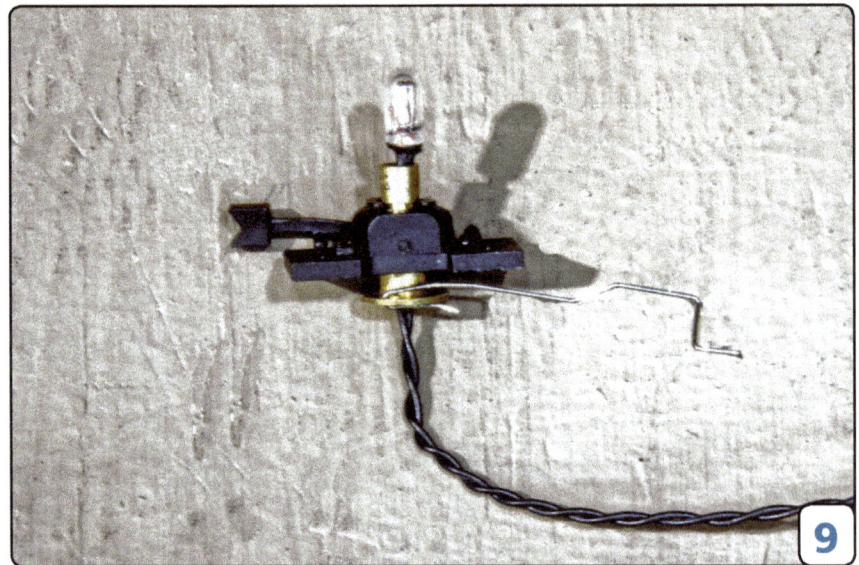

Photo 10 shows how to begin installing the lighted switch beacon to the ties on the switch. Note the little Z-shaped bend in the crank wire seen in Photo 5. Your kit may have the wire with only the first 90-degree bend at the top of the wire, with lots of excess length wire after the bend. It is that way so the kit can also be used on other switch makers' switches as well. If yours doesn't look like what you see in Photo 5, simply add the last bend, and cut off the excess wire so your crank wire looks like what you see in Photo 5.

Once that is done (if necessary), work the little Z shape into the hole in the throw bar of the switch, as shown in Photo 10. Also pass the twisted pair of wires down through the large hole you made in the table top between the ties (refer to Photo 4).

Now comes the tricky part! Work the switch stand and its attached crank wire so that the beacon easily rotates the full ¼ turn as you activate the switch motor back and forth. The goal is to make sure that the switch points make the full travel from fully closed in one direction all the way over to fully closed in the other direction. Your second goal is to make sure that the rotating beacon does not prevent the switch from fully closing in both directions. I found that in some cases on some of my switches, it became necessary to open up the hole in the switch throw bar to .060, or exactly 1/16″ using a 1/16″ drill bit Do use a power drill! Mount the 1/16″ bit into a finger-held drill chuck and slowly open up the hole. That will prevent any damage to the switch throw bar.

Once you have determined that the switch is performing perfectly, take a pair of long nosed pliers. Firmly grasp one of the railroad spikes in the tip of the pliers with the tip of the spike pointed out the end of the long-nosed pliers, and press the spike straight down through one of the two holes on one side of the switch stand base and into the wood tie. Check the function of the switch again; then add another spike on the other side of the switch stand base. Once again, be sure to check the movement of the switch points.

Work on the first of these switch stands may be a little frustrating, but after you see how everything works, you can breeze right through the rest of the layout. For me, it became much easier once I changed my priorities to first making sure that the rotation of the beacon was not inhibiting the movement of the switch points. By slightly bending the throw rod or slightly enlarging the hole in the throw bar, everything worked much better. Steve Brenneisen, at Ross Custom Switches, provides a diagram showing how to put bends in the throw rod wire, as well as other tips and tricks he uses to make it work better.

Only now do you need to make sure the location of the switch beacon is squared-up to the location of the track switch. By loosening the set screw on the rotating beacon, you can set the beacon until the red marker (or red light) tells the engineer that he is taking the turnout position on the switch, and the white markers (or green light) tells him that he is set to go straight through the switch. When you complete those adjustments, it should look something like what you see above in Photo 11, looking straight down on the top of the switch beacon.

Note that four spikes are provided in the kit. I think more than two (one on each side) is overkill. After I got two of my four in, the switch beacon was very firmly mounted. Besides, if you're as clumsy as I am, you'll lose the other two spikes just trying to get the first two in!

The example switch I'm showing you in Photos 12 and 13 is really a wye, not a standard turnout. I want my engineers to know that when the wye is lined to the right, that is the normal direction. So I have set my beacon to show green when the wye is lined to the right, and red when the wye is lined to the left. The directions provided in the kit from Steve Brenneisen differ somewhat from mine, but I think either his way or mine will serve you well. In my case, I already had the switches and the switch machines down and ballasted, so there was no "re-moving the switch machine first," as Steve indicates in his directions.

Also keep in mind that these lighted switch stands can also be used if you have manually operated switch ground throws set up. There's nothing preventing you from being able to have the direction of the manual switch indicated, just as it is for your automatic switches. Bottom line: it all makes for more realistic operating sessions with your friends.

CHAPTER 39 - Aging the Right-of-Way

In the summer of 2019 I had the thrill of seeing the restored Union Pacific No. 4014 Big Boy head back to its home in Cheyenne, Wyoming, from West Chicago. My train friends and I decided to go out somewhere west of Chicago and find a nice, quiet, small town grade crossing to observe this beast go high-balling by in all its glory. We picked a small town just west of DeKalb with a nice country road grade crossing on the GPS map. We thought that would provide us with an uninterrupted view of this piece of history.

When we finally got there, it seemed that most of rural Illinois also picked this spot; so we waited, along with the hundreds of our newest best train friends. The train was understandably running a little bit late, probably due to all the railfans lining the tracks all the way out from Chicago.

When I get a bit of idle railfanning time on my hands, I do what most true model railroaders often do: I begin to take a close look at the tracks and other parts of the railroad right-of-way around me. I compare what I see with what we all tend to build on our model railroads. The first thing I noticed on this particular day (Photo 1) was that not only were the sides of the rails rusty, but the track ties to which the rails were affixed had a rust colored appearance as well. This overall rust color appearance is due to all the brake dust and metal powder given off by brake shoes on metal wheels.

In Photo 2 you'll notice something else. The more heavily traveled mainline (the far track in this photo) has a heavier coating of the rust color. Even the ballast itself where it is close to the rails of that track has that rusty appearance.

As soon as I got back home, I took a close look at the track on my own layout (Photo 3). Wouldn't it be interesting to see if I could simulate that rusty brake dust look on my own right-of-way?

I have long been a fan of Floquil's #F110007 Rail Brown paint to brush on the sides of the rails of all my Gar-Graves and Ross track to simulate the naturally rusty appearance of the rails. The problem now is that Floquil paint has all but vanished off the store shelves, along with many other railroad colors and brands.

But rust is rust, right? Well, maybe not! I started to look closely at the photos I took that railfanning day, and I realized that the rust on the sides of the rails was actually browner than the rust dust on the ties and on the ballast. I found an acrylic paint product made by Vallejo Model Air paints called Light Rust that looked promising (#71.129 left side of Photo 4). This paint is already the right consistency to be sprayed through an airbrush right out of the bottle. Even though it calls itself Light Rust, it is a bit too orangish for my liking. I mixed it with Vallejo's #71.113 Dirt (right side of Photo 4) to get it to the muted rust color that I personally like. Your taste may vary, so try some experimenting on your own before you do this on your own layout.

To achieve the rust dust effect on your ballasted track, you will once again be looking at the perfect opportunity to purchase and use an air brush. The price continues to go down on this wonderful tool. A quick glance at the Paasche'

website online has complete systems with airbrush gun, paint jars, tools, spare tips, and even the compressor for $129 (www.paascheairbrush.com). Walmart even has a basic off brand airbrush system for $43!

If none of that moves you, take a look at Photo 5. Here is an aerosol add-on system from Preval that will let you spray any manufacturer's paint for about $6.00. It works, but I wouldn't recommend it for this project. Here's why.

The key to adding this weathering effect to your track and ballast is knowing when to stop. This truly is one of those situations where less is more. I made a little test board with some scrap track and some ballast glued down to try out my hand at air brushing some rust dust onto the ballast and ties, and found that there is a natural tendency to air brush too much paint onto the project. I quickly learned to apply very little (Photo 6); then to let it dry first; and only then to check my handiwork. I also found that thinning the paint even more and increasing the air pressure higher, made the finished product look even better. Increasing the air pressure is something you simply cannot do with the add-on aerosol system.

The key to applying this rust dust effect is to keep the air pressure high and hold the airbrush tip very close to the base of the rail, as shown in Photo 6. That little pocket created by the rail and the ballast allows the airbrush to spread the paint color very lightly and keeps the paint thinly applied onto the ties and the ballast right at the base of the rail. It also gives that effect of the rust dust being just a little lighter in color than the rusted rail itself.

Compare closely Photos 3 and 7. Photo 3 is the before photo with the rust-painted rails and the pristine gray ballast. Photo 7 shows my effort at spraying the ties and the ballast ever so lightly. That is how I want my rust dust to look. It is subtle, but still noticeable. Also note that it is indeed not as orangish as the real thing in Photo 3. I can't quite decide which one I like better, but the less orange look is winning out with me.

You may want to make yours just like the paint color in the Vallejo Light Rust bottle. Whatever you do, try some painting on a separate test board before you spray it on the finished ballast on your layout. It just isn't something you can get back off the ties and ballast or paint over.

In Photo 8, I purposely made the amount of rust a bit more on the far rail so I could compare which one I liked more. It turns out I like the slightly heavier rust dust rail more than the close one. Stopping and studying the end effect on your test board is very helpful for determining which way you like it.

Now take a look at Photo 9 below. This isn't the finished product yet, because there is still trackside scenery and signaling lights to be added, but one thing does stand out. The beauty of a model railroad is in the details! The track looked good without weathered ballast, but the addition of those finishing touches made it look better. The added rust on the sides of the rails was just one more detail that makes the scene more believable. The plastic rock material looked pretty good when it was being put on, but wow, it sure looks a lot better with the overhead road bridge and the

support beams in place. Trackside vehicles and structures all add dramatically to the scene, and now the hint of some brake dust on the right-of-way adds even more. That's why most model railroads are never finished in the minds of the modeler. You can still see a tremendous variety of things to add to the scene in the future.

CHAPTER 40 - In-The-Floor Wire-Ways

Back in chapter five I showed you how to make hinged sections of your layout that will allow you to access remote areas or even cross completely through your layout to gain access to a closet or some other room.

In Photo 1above, the two levels of my layout hinge up or down to allow me to pass through the layout to get to the closet behind it.

Photo 2 shows the upper layout level hinged up and the lower level hinged down, permitting the door to the closet to open out.

The obvious problem is that any wires needed to cross that gap must find a way to do so without getting in the way. Since that is a tile-covered concrete floor, we can't very well chop up the concrete to put the wires under the floor. So we'll do the next best thing. We'll just make a slightly raised false floor to protect the wires that need to cross from one side of the opening in the layout to the other.

We don't need much room; only less than an inch in height would do the trick. The solution is elegant and simple. Using some scrap 1x2s and some 1/8″ Masonite left over from making the scenery backdrop, covered in chapter two, cut a piece of the Masonite big enough to completely fill in the floor opening for the walk-through between the two parts of the layout. This piece of Masonite will be mounted on the thickness of a few 1x2s spaced evenly apart to support the weight of someone walking on the new subfloor (Photo 3).

It will also be necessary to make a ramp on both the front and the back of the raised floor to allow easy access to the raised section without a trip hazard. In my case, I made my ramps only about 8″ deep on the front and back of the raised floor. Space the 1x2s on what will be the raised portion of the Masonite with one edge of the front and back 1x2s extending out from the underside of the Masonite about 1/4″, allowing you to make a landing for the ramp pieces to attach to.

I spaced out my 1x2s under the floor piece about 4″ or 5″ apart. This will provide more than enough support for the thin Masonite floor. The spaces in between these 1x2s will be where the wires will run beneath the walkway. Note in the photo that the ramp on one end of the raised floor where the ramp will extend into the closet door is cut narrower than the other ramp.

Photo 4 above shows the entire assembly turned over right-side up. Simple #6 x 3/4″ flat head wood screws mounted through holes drilled into the Masonite are used to locate and attach it to the 1x2s. Note also the two ramp pieces of Masonite mounted to the leading edges of the 1x2s beneath the raised floor at the front and the back edges. To give the ramp pieces some necessary support, locate a final length of scrap 1x2 beneath the slanting Masonite ramps and attach with some more wood screws. Finally, I applied some spackling compound to all the screws and sanded the surface to prepare it for painting.

Photo 5 shows the raised floor assembly in place on the floor between the black painted legs of the rear upper portion of the layout. Note also that in my case I cut a significant amount off the bottom of the closet door in the back. The door needs to be a little higher to clear the new slightly raised walkway floor. But in my case I had an additional problem. I had to make the opening much larger than needed to allow for some air flow through to the dehumidifier in the closet behind the door as well.

In Photo 6, I cut some additional plywood for panels to mount on either side of my raised walkway to clean up the appearance as well. This is purely optional. I just wanted the finished project to look good as well as being functional. There is nothing worse-looking than a bunch of wires hanging out all over the place. The two plywood panels will be attached along their back vertical edges with piano hinges, allowing the panels to swing open for access to the wire ways under the layout when the project is finished.

Photo 7 shows all the plywood pieces painted with a fresh coat of flat black paint, awaiting the attachment of the two piano hinges in the back.

Photo 8 shows the right door with its piano hinge installed. Attaching a simple magnetic catch to the door and the front leg of the upper layout frame keeps the door closed until needed.

Photo 9 shows the access door opened to see the attachment of several wire clips on the rear leg of the upper portion of the lay-out, covered in chapter four. All wires running under the raised floor now route over to the back of the opening and up the wire way. That cleans up the opening to afford me easy access to run wires on past the walkway. Dimensions for this project will vary depending on your own application of this idea. But by using some simple 1x2s laid over on their side to support the thin 1/8″ raised Masonite floor, you will create a full 3/4″ height of free and open space beneath the floor to run as many wires as you will ever need from one side of the layout to the other. The full height of the raised floor is a mere 7/8″, making its existence practically unnoticed.

This project may take you a little extra time, but it sure beats chopping up the concrete floor to install a conduit!

CHAPTER 41 - Keep It Simple: The Lowly Wire Nut

There's nothing more important to a smoothly operating layout than cleanly getting power to the track. That was true 50 years ago, but is even more true today. This era of both digital and radio signals moving from the rails to the engines requires nothing but the most efficient method of getting both the electricity and the digital signal from the source to the train. Our trains run on relatively low voltage (0 to 24 volts), which means that any wire connection must be nearly perfect to prevent a loss of voltage or digital control signal to the track.

Back in the day when we controlled train speeds by varying the voltage in the track, if you were running the train at a very slow speed (a voltage of, say, 6 to 8 volts, as an example) the loss of as much as 1 or 2 volts due to track joints would result in a very noticeable speed change in the locomotive. Once the locomotive went a few track joints away from where the wire was attached to the center rail, you would see a noticeable drop in speed. For that reason, we added another connection from the AC+ wire to the center rail every few track joints to prevent the voltage loss from showing up in the speed of the trains.

I've always believed that nothing beats solder connections when it comes to the wiring on train layouts. As many of you who have followed my articles over the years already know, I'm quick to point out how much better a solder connection is compared to any other type of wire-joining method. But I've also learned over the years that you don't always need perfect electrical wire connections.

Solder connections are the perfect method for transmitting power from wires to rails. There is also no substitute for solder joints between wires and rails when it comes to good digital signal transmissions used by command control devices such as DCS and DCC as well. Digital signal strength can be easily weakened with almost any other kind of connection except a good solder joint, and I still very much prefer only that method of attaching wiring to track.

Nowadays, with DCS, TMCC, and DCC controls, you only need a single attachment of the AC+ wire to the center rail, and we apply full voltage to the center rail from the transformer. Through DCS, DCC, or TMCC we instruct the engine to go down to the center rail to get only the voltage it needs to go a nice, slow scale speed—such as 5, 10, or 15 mph, or any other speed we specifically instruct it to go. Sure, we may have a 2-, 3-, or 4-volt drop in the center rail over a distance of 75 or 100 feet, but who cares. We only want or need some relatively small voltage amount (maybe even up to 15 or 16 volts) to go the speed we want; but since we put the full voltage into the track to begin with, we can now afford a 3- or 4-volt drop in the center rail with no affect on the train at all.

The other thing besides voltage that rides that center rail is the digital signal, the means by which we talk to the engine. For that reason I still promote nothing but soldering the wire to the rail whenever possible. It is very easy to lose digital signal strength through simple pressure connections.

But hooking up accessories is a different matter. Accessories perform a simple function at a specific voltage, with no digital electronic tricks being involved. And each accessory needs at least an AC or DC+ and an AC or DC- wire hook up. In many or most cases, it needs more than one set of such wires depending on all the things the accessory does. For instance, if you are controlling a Ross or GarGraves switch, you need one AC+ wire and two different AC- wires to determine which direction the switch is thrown. If you add a lighted switch stand, you will need another A+ and another AC- wire for the light bulb in the switch beacon. If you want the switch to be non-derailing like the old Lionel switches were, you need still two more wires—one each from an insulated outside rail to the switch machine's control wires. Lastly, you need at least two more AC- wires from the switch controller (or AIU control box) to the switch machine, and one AC+ wire to the switch machine.

I don't know if you've been counting, but that's at least 10 wire connections thus far for only one switch. By the time you add in connections for extending wires to other locations, you can easily average 16 to 20 wire connections per switch. My layout has 35 switches, so I can easily foresee 500 or more connections for wires just for the switches. When it comes to soldering wires, that's simply too much time required for making wire connections just to make switches work.

For wiring-up accessories, there is an easier way than soldering. Introducing. . . Ta-Da. . . the wire nut (Photo 1)!

Wire nuts come in a long list of colors, each one representing relative size from one to the next. For our purposes in the train layout world, we're primarily concerned with only the five colors shown in Photo 2, with gray being the smallest one and red being the largest.

This little plastic device is color coded for both the number of wires that can be joined within the wire nut, as well as the number of different sizes of wires that can be joined within the same wire nut. I bought the ones seen in Photo 3 at a local Lowe's store in packages of about 25 or 30 (depending on size) for around $2.98 per package. The package wrapping shows what size wires should be used with a particular color, as well as how many different-size wires can be joined within one wire nut.

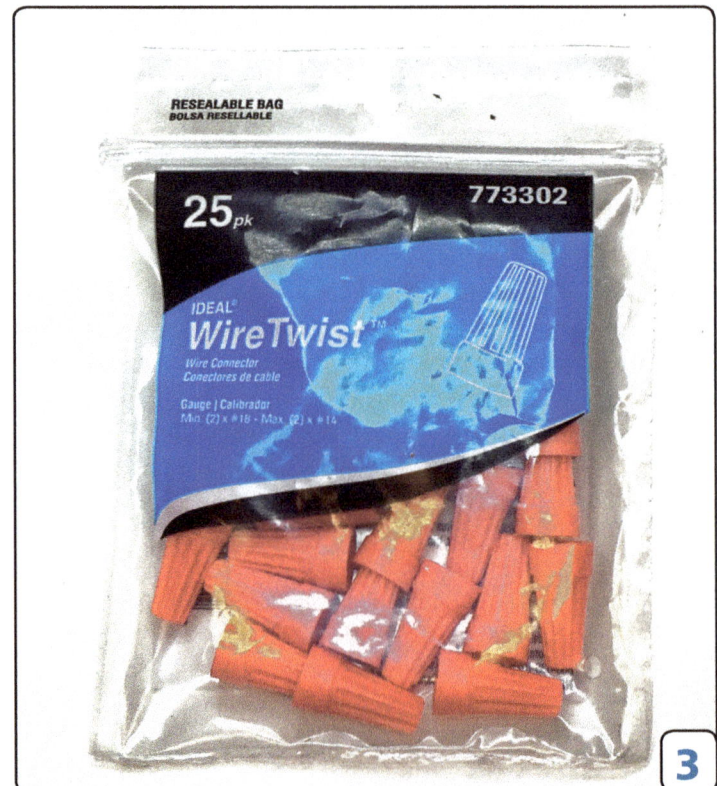

Chapter 41 *Building A Layout* by Jim Barrett

The actual anatomy of the device is noteworthy. While they are plastic on the outside, the better ones have a metal spiral insert on the inside, as seen in Photo 4, which acts like the threads of a screw turned outside in. Check to see that the wire nuts you purchase are made with this metal spiral insert built into the plastic shell. Cheap ones are made without the metal lock included.

If you look closely at the photo, you will see that the metal spiral decreases to a smaller and smaller cone as you go deeper into the wire nut. This forms the all-important lock on the strands of the stripped wire ends as they are screwed into the wire nut.

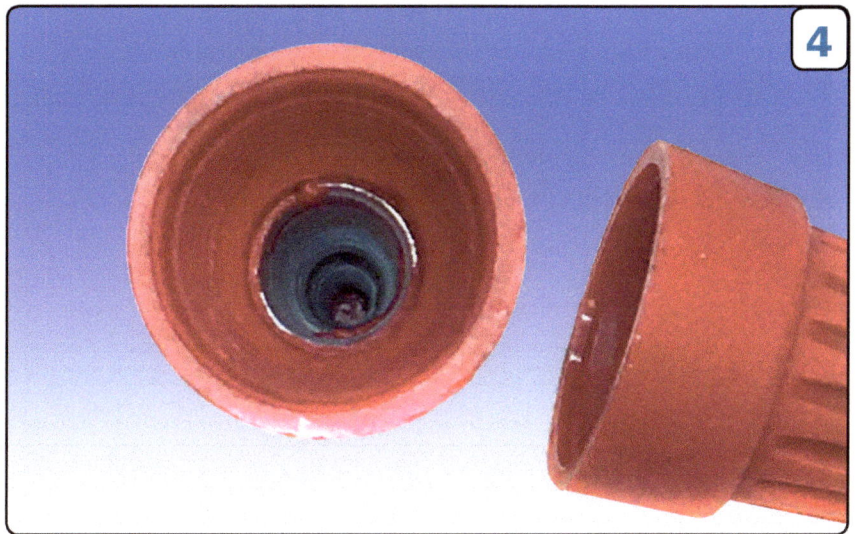

Even with the smallest size (the gray wire nut shown below in Photo 5), there is still a small, spiral locking mechanism built into the device. I included the coin in the photo to show the relative size of the wire nut.

For most train layout accessory wiring you will be using primarily the gray and the blue wire nut colors. Photo 6 shows two green 22-gauge wires stripped and ready to be joined with a gray wire nut. How much insulation you strip off depends on the wire size, the number of wires being joined in the same wire nut, and whether there is more than one wire size being joined in the same wire nut. In the example shown in Photo 6, I stripped off about 9/16" of insulation of both 22-gauge green wires shown.

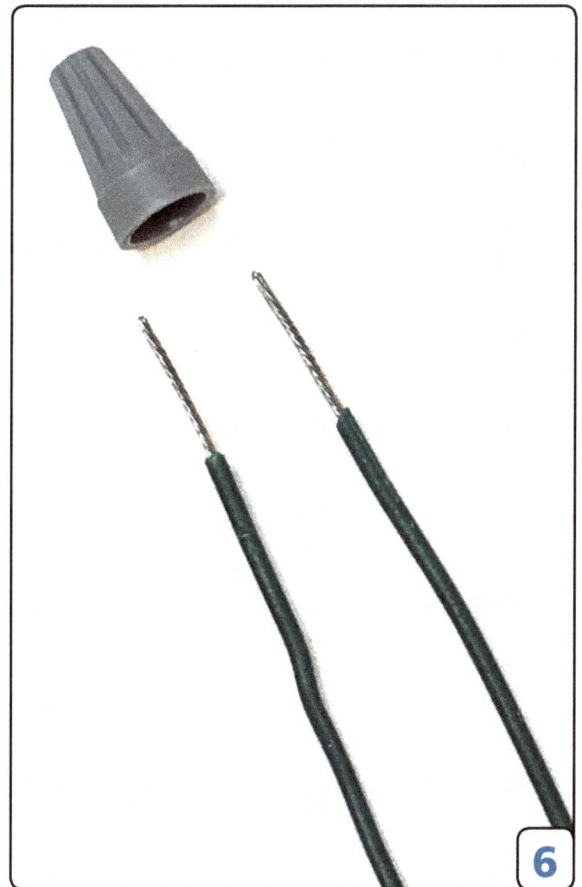

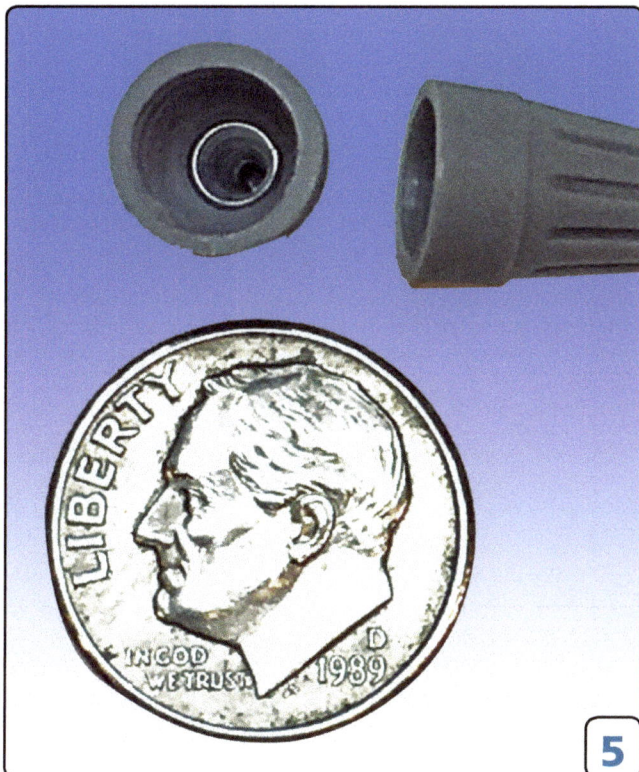

After removing the insulation, gently twist the wire strands together so they look like what is shown in the photo. Then twist the ends of the two wires together and check to see that the resulting stripped ends of the wire are not longer than the depth of the wire nut itself. If they are, go ahead and trim them off with a wire cutter.

Note in Photo 7 that many times you may need more than two wires joined together in one wire nut. Always be sure to check the guideline specifications of the wire nut packaging to make sure you are not putting more wires into one wire nut than the guideline allows. If you do have too many wires, go up to the next size in wire nuts.

Once the wire ends have been trimmed to length, gently screw on the wire nut, turning the nut onto the bare ends of the twisted wires in the same direction as the wire ends were turned. When complete, the result should look like what is seen in Photo 8, with no bare wire extending out from the bottom of the wire nut.

Be careful not to over tighten the wire nut. Working with smaller wire sizes in particular, it is easy to over tighten the wire nut and break off the stripped ends of the wires within the nut.

Many times in accessory wiring you will have to join wires of two different gauges, especially when wiring switch beacons and other small lights. Photo 9 shows a 22-gauge green wire and a very tiny (about 34 gauge) black wire from the light bulb. When twisting these two radically different wire sizes together, it is more a case of wrapping the smaller wire around the larger wire. When this happens, you will need to have the smaller wire stripped to a longer length than the larger wire.

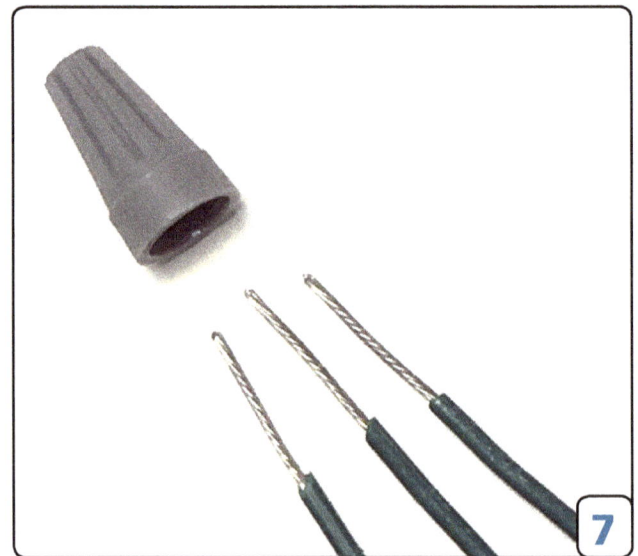

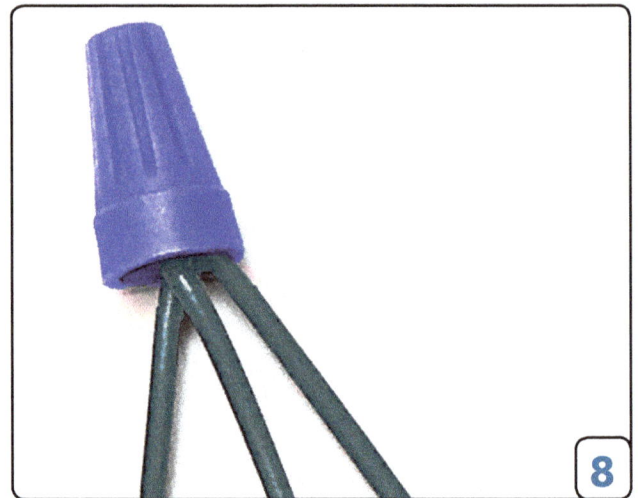

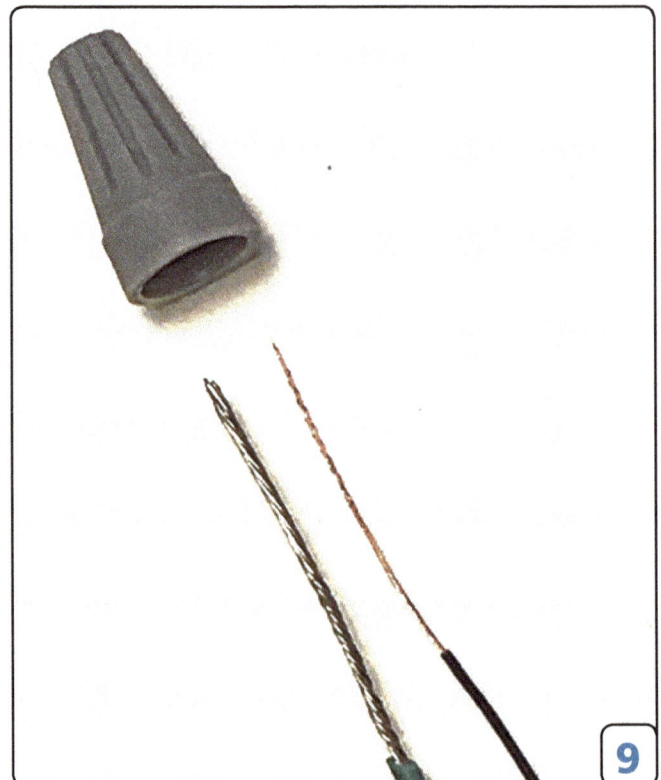

Another factor to consider is that the result of the paired 22-gauge and tiny 36-gauge wire will probably still be too small to grip into the small gray wire nut. The solution for this is to make the twisted pair of wires twice as long as you would normally need, then double them over as shown in Photo 10 before inserting them into the wire nut.

The finished result should look like what you see in Photo 11.

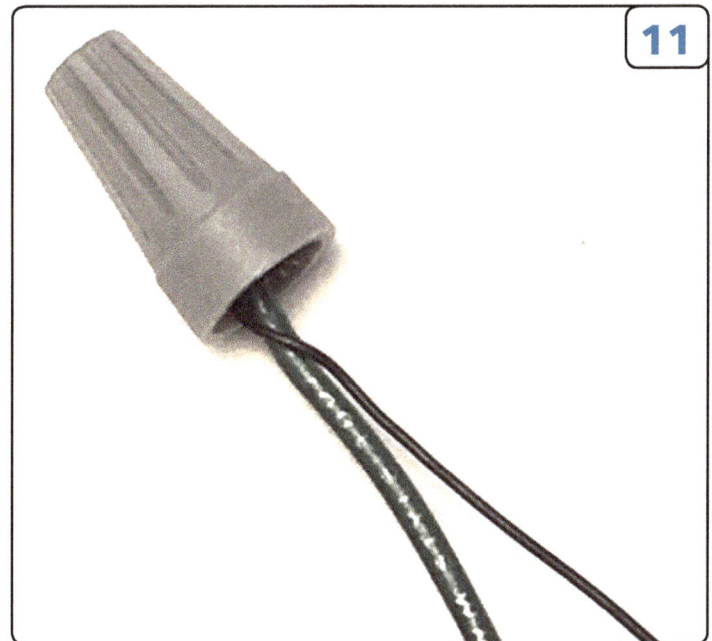

Photo 12 below shows two 22-gauge green wires and one 18-gauge red wire. Once these three stripped wires are ready for a wire nut, it will be obvious that they will not fit nicely into a gray wire nut.

Go up one size to a blue wire nut and they will all fit together and get along nicely (Photo 13).

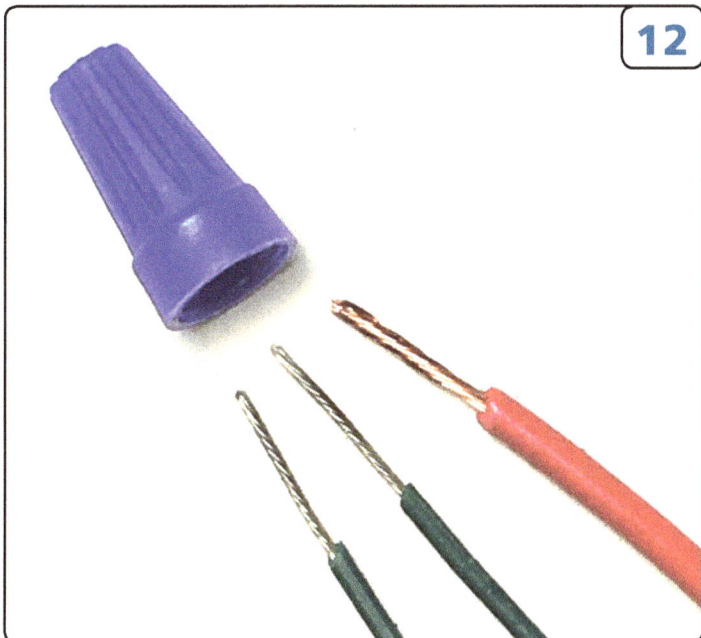

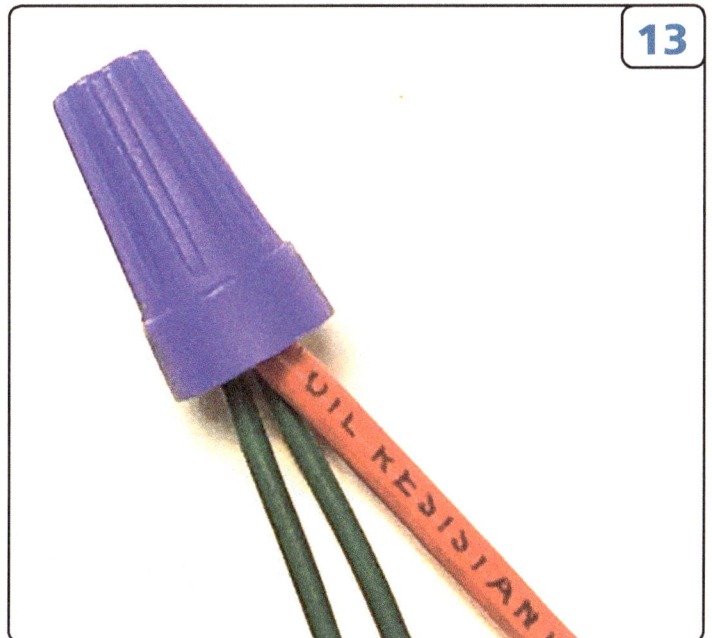

Once you get above 20-gauge wire, the wire nut sizes need to increase rapidly due to the increased amount of bulky wire housed within the wire nut. If I remove the red 18-gauge wire and replace it with a black 16-gauge wire, an even larger orange wire nut is needed to make the connection (Photo 14). Interestingly enough, that one step up in wire nut size will even let you add the red 18-gauge wire back into the mix (Photo 15) without causing any problem.

Wire nuts are not very good for wire connections where a digital signal is present. Electrically speaking, a wire nut is a pressure connector (joining two or more wires through a pressure contact inside the wire nut). Digital signal strength is easily diminished or lost through pressure connections, and is never lost through a proper solder connection. But wire nuts are good for simple power connectors for any and all accessories. They are also very forgiving. If you find later that you have to add a wire into an existing connection, simply unscrew the wire nut, add the new wire in, and reconnect with either the same wire nut or the next size up, as needed.

There are a couple of other good points for using wire nuts as well. You need only two tools—a small pair of wire cutters and a wire stripper—and you don't need any electrical tape. Give 'em a try!

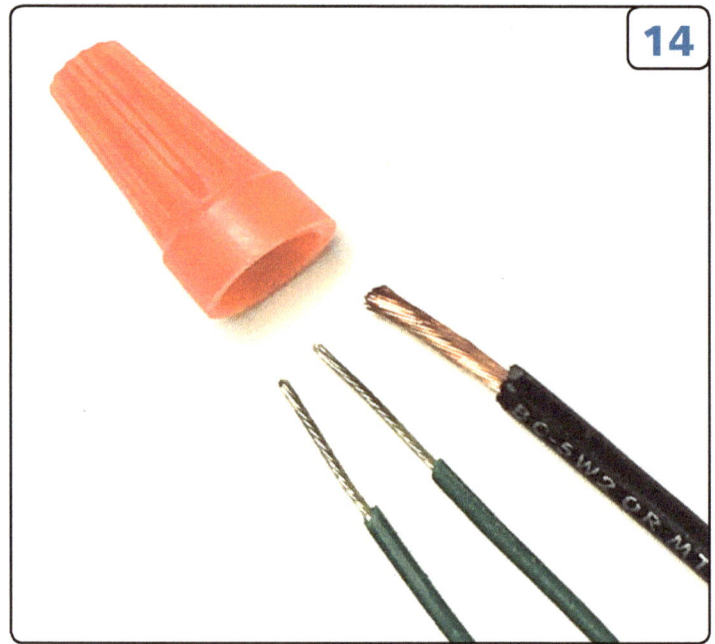

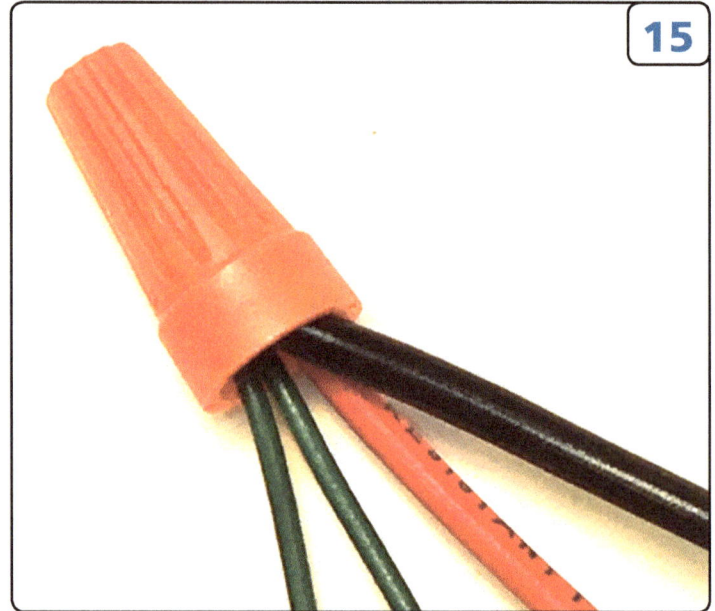

WIRE NUT SIZING CHART

WIRE SIZE	22-16	22-14	22-14	18-12	18-10
MINIMUM	1 #20 + 1 #22	3 #22	3 #22	1 #14 + 1 #18	1 #12 + 2 #8
MAXIMUM	2 #16	2 #16	2 #16 + 1 #18	2 #14 + 3 #16	3 #10

CHAPTER 42 - Keeping Things Clean

If you haven't already thought about it, once you get your layout finished (if there really is such a thing as finished), you will have quite an investment of time and money in its construction. That being the case, you will want to preserve its finished appearance for as long as you can.

Nothing makes a layout look old and ignored more than an accumulation of dust and dirt over a period of time. The problem is, most of us don't give that more than a passing consideration until we actually notice that the layout is starting to look old, dreary, and drab. By that time, it is already too late in far too many cases. The best time to think about how to keep a layout looking fresh is before you ever start building it.

The first sign that a layout is getting drab and a little seedy looking is when we begin to notice the accumulation of actual dust itself. Lots of layout owners say to me, "I never clean my layout because I want it to have that natural weathered and dusty look." Trouble is, real dust doesn't have that "natural, weathered and dusty look." That's because real dust doesn't scale down to believable scale dust. What the eye wants to perceive as a dusty old building at 1:48 scale is really a painted surface that is dulled down to a flat, softly textured color. Photo 1 is a picture of a general store that resides on my layout. Note that what looks like an accumulation of dust over the years is really a painted surface, with Testors Dullcote applied over the top of the final paint color. The building itself is actually very clean, and as free as possible of train room dust.

Real dust ends up looking like. . . well. . . real dust. It doesn't look like weathered buildings; it looks like dirty model railroad structures. Real dust gets full scale human fingerprints in it, or ugly evidence of half-hearted attempts to remove same. Then it doesn't look like real anything.

The better modeling trick is to create the appearance of scale dust on a building surface, which won't come off, using Testors Dullcote or other equivalent gloss removers as a finishing touch. Even the shiny surfaces of things like automobiles and other machines should generally not look like they have shiny surfaces when viewed from a distance. The next time you are on a plane flight, notice when you are coming in for a landing that as you get close enough to the ground to make out cars and trucks easily, there is no real shine on the surfaces of these vehicles. The only thing that stands out is the color of the vehicle, not that it has a shiny surface. You can easily achieve the same effect with the models on your layout by simply spraying them with a light coating of Dullcote to remove the shine. Getting rid of the shine is, after all, the first step we are after when we try to weather our locomotives and rolling stock.

Bob Bartizek notes:

"Dust typically comes off the concrete basement floor. Just stamp your foot hard on a concrete floor and look at the dust cloud it creates. Dust also gets shed from concrete block basement walls. And, if the ceiling is unfinished, dust will sift down through joints in the flooring upstairs, or from where the flooring meets the floor joists just above the layout. I applied an epoxy stain/sealer to the concrete floor, installed sheet plastic vapor barriers on the inside of all the wall studs to seal off the concrete basement walls, and spray painted the ceiling joists and everything above with a thick coat of black paint. The paint effectively sealed the sources of overhead dust. The floor of my train room was carpeted in all of the aisles. Tack strips were glued to the floor and standard wall-to-wall installation methods were used."

This system, Bob notes, effectively controlled the amount of general dust that made its way into the room. Frequent carpet cleaning in the aisles of his train room removed any newly tracked-in dust; and as a result, the amount of dust that settled on scenery and trains was kept to an absolute minimum.

Also give consideration to getting a dedicated vacuum cleaner just for your train room. Keeping the filters clean is much easier when you know what jobs the vacuum cleaner has been doing. Get one with a good air filtration system so that you are actually capturing the dust instead of simply redistributing it when you use the vacuum. It is much easier to depend on a good vacuum cleaner to do its job when you know that it hasn't been doing other jobs around the house, such as cleaning out the bed of the family pickup truck. I would venture to say that one of the most common sources of dust in train rooms is clogged filters, or even no filters, on the vacuum cleaner being used to clean the train room to begin with.

You may have areas on the layout that will allow you to use a vacuum cleaner with a hose attachment directly on the layout. The trick is to use a vacuum with a weak enough suction so that you won't end up damaging fine details. Some small shop vacs have a device on the nozzle fitting of the suction hose that will allow you to vary the amount of suction so you can use it around delicate areas. There's nothing worse than carefully vacuuming around a beautiful street scene and suddenly seeing the town's mayor and a couple of other townsfolk being sucked into purgatory!

A mini vacuum cleaner is handy; but because they are battery operated, they can't get much done without constantly changing batteries or recharging

The best of all worlds is a step down kit like the one pictured in Photo 2. If you do a Google search for "Stewmac. com" and then enter "0523" in the "search for" box, you will see such a kit offered for as little as $11.89. This mini hose plugs 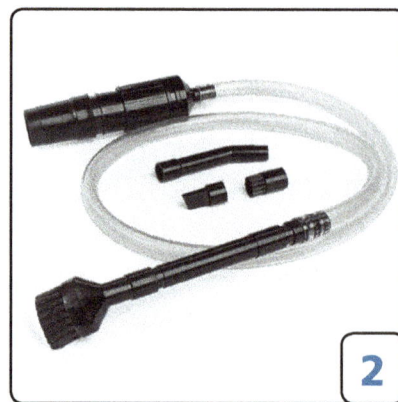 right on to the end of a standard vacuum hose nozzle. The beauty of this system is that the additional small hose included makes it much easier to control the brush end of the vacuum, thereby allowing you to get down into small places on the layout. At that price, it is less than a replacement mayor and one or two other townsfolk!

Consideration should also be given to why dust gathers on trains and layout surfaces in the first place. Depending on what part of the country you live in, humidity can be a constant problem for trains. It is already a significant problem when it comes to the operation and preservation of trains, but it also is a major problem in keeping layouts clean. Humid environments mean that trains and scenery live in an environment that constantly provides a fine, moist surface, which not only attracts dust, but makes it stick to the surfaces that it gathers on. Once that happens, the dust is not easily brushed off and with another cycle of drying and humidifying, will now attract an even more difficult layer of dust to remove. Humidity is probably the most common and annoying problem in attracting and retaining dirt and dust on your layout surfaces.

The most important device you can install in a train room (or your whole house, for that matter) is a dehumidifier to control humidity swings in the air in your train room. By controlling humidity changes, you not only control the expansion and contraction of materials used to build your train table, but you also manage your layout's tendency to attract and retain dust and dirt.

Dust also comes from loose scenery materials used to build your layout. In general, it's a good idea to make sure that there is nothing loose on your layout. I have a tendency to leave ballast around switches and operating accessories loose. Ultimately, that is another source of dust, so I now carefully make sure that all ballast, grass, gravel, and other loose scenery materials are fastened down to the layout using a dripped mixture of white glue and water applied over sprayed wet water, which is water mixed with a drop or two of liquid dish detergent mixed in. OGR Publisher Emeritus, Rich Melvin, pointed out to me that this technique also lets him clean all those surfaces with a mini vacuum cleaner head without disturbing any of the fine details.

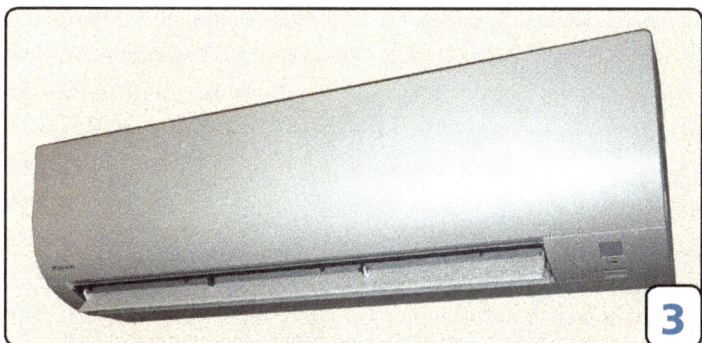

Air ducts are a source of dust from other areas of the home. OGR Publisher Alan Arnold built his layout in a very spacious room that was a former church. His layout room is separate from any other part of his house. It has no windows that can be opened, and it has an installed heating/cooling unit that uses the air in that room exclusively. The system, shown above in Photo 3, is called a mini-split. It sits on the wall, up near the ceiling of this cavernous room, and requires no ductwork. The unit has an outside sensor that senses the outdoor air temperature, determines what to do inside, and adjusts the temperature of the large room inside by heating or cooling the room air. It gently circulates the air in the large, cavernous room, without using any air ducts. The mini-split has internal filter to clean the air. They are small and easy to replace, and because there is no ductwork, the air stays very clean.

Another consideration is, sadly, smoking locomotives. Active smoke units in locomotives deposit a fine vapor mist on all surfaces. If you are like me and love to see those steamers emitting monstrous smoke plumes as they exit the tunnel portals, then you will likely have do a great deal of extra cleaning on the layout. Removing the dust that accumulates from smoke unit residue is a major problem that must be attended to, or your layout's wonderful scenery details will soon become drenched in dust and dirt that is virtually locked into the scenery. I use smoke units sparingly only when new visitors are over to see the layout, and I shut them off after a very short time.

The final dust prevention element to add into your home and train room is a very good air cleaning system. The majority of homes and train rooms are heated and/or air conditioned with a duct air handling system. Typically, these systems recirculate air that is already heated and/or cooled and combine it with some minimal amount of outside fresh air. These ducted air systems are frequently already outfitted with air filters and air cleaning systems, which if you haven't looked into it in the past five or ten years, have come a long way. Check with your preferred HVAC (heating, ventilating, and air conditioning) professional to see what is offered now compared to what you have currently in your existing system. Upgrading your existing system to a new and more efficient system with easily replaceable filters definitely will reduce the amount of dust in your whole house to near nothing. I had a new air cleaning system (Photo 4) installed into the duct work of my house when I moved in six years ago, and it has practically eliminated the need to routinely clean the house. Train layout dust has all but disappeared.

There is no new miracle cure for dust, but there are much improved filters that do a far better job of removing dust particulates as the air is being circulated throughout the home. As you can see in the photo, it can be added to any existing system and requires little or no additional space in the duct work. In my case, they put the entire filter system in the space between the lower end of the cold air return duct (shown on the right) and the furnace. I took one additional step: recommended filter changing times were every six months; but when I increased that to every four months, it was well worth the effort. Replacing the filter cost $25 and takes ten minutes. Once I had done that, it seemed like the last remaining dust in the house disappeared.

Another tip offered by Bob Bartizek was a system for removing dust that he brushes off the roofs of passenger cars and other rolling stock, as well as the roofs of small scenery structures on his layout.

"I use a new, small paint brush (about 2″ or so), or sometimes a shaving brush, and dust the roofs of passenger cars and any flat rooftops on structures.

I brush the dust into a paper towel that I have sprayed lightly with Endust or a similar product. The sprayed paper towel acts as a dust magnet to capture and retain the dust removed by the dusting brush. In 15 years, using this method I never have had much of a dust buildup."

I thought Bob's idea was so good that I tried one little modification to it when attempting to remove dust from detailed steam locomotives and tenders. I sprayed some Endust on a 3x5 index card and kept it close to the locomotive (butted right up against the edges of the model) as in Photo 5. As I brushed cervices and small crannies around detailed parts of the locomotives, tenders, and cabooses—using a new, dedicated artist brush—sure enough, the dust was captured by the index card, and the model was thoroughly and easily cleaned. Remember, the trick is to capture the dust, not rearrange it to some other place.

These are only a few examples of good cleaning ideas. The bottom line here is top keep the layout clean without accumulating a bunch of full scale dust!

CHAPTER 43 - As Seen in a Different Light

From the time of Thomas Edison onward, we've judged the brightness of a light bulb by using the term watts. For instance, a 60-watt bulb was brighter than a 40-watt bulb; a 100-watt bulb was brighter than a 60-watt bulb, and so on. That has been the way we judged how bright the light was on our layouts (or on anything else, for that matter) from roughly 1879 until just a few years ago.

The problem is, we all got lazy and comfortable with a slight misunderstanding concerning what the term watts really meant. It wasn't our fault. We actually had no need to measure the brightness of a light bulb in any other way because light bulbs were all made the same way. How many watts of electricity was the only way to change or evaluate the brightness. The term watts and the brightness of a light bulb went hand-in-hand. Simply put, the brightness of the light bulb increased in direct ratio to the amount of current that was used to light the bulb.

Ah, but that was then, and this is now! With incandescent light bulbs, the real definition of watts is a measurement of how much electrical current is flowing through the filament of the light bulb to get to a certain level of brightness the light bulb is producing.

Now, however, there's a new kid on the block. This "new kid" is something called Light Emitting Diodes, or LEDs. Originally, LEDs were not even considered something to think of as light producing as much as they were just little ways to indicate whether something was turned "on" or not. They were the tiny little red or green light indicators used on nearly every electrical device we now use in our world.

But something absolutely fascinating has evolved in the past few years. Technology has found ways for the LEDs to emit more and more light of any color you'd like until they have now become an alternate way to actually produce light, eventually replacing Thomas Edison's incandescent light bulb forever. The most remarkable thing about the LED is that they produce light so efficiently that they use far less electricity to produce the same amount of light as emitted by an incandescent bulb.

But that resulted in another problem. What do we use to measure how much light an LED produces compared to an incandescent light bulb? It can't be watts like we traditionally used because the brightness of a 50-watt incandescent bulb can be exactly duplicated with a 7-watt LED bulb. Think about that! The brightness of the two bulbs are equal, but the amount of electricity they use to get there can save you up to 86% on your electricity bill simply by switching from incandescent bulbs to LED bulbs.

The new term used to measure the brightness of light produced electrically is called lumens. A quick trip down the lighting aisle of a Lowe's, Home Depot, Menards, or any other big box store will give you a great education on this term. Now the packaging for a light bulb and/or an equivalent LED notes the watts it uses to make the light, but also the amount of lumens the light puts out. As an example, take a look at Photo 2 showing an LED light bulb that produces the equivalent amount of light as a 50-watt incandescent light bulb. It identifies itself as a "50W Replacement" light; but because it is an LED, it only uses 7 watts of electricity to produce that much light. In the lower left corner of the packaging it also states that the amount of light is now measured as "500L"(lumens). So now we have some understanding of the terms watts and lumens. An incandescent 50-watt bulb and a 7-watt LED bulb each put out about 500 lumens.

Don't be confused by another energy-saving light that is also available. There is something called a halogen light (Photo 3), which is a technology that has been around much longer than an LED. It does save some electricity, but it is still not anywhere near as efficient as an LED light. As you

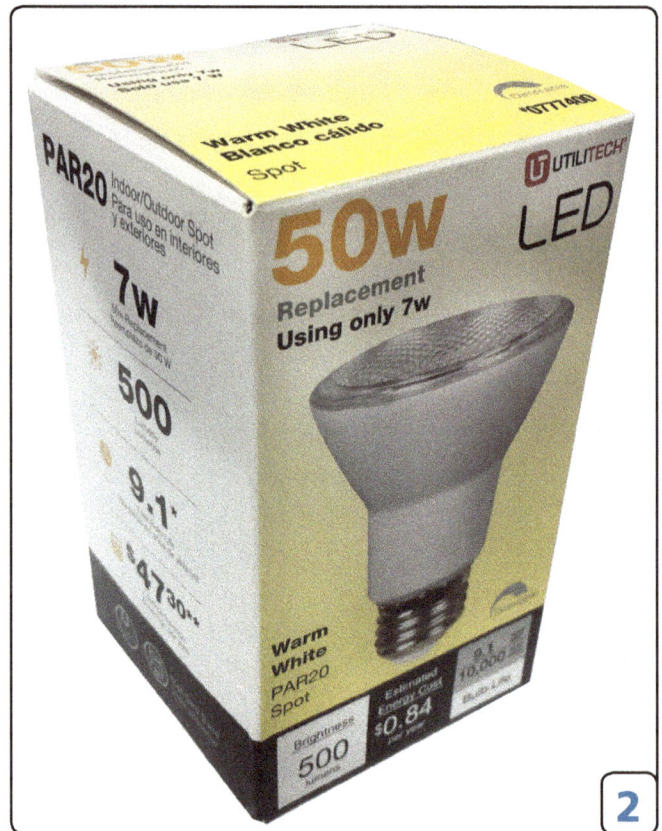

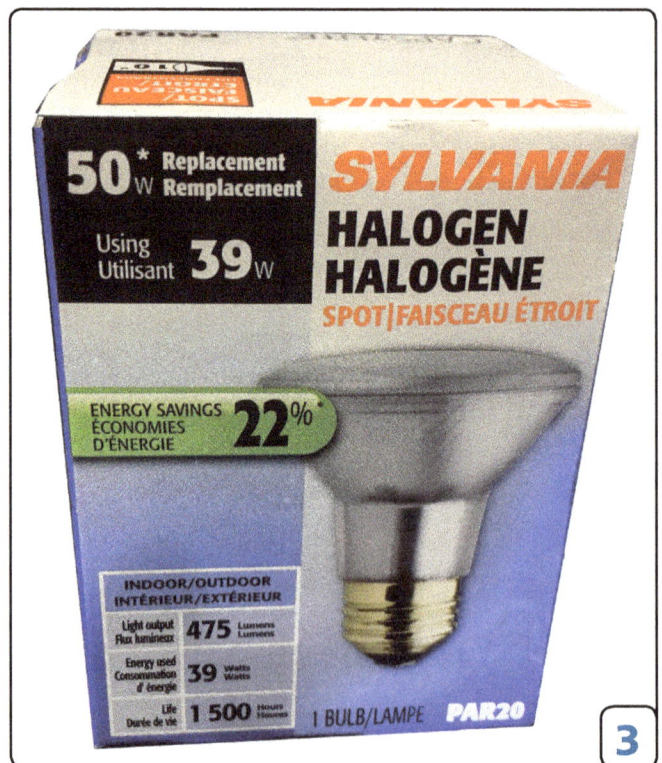

can see by the packaging, it only produces about 475 lumens, as compared to 500 lumens from an equivalent LED. Furthermore, it saves only about 11 watts per 50-watt-bulb equivalent, as compared to a 43-watts savings with the LED light.

There is a third term we need to learn about. Have you ever noticed that the colors of things you are already familiar with sometimes look very different depending on what the source of light is? Photographers have long known of this effect due to the many different types of lighting used in photography. Some lights make things look slightly blue, while others make the same image look more warm, or soft. There is a reference to that on the LED shown in Photo 2, where it says "Warm White."

The technical term used to define the color of light produced is "color temperature." However, that has nothing to do with the actual heat being produced by the respective bulb. When it comes to light-producing devices, the term "color temperature" refers to the actual color of the light it produces. Color temperature is measured in degrees Kelvin, or simply K. That is what determines how the overall color of an image is going to appear. Have you ever noticed how things look more blue when illuminated under standard workshop fluorescent light? That is because the color temperature of the light put out by standard fluorescent tubes is different than what is put out by standard incandescent light. Some fluorescent tubes are color-corrected for this and are engineered to put out a warmer light than standard fluorescent tubes. Commercially, they are often labeled as warm white or kitchen and bath light.

Okay, let's review. Temperature, as it applies to lighting, is measured as kelvin, or simply K. That number is how you deter-mine the overall effect that is going to be produced by the lighting product you are going to use. Photo 4 shows the packaging on a pair of standard 48″ long fluorescent tubes (the ones shown are the smaller 1″ diameter tubes) like the ones commonly used in work-shops or laundry rooms. They are called a cool white tube because, as they show on the little scale, they put out a 4100 K (degrees kelvin) light value, which is cooler or bluer than a warm white tube. To reduce all that jargon to the simpler kelvin temperature ratings, we consider a warm white tone to be anything in the range of 2700 to 3000 kelvin, or K. A light in the range of 4000K to 6000K would be referred to as a cool white light.

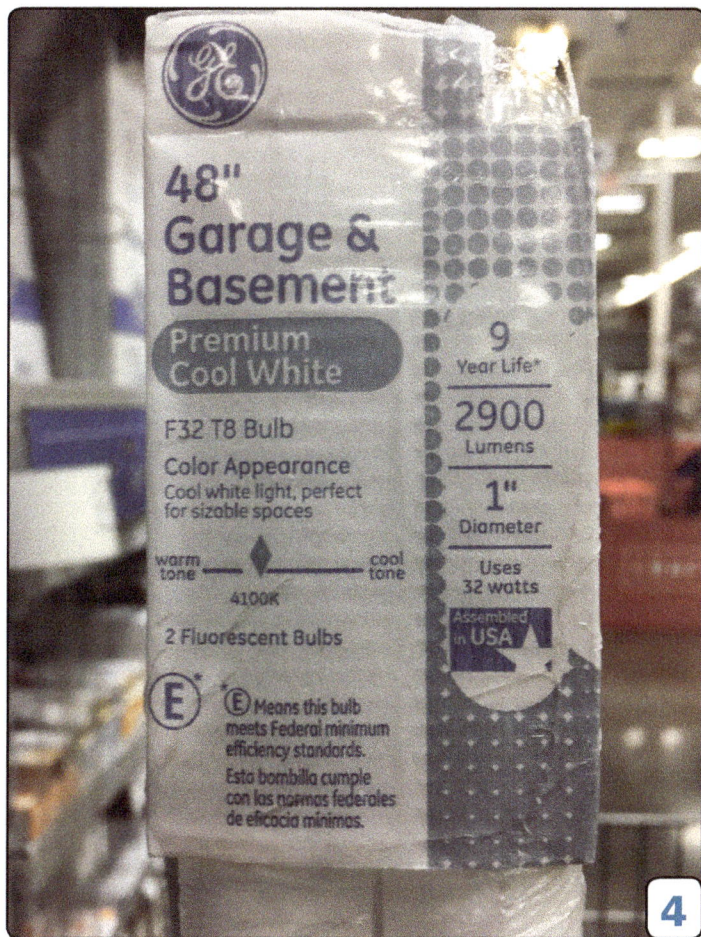

Photo 5 on the next page is the same group of images I used at the opening of this chapter, with the color temperature (kelvin) ratings of the light used to make the four different appearances. This will give you a clear example of kelvin temperature rating on light and what the result will be on objects on your layout. The warm white temperature range between 2700 and 3000 kelvin gives things a warm tone, more like the color your eye would see with incandescen lamps. The higher number K ratings shown (4000K to 6000K) are the bright and cool white color tones given off by standard commercial fluorescent tubes. The higher numbers are also closer to the color of sunlight.

2700 K - Warm White **5a**

3000 K - Warm White **5b**

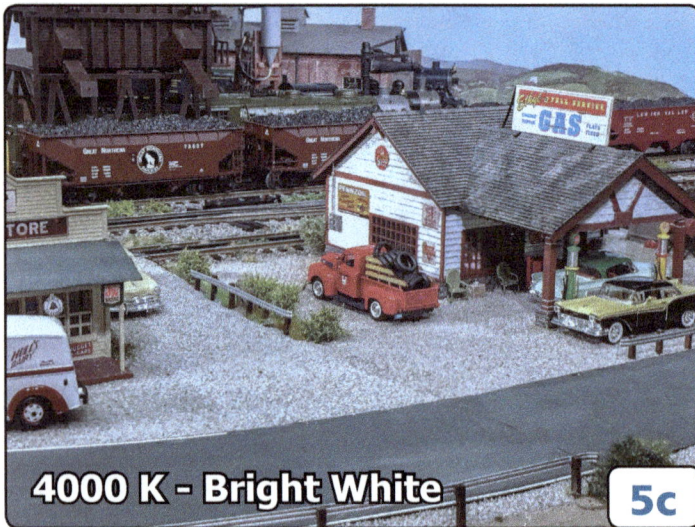

4000 K - Bright White **5c**

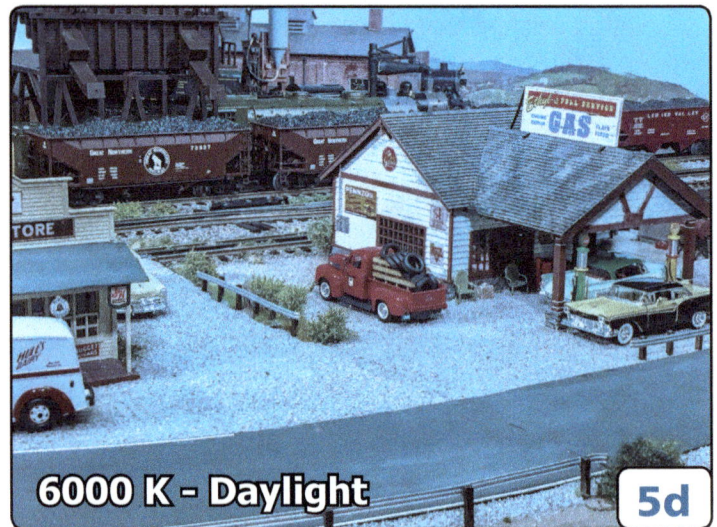

6000 K - Daylight **5d**

There are LED tubes available now to replace fluorescent tubes. Photo 6 shows the end of a 48″ long, 1″ diameter LED tube that exactly replaces a fluorescent tube of the same dimensions. The fluorescent tube pictured in Photo 4 uses 32 watts of electricity to produce 1900 lumens of cool white brightness. The LED tube uses only 18 watts to put out 2000 lumens of 3000K (or warm white) light. But here comes the best part.

The expected life of the LED tube is 50,000 hours! Let me do the math on this. If you burn the lights in your train room an average of four hours every day for five nights every single week, you won't be replacing tubes for about 48 years! And the amount of electricity you will use will drop by 43% as well.

Until recently, one catch was that a slight amount of rewiring was needed on your overhead light fixtures to convert them to be able to use LED tubes, but even that has gone away now. If you Google "Luxrite 4FT LED Tube Light, T8, 18W (32W Equivalent), 3000K Soft White, 2000

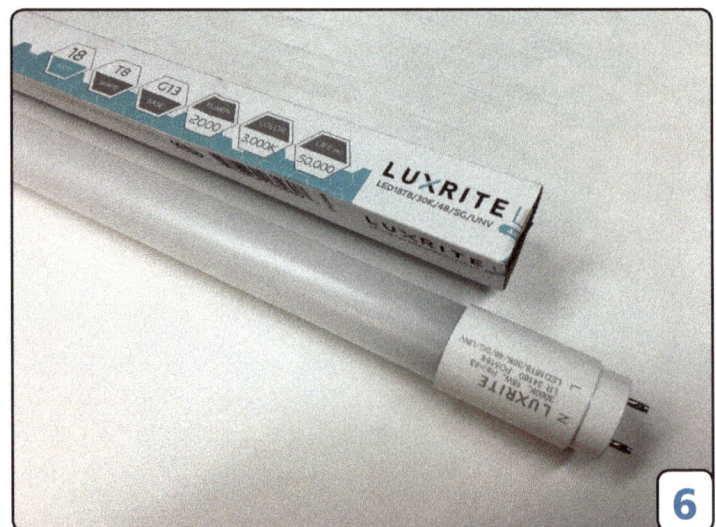

6

Lumens, Fluorescent Light Tube Replacement, Direct or Ballast Bypass," the 25-tube pack displayed will sell for about $314, or about $12.56 per tube. Just remember, you will never need to replace them for about 48 years. That makes the $12.56 look pretty darn good compared to five or six standard fluorescent tube replacements over that same time period.

My layout room has both 4′ fluorescent tubes and track lights for regular screw-in bulbs. I did this because I wanted to be able to dim the lighting on the layout to produce any number of effects. Fluorescent tubes (and 48″ LED tube replacements) don't dim, but incandescent as well as LED light bulbs do dim. That's what the track lights are for. Back before LED bulbs, when I installed my track lights, I bought and installed a commercial grade light dimmer (Photo 7) that would handle 2,000 watts, or a total of about 40 incandescent bulbs.

A dimmer like that one works by holding back the watts that don't make it to the light bulb and converting them to heat. On a commercial grade dimmer, that heat is absorbed in the fluted heat sink base shown under the faceplate of the dimmer switch visible in Photo 7. I quickly found out that dimming down as many as 40 incandescent bulbs produced a great amount of heat in the finned baseplate! To be on the safe side, I cut back the number of lights being dimmed to only 25. That did cut the heat down, but it sort of defeated my purpose of using a dimmer in the first place. I wanted to use a large number of "spot" bulbs as compared to "flood bulbs" to highlight interesting scenes on the layout. The result was there wasn't enough overall light on the layout to satisfy me. When 7-watt LED lights came out, that changed things dramatically. Now, I could use as many as 175 LED lights if I wanted to and have no more total watts than 25 incandescent lights on the dimmer. Wow!

That one change allowed me to convert to ONLY "spot" type LED bulbs and still have more than enough light for the entire layout. And they could all be dimmed from intense noonday sun to dusk or dawn light simply by turning the dimmer wheel. Since my overall number of LEDs was still only about 75, as compared to 35 incandescent bulbs, my total energy consumption was still down by 70%. I love it when technology works in our favor for a change!

So let's do a short review relating to watts, lumens, and color temperature.

Back when we only had incandescent and fluorescent lights to deal with, we only used to think about lighting in terms of watts. Now, with LEDs replacing both standard light bulbs and standard fluorescent tubes, we need to think about watts, lumens, and color temperature. Watts is how much electricity they use, lumens means how bright they are, and color temperature relates to the color of the light that is produced.

On a broader note, don't just think about this in relation to your train layout. Think about converting absolutely everything in your home to LEDs. The more you do, the more you save!

Chapter 43

Building A Layout by Jim Barrett

CHAPTER 44 - Control Layout Lighting with an AIU

As the installation and use of DCS (and TMCC) becomes more and more prolific on our O gauge layouts, I am continually amazed at how many of these same creators of dazzling train empires willingly put down their DCS remote just to pick up some other kind of remote or manually manipulate toggle switches just to show off the lovely lighting effects on their layouts.

Ladies and gentlemen, that is a completely redundant effort, and is totally unnecessary to do! Not to mention the fact that use of the word "redundant" when it comes to lighting means (to me anyway) that you just nearly doubled your tedious electrical wiring efforts for no good reason. Those of you who use the MTH DCS system to control your trains for some reason miss the fact that the AIU (the Accessory Interface Unit) of the DCS system is already there,

ready and waiting to manage your layout's lighting effects as well, without the addition of any other method of controlling lights on your layout at all.

With the DCS system, a TIU (Track Interface Unit) with the addition of a single AIU allows the operator to control the function of 10 track switches and 10 accessory functions. Due to the flexibility of the DCS system, it is possible to use as many as five AIUs together daisy chained from one TIU. Mathematically, that makes it possible to control up to 50 track switches and 50 accessories from one TIU. If that isn't enough, the DCS system still has the additional capacity to operate as many as five TIUs on one layout. The mind boggling truth is that the DCS system can handle up to 250 track switches and 250 accessory connections—all controlled by a single remote!

Now it is quite obvious that one person trying to control a layout that complicated with one remote would far exceed the definition of fun. I point this out only to underline the fact that the DCS system has room to individually control what nearly anyone could ever want, and most of us maybe never even thought of doing. It also has the ability to control groupings of scenes or sets of action together, which greatly simplifies things for you, too.

Here's an example. I've traveled and photographed many layouts over the years, and one thing I've noticed is that nearly every layout has a greater need for switch controls that they do for accessory controls. That means that regardless of how many AIUs you employ to handle the track switches, you will probably have an abundance of unused, extra accessory control ports available to you. Why not use those extra accessory ports to manage your layout's lighting in a spectacular way? Spectacular means that you can not only use the DCS remote to turn your layout lights on and off, but you can also use the DCS system to preprogram certain sequences of lights that you wish to turn on and off depending on time allotted for evening and night scenes. Some of you may already know that you can preset the AIU's sequence of operating track switches, but did you know that you can use the same method for sequentially controlling the turning on and/or off of layout lighting, as well? It's relatively easy to use the AIU to program your own preferred sequence of illuminating or turning out those lights to create easy, progressive night scenes.

My late friend Barry Broskowitz published a definitive book on how to best use the DCS system titled The DCS O Gauge Companion that he researched and continually developed over the years for layout operators. If you don't have a copy of his book, it's available on Amazon. Search on Amazon for "DCS Companion 3rd Edition" and you will find it. Make sure to include the words "3rd Edition" in your search. There are still some copies of his 2nd Edition available, but they are outdated. It is well worth your investment to have this handbook on the DCS System.

In this book Barry points out that it is very easy to add individual accessories into the system, complete with their own names showing up on the screen of the operator's DCS remote. My thinking is, why not group together lights from building backdrops? As long as you limit the number of watts per group to 60 or 80 watts per accessory channel, you are well within the limits of the electrical relay. If you figure that a grain-of-wheat light bulb (like the one shown in photo 5) is about one half to one watt per bulb, there is certainly less than 80 watts worth of electricity flowing in one group of buildings. All you need to do is to give some

name to a set of buildings and control them through a port in the AIU. On my layout I've got 50+ track switches, so that means I'm using five AIUs to control the switches. That also means that I've got 50 accessory ports as well. I should be able to control any lighting combination I can imagine!

That's my own standard: not to exceed 80 watts per relay loading in the AIU, even though the MTH personnel tell me that the individual relays in the AIU can handle a higher loading than that. I prefer to error on the side of caution, and limit the loading to only 80 watts or less per accessory port. If you consider that grain-of-wheat bulb in photo 5, that means you can hook up at least 100 or so bulbs without causing any undue strain on the relays in a single accessory port in the AIU.

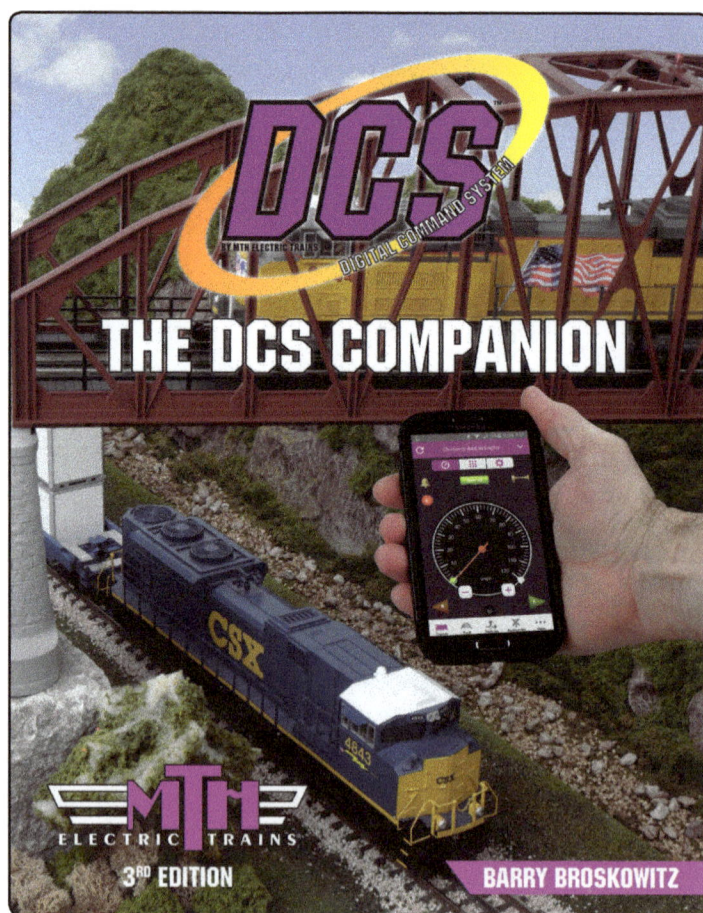

The DCS Companion, 3rd Edition, written by Barry Broskowitz Available at amazon.com.

Photo 1 at the beginning of this article shows an array of building fronts being used as a scenic backdrop on part of my layout. In Photo 2, look what a difference it makes when you remove those Ameri-Towne building fronts (or backs)! My friend (and expert O gauge layout modeler) Bill Bramlage has shown me how to build groups of building flats together as a single module (as shown in Photo 3).

Photo 4 below shows the same three buildings, but from the back side with all the lights and wires installed right at your workbench, before you even take it into the layout.

Note in Photo 5 how carefully he locates the light bulb. Bill points out to make sure that you don't let the bulb touch the window material or the venetian blind graphic material either. Note also that he sparingly uses those grain-of-wheat light bulbs mounted above only certain windows. Note that there are only six or eight bulbs total randomly mounted in the windows of the building module. Adding subtle lighting sparsely is all that's needed to create the effect of a well lighted building.

Another one of Bill's favorite tricks is to bring all the bulb wires together down to a short piece of N gauge track and use the track as a buss bar for all the lighting in the module. Then he attaches only one pair of wires from the N gauge track buss bars down through a hole drilled in the bottom of the module frame. I add a strain relief knot (Photo 6) in the wire to keep the wire from pulling on the tiny gentle wires or the N gauge buss bars inside the module.

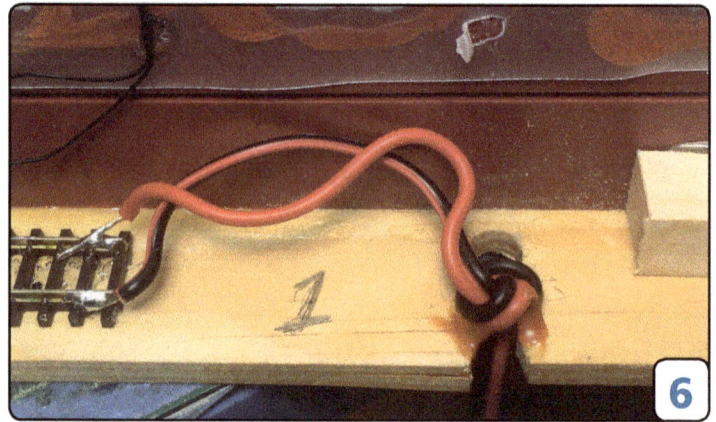

The end result is a single pair of wires coming out of the bottom of the module and going through the table. Seen in Photo 7 is the finished module installed at the back of the layout up against the wall.

Four additional modules are installed to finish out the back wall as shown in Photo 8.

Here's a real modeler's time saver tip: make that single pair of wires extending from the bottom of each building module at least as long as you need to get through the surface of the train table and reach all the way out to the front edge of the train layout (Photo 9). That will allow you to make all your connections from an easy access position outside your layout at the front edge. It's always so much easier to make electrical wiring on your layout from the comfort of a chair out in the train room instead of crawling under the layout to work on wiring overhead.

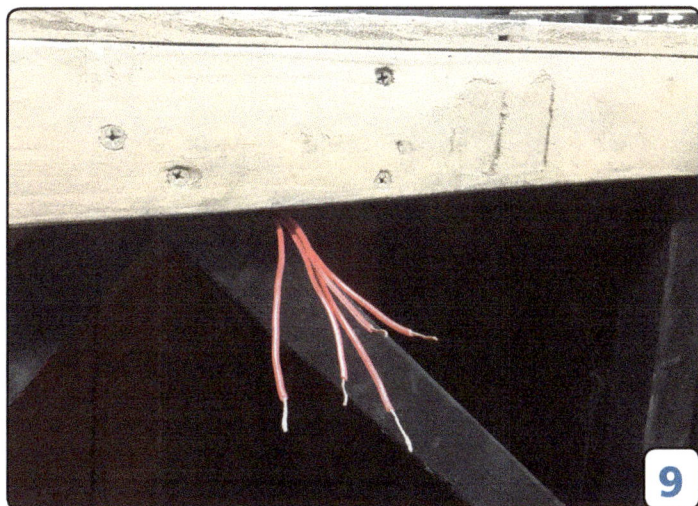

In my case, each of the modules has one red wire and one black wire coming from the module. All the black wires are joined together and attached to a single AC(-) or Common bus wire running under the table that connects to the AC(-) or Common posts on all transformers on the layout. The result is that half the wiring for each and every accessory requires only one wire to get to the transformer's AC+ or Supply wire. Each AC- or Common wire runs only from the accessory to the nearest AC Common buss wire under the table.

Photo 10 shows an MTH AIU or Accessory Interface Unit.

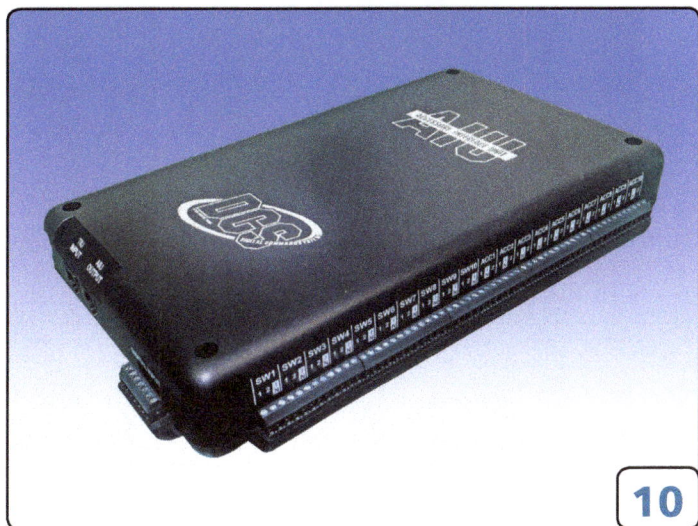

And if you ever wanted to know what's inside an AIU, take a look at Photo 11. You can see that the AIU consists thirty relays, all soldered to a motherboard. You can control each and every one of them with your DCS remote, or via the WiFi App.

Photo 12 shows that two wires go to each port for an accessory. One is an AC+ supply wire, which comes from the transformer to the AIU, with the accessory voltage you are going to use for what you want to operate. The other wire goes from the AIU to the accessory. In the photo, the supply wire from the transformer is connected to the IN terminal port on the AIU, and the wire going from the AIU to the accessory is connected to the 1 terminal port. In the photo, both of these terminal ports are at ACC10, or accessory port #10, of this AIU. The booklet that comes with the AIU will tell you how to make these connections and how and when to insert the name of the accessory into the DCS remote.

Depending on the size of your layout, you may need to only control one or two accessory ports to turn on all your lighting accessories. If you need more than that, or if you want to use more than just two to be able to turn on some lights at different times than others, then you can easily set up something called a Scene in DCS. Setting up a Scene simplifies turning on many things at the same time by teaching the system to control many different accessory controls with the simple touch of just one button on the remote. Using the Scene command will let you possibly control all the background lighting, all the building lighting, and all the accessory lighting—all from a single one-button command, if desired.

On my layout, I may end up using 30 or more accessory ports, which will allow me to create a progressive lighting scene by grouping buildings all over the layout in small bunches. That will allow me to teach the system the use of the Scene command to progressively light up the whole evening scene gradually, building by building, until all the lights are eventually on.

The details on how to make this happen with the AIU are in the booklet that comes with the AIU and also with Barry's book. It involves first connecting all individual lighting groups as we just detailed above, then setting up a Scene command on a single key of the AIU that will group all the lighting effects you have already added into the system. From that time on, a single press of the scene key for that single scene will sequentially light up your whole layout.

Ironically, that's how "more complicated" gets to be "more simple"! 🚋

CHAPTER 45 - The Lessons I've Learned

After 55 years of teaching carpentry, building professional scale models, and constructing train layouts, you would think that a guy would have learned everything there is to know about how to do it correctly, wouldn't you?

Wrong!

But one of the greatest things about this hobby is that no one has a monopoly on the only correct way to do something. That especially applies to me. For the past six years I have tried to document things from the start of my layout construction to the present, covering some of my favorite ways to build an O gauge layout. But along the way I've discovered many times how I could have done something a bit differently—or just plain better—as the result of things I learned after the article went to print.

Over the past half-dozen years, many of you have approached me at train shows or written to me with suggestions on how you have solved the same problem with results at least as good as I've had, and many times even much better. This final chapter of this book will cover a few things I've learned "after the fact," so to speak.

In the chapter two I showed you how to build a scenic panel to be mounted all around the back wall of the train room. That included covering a large glass block window in the wall (Photo 1). I thought merely covering the window with black foam core board on the inside would eliminate the solar heating effect (Photo 2), followed with putting up the Masonite panel to cover the window opening (Photo 3). What I learned was that solar heating happened anyway.

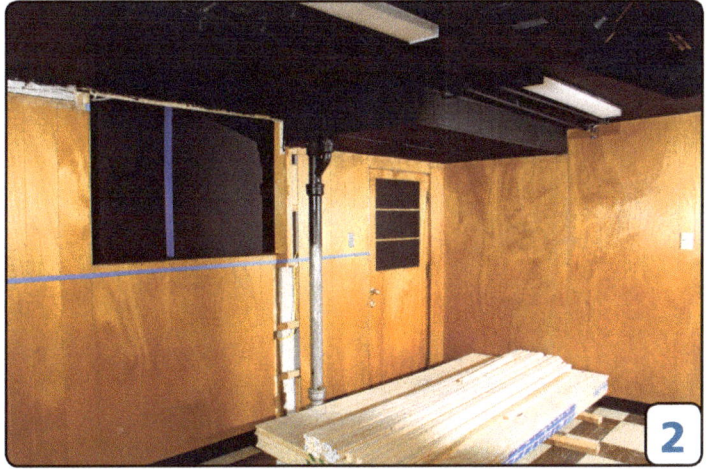

The dead air space between the black foam core board covering the glass block windows and the Masonite scene panel still heated and cooled, depending on the season. That made for unwanted warping and bulging in the scene panel, which was the thing I was trying to eliminate to begin with.

Eventually, I had to remove the scene panel and add some insulation material between the black foam core board covering the inside of the glass block window and the Masonite scene panel. I trapped the insulation in place with some tape and put the Masonite scene panel back in place. Now the heating and cooling effect was eliminated, and the scene panel behaved much better.

In chapter three I showed you how to prime and paint the blue sky backing on the Masonite panel backdrop using flat, water based interior house paint, then adding clouds onto the blue background using some templates and common home improvement store aerosol spray paints (Photo 4).

My friend made a test board (shown propped up in the front); and I determined that I wanted my blue sky lighter than the test board, so I used a lighter shade of the same blue paint. The finished product is shown on the wall behind the test board.

Well, what happened is that I didn't account for the effect of the room's fluorescent lights over the years. The blue that I used as the color of the sky faded to an even lighter blue. If I had it to do over again, I would have used the stronger blue on the test board to begin with. That would have probably faded to the blue that shows on the wall behind it in a couple of years.

Another valuable lesson learned is that if your train room is also a main thoroughfare in your house, the constant saturation of lighting will indeed fade most colors a little, if not a lot, depending on what kind of paint is used, and how much time the lights will be left on unnecessarily in the room.

In chapter 36, I showed you how to make a matching piece of the rock wall removable (see Photo 5) so that it could easily be removed and set aside, thereby allowing the operator to go inside the layout to perform any necessary maintenance.

An example of where this is needed is shown in Photo 6. This is where the lower level track is on a hinged panel that drops down to allow you to perform maintenance on the layout. Also, the upper level panel hinges up and out of the way, so I can move deeper into the layout to get to the back. The rock wall is permanently connected to the upper and lower levels of the layout on both sides of the opening.

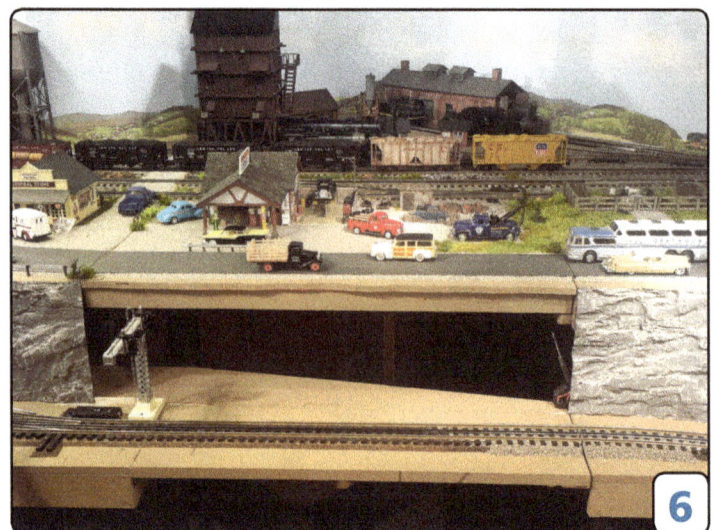

Photo 7 shows a piece of Styrofoam cut to fit in the opening. I explained that putting down a piece of balsa wood on the bottom layout level was a good way to keep the Styrofoam from being pushed too far back into the opening.

Using a hot wire foam cutter (Photo 8), I contour cut the Styrofoam to fit against the edge of the wood on the second deck of the layout. I then contact cemented the plastic sheet of rock wall material onto the Styrofoam backing (shown turned on its face in Photo 9). As you can see from the photo, the idea was that the plastic sheet of rock wall material would fit overlapping the rock wall at both ends of the removable piece of Styrofoam insert.

What actually happened was that the finished assembly of the rock wall plastic sheet and the Styrofoam backing had no way to tightly fit into the opening and stay put! No matter how I tried, the removable assembly of rock wall was always removing itself due to the vibration of trains or nearly any other motion around it. So here is the "fix." After the Styrofoam insert is cut to fit between the two levels (refer back to Photo 7), and the finished front shape is cut into the surface with the hot wire (see Photo 8), and before the plastic sheet of rock wall material is contact cemented onto the Styrofoam insert piece, one more operation needs to be performed.

At two or three places selected randomly along the top level plywood that hinges up, drill down with an 3/16″ drill bit completely through the plywood and into the pink Styrofoam. Get some scrap pieces of 1/8″ square basswood sticks (such as the material you used to make posts for guard rails), and gently slide them down into the holes in the plywood and into the Styrofoam. Cut them off so they stick up about an inch or so above the upper deck plywood, use them as sign posts, and glue something creative onto them. Now you have easily removable locking sticks that can be slipped out of the holes, allowing you to easily remove the rock wall insert!

At the bottom of the rock wall, add a couple of sticks directly in front of the rock wall to keep the base of the assembly pinned tightly in at the bottom. Mark the location where you want them, drill the holes, and then add some more sticks.

Lastly, feather both ends of the plastic rock wall that extends out over the vertical edges of the rock wall on the layout, and glue the plastic sheet of rock wall material onto the face of the Styrofoam insert. Be sure to glue no more than the bottom half of the plastic rock wall material onto the Styrofoam insert. That will be enough to keep the upper half of the rock wall material sprung tightly up against the upper level of the layout.

These are just a few of the lessons I've learned as I built my O gauge empire. I hope they helped you build your O gauge world!

Jim Barrett
April 3, 1946 - October 29, 2020

About the Author

***O Gauge Railroading* magazine's
"Backshop Foreman"
Jim Barrett**

Jim Barrett was born on April 3, 1946, in Mitchell, Indiana. His parents ran a photography studio, and Jim learned his way around a camera and a darkroom at an early age.

Jim taught high school industrial design for several years before taking a position as a design engineer with Kenner Toys. After several years with Kenner, Jim went to work for the General Electric Turbine Engines Division in Cincinnati, working on the designs of GE Aircraft engines.

Jim began working with O gauge trains as early as 1953, sitting at the right hand of repair techs in a Louisville KY train store. He became familiar with trains from all the manufacturers, learning what makes our model trains "tick".

Jim's lifelong pursuit of O gauge trains resulted in him building countless O gauge layouts on contract. Starting in 1989, Jim wrote articles for *Switcher* magazine, the quarterly publication from the Lionel Operating Train Society. This work led him to meet Myron Biggar, publisher of *O Gauge Railroading* magazine, on one of his many (60+) trips to the York Pennsylvania TCA Train Show.

In 1993 Jim became a video personality, working with Myron and Rich Melvin to produce the now-famous ***"Jim Barrett in the Backshop"*** video series.

In August 2002, Jim became part owner of *O Gauge Railroading* magazine, along with Fred Dole, Ed Boyle and Rich Melvin.

Jim's first ***Backshop*** column appeared in Run 148, the August 1996 issue of *O Gauge Railroading*. His last column ran in Run 315, the December 2020 issue of OGR. That column is chapter forty-four in this book. Jim's body of work, spanning twenty-four years, is a lasting legacy to his passion for this wonderful hobby.

EPILOGUE

by Rich Melvin, Publisher Emeritus
O Gauge Railroading magazine

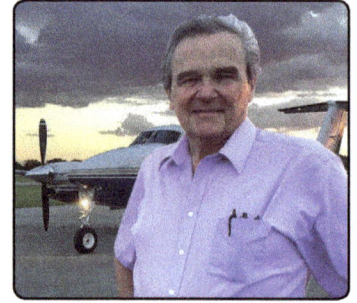

Rich Melvin, Publisher Emeritus
O Gauge Railroading magazine

Jim Barrett...what a great guy.

I met Jim in 1993, when former *O Gauge Railroading* owner Myron Biggar wanted to produce a video series for the magazine. Myron had hired my video production company to produce those videos. Myron introduced me to Jim, who was to become the host of the *"Jim Barrett in the Backshop"* video series. I was immediately struck by Jim's genuine friendliness and affability. He was the classic "nice guy." There are those times in life when you meet someone, and within the first few minutes of meeting them, it seems like you've been friends for years. That's how it was with Jim and me.

I got to know Jim better as we started working on the Backshop videos. Jim had never done any video work before, but he had been a teacher. He had no problem speaking extemporaneously to a camera, but he was unfamiliar with the video production process. It was here that I saw how much Jim was committed to making truly good videos that would be understood by his audience. I had only a single video camera at the time, but we needed to shoot both wide shots and close-ups of whatever Jim was working on. That meant that Jim basically had to do everything twice, once on a wide shot and again on a close-up. To a lesser man, undoing ten or fifteen minutes of intricate, careful work just to have to do it all over again would have been a terrible source of frustration. Not for Jim. It didn't bother him at all to have to do things twice, or to have two examples of whatever we were working on ready for the video. His focus was always on his audience, and his concern was always that his audience would understand whatever it was he was teaching. Those videos have stood the test of time, and they show what a great teacher Jim truly was.

Jim endured some tough times in his life. In the mid-2000s Jim went through a difficult divorce, and he lost his house in that proceeding. He recently lost his second wife, Karen, to the ravages of Alzheimer's disease. And yet, every time I talked with Jim during those tough times, he was always upbeat, happy, and positive about the future. Jim was definitely a "glass is half-full" kind of guy.

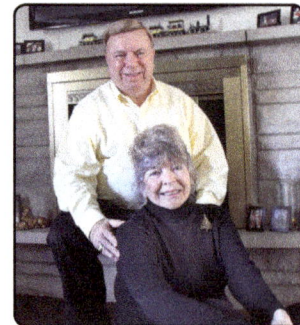

Jim and Karen Barrett

In the face of all this adversity, Jim's salvation was the model train hobby! His unending passion for this hobby sustained him through those tough times. When he lost his house in the divorce, Jim moved to a new house and immediately began drawing up plans for a new layout. That layout became the inspiration for his Backshop columns from its beginning in 2013 to his final column in October 2020. It is a tremendous body of work that is preserved in this book.

When Jim Barrett died on October 29, 2020, *O Gauge Railroading* lost a great partner and writer. The hobby lost a wonderful ambassador. In many ways, Jim was larger than life. His big smile; his never-ending words of encouragement; his always-positive attitude; his knack for making complicated things easy to understand; his character; and his just plain friendliness made him an unforgettable class act.

I will miss my friend Jim...he was a great guy.

Rich